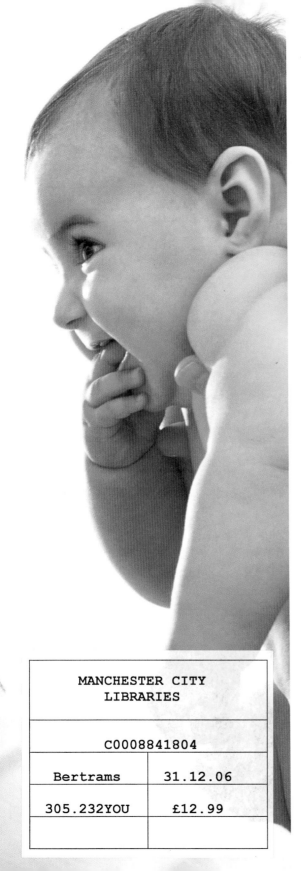

Contents

HOW BABIES LEARN

THE SECOND YEAR

HOW TODDLERS LEARN

THE THIRD YEAR

HOW TODDLERS LEARN

A message to parents from Johnson's®

For more than 100 years, Johnson & Johnson has been caring for babies. Our baby products help mothers and fathers soothe, comfort, and nurture a deep, loving bond with their child through everyday care.

Building on our commitment to children and families, Johnson & Johnson established the Johnson & Johnson Pediatric Institute, LLC. This unique organization promotes continued learning and research in paediatrics, infant development, and pregnancy, building programmes and initiatives for professionals, parents, and caregivers that shape the future of children's health worldwide.

Through science, we continue to learn more about our youngest and their physical, cognitive, and emotional development. Parents and caregivers want advice on how to use this learning in their daily lives to complement their basic instincts to love, hold, and talk to their babies.

Good parenting is not a one-size-fits-all formula. With JOHNSON'S® *Child Development*, we hope to support today's families with the knowledge, guidance, and understanding to help them bring forth the miracle embodied in each and every child.

The first six months

When you hold your newborn baby in your arms, it's impossible to imagine him as a strapping six-month old. But it won't be long before he's sitting in a high chair, throwing spoonfuls of fruit puree around, and interacting with the family as though he's always been there. How does your baby cover so much ground in such a short space of time?

Your baby's development

Your baby naturally develops at a quite incredible pace – but at the same time every achievement that he makes, every new milestone that he passes, is intricately bound up with all you do to make sure he is happy, secure, and loved.

The most important point to remember as your baby grows is that babies develop at different rates. Like all babies, your newborn will smile, lift his head, babble, and grab things at specific times – but your baby is also unique. He won't do something just because a book says he will or because you want him to. The "right time" will be when he is ready. Charts and books like this one can only offer general guides to how babies develop. You cannot speed up the developmental timetable, but if you are giving your baby lots of love and care, you are giving him exactly what he needs: the wherewithal to develop at his own pace.

All he needs is love

Your baby's development doesn't happen in isolation from the rest of the world; he can only learn and progress by being part of it. Having you, your partner, siblings, friends, and family members there is fundamental to his learning and developing.

Not only does he learn by example, he needs acknowledgement, love, and encouragement from the people around him in order to reach his full potential. So by doing what comes naturally – cuddling him, talking to him, going to him when he cries, and interacting with him – you are giving him a sense of security and confidence that allows him to blossom.

You are developing, too

As your baby learns to do more and more, your skills as a parent will adapt to meet his new needs. By your baby's four-month birthday, you will probably have established a daily routine for him, revolving around feeding, napping, going for a walk in the park or to the shops, bathing, and going to sleep at night. A routine will help you both feel secure and confident, and will provide the foundations of your life together as a family.

The development process

Development is rarely a linear process: occasionally your baby's development may seem to take a step backwards. For example, he may have slept through the night for several weeks and then suddenly start waking up every three hours again for no obvious reason.

Such seemingly backward steps are perfectly normal – in fact, they are often a sign that he is about to take a developmental leap forward. You may find that a week or two down the line, he's considerably more alert and responsive to people and events around him, or is sleeping less during the day than before.

Playing is learning

Playing with your baby is not only fun, it provides the fabric of your baby's learning experiences. Every time you play or interact with him, you are not simply entertaining him; you're teaching him invaluable lessons about himself, about you, and about the world.

For example, by shaking a rattle for your new baby, you are helping him learn to focus, as well as introducing him to the concept of cause and effect – after a while he will begin to understand that shaking the rattle is what makes the noise. And by playing "This Little Piggy" on your two-month-old's toes, you are introducing him to the delights of anticipation (in this particular case, the tickle at the end) as well as the nature of counting rhythms. A game of hide the teddy with your five-month-old helps him get to grips with complex concepts, such as the fact that objects exist even when he cannot see them. Of course, all the time you are playing these simple games with your baby he is developing his own sense of humour, and letting you know just how funny he finds your jokes!

About this book

During these thrilling six months of change, your support, encouragement, and love can do more than anything else to help your baby blossom. But understanding how your baby develops is vital to helping you tune into his needs and give him what he wants.

Section 1

The first half of this book tells you all about how your baby's development will affect both his physical and his emotional needs. For example, why does your five-month-old keep waking at night when previously he slept through? How important is it that he learns to roll over or grab hold of things at a certain age?

Being one step ahead in terms of knowing what to expect from your baby will help you understand him so you can respond in the best and most effective way possible. And being able to meet his needs in this way will not only help him feel loved and valued but boost your confidence as a parent too.

Section 2

The second half of this book contains a wealth of information about how and when your baby is likely to reach each new milestone. Although the information is organized by month, it's important to remember that the time scale is flexible. Babies develop at different rates, and your baby will progress at the speed that's right for him.

However, babies' skills progress in a predictable sequence because a certain amount of growth and development has to take place before a new skill can be acquired. So don't expect your baby to sit up without support, for example, before he's strong enough to support his own head.

Once you see your baby trying to do something new, there are lots of things you can do to try to encourage him along the way, and this section includes ideas for games and activities you can play with him. Giving your baby the right kind of stimulation will build his confidence and self-esteem and will help give him the best possible start in life.

The birth

It's hard to say exactly what your baby feels as she is transported from the cosy comfort of the womb into your arms, but if your pregnancy has reached full term she should be well prepared for survival in the outside world.

The effects of birth on your baby

The transition from your womb to the birth room triggers a number of changes in the way your baby's organs function, placing new demands on her body.

The most significant of these is that she now starts to breathe for herself. While in the womb, her lungs were filled with amniotic fluid, but this is usually expelled during labour because of the compression as she passes through the birth canal. This leaves her free to take her first gulp of air, and as she does this her blood circulation will quickly adapt to ensure that there is enough oxygen in her body to cope with life outside the womb.

Babies born by Caesarean section sometimes need help to clear their lungs because they haven't been "squeezed out" in the birth canal. The effects of anaesthesia can also cause temporary breathing difficulties and, if your baby was born under general anaesthetic, she may be as drowsy as you for some hours after the birth.

What is she feeling?

The sudden sense of space and air on your baby's skin will be a shock to her senses, which will have already been highly stimulated by the birth. In fact, newborns are often more alert during the first moments after being born than at any other time during the first few days.

If you are not too exhausted from the labour and your baby is alert, take advantage of this special time. She will be very responsive to your touch, voice, and warmth. Stroking her, cuddling her, talking to her, and letting her suckle will facilitate a loving bond between you. These early moments are a wonderful opportunity for you and your baby to get to know each other. But on the other hand don't worry if you don't get the chance to do this straight away: there will be plenty of time in the coming weeks and months.

Birth weight

One of the first questions people ask when a baby is born (after they've asked what sex it is) is: "How much does she weigh?" Birth weight is considered important because it can give a general indication of a baby's vitality, but healthy babies come in all shapes and sizes. A petite baby weighing 3kg (6lb 9oz) can be as vigorous

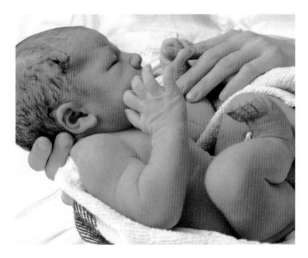

and sound as one who weighs a strapping 4kg (8lb 13oz). There are no hard rules about weight, although a baby under 2.5kg (5lb 7oz) may cause concern, because it may indicate a lack of nourishment in the womb, or some other complication of pregnancy.

Your baby will be weighed just a few minutes after birth. Many factors will affect this reading, including your own health and birth weight, your diet during pregnancy, placental function, genetics (larger parents usually have larger babies), gender, and race.

Your baby will probably lose weight in the first week after the birth – a drop of around five to eight per cent of her birth weight is perfectly normal. Her body has made a sudden adjustment from a dark, peaceful, watery environment to a bright and noisy world where she breathes air and has to feed through her mouth rather than get nourishment automatically.

By around two or three weeks, your baby will probably have reached her birth weight again.

The Apgar test

As soon as your baby is born, a delivery nurse or paediatrician will evaluate her to check her well-being. This Apgar test – named after its creator, Virginia Apgar – is done one minute and five minutes after delivery and helps medical staff ascertain whether your baby needs any immediate extra assistance to adapt to her new environment. The following things are measured:

★ heart rate

★ breathing

★ muscle tone

★ reflex response

★ colour.

This test is only an indicator of your baby's general health at birth. It cannot predict how healthy she will be as she grows up or what sort of personality she will have.

Understanding the Apgar score

Each category is given a score of 0, 1, or 2. A score of 2 indicates a good response in the particular area measured. For example, a heart rate over 100 beats per minute would provide a score of 2, as would good respiration, lots of activity, a lusty cry, and a pink colour.

These scores are then totalled to give the overall Apgar reading (a possible maximum of 10 points).

The vast majority of babies have an Apgar score of 7 or more; only rarely does a baby score a perfect 10. If your baby's Apgar scores are very low in most of the areas measured (for example, if her respiration is irregular, her heart rate is low, and she is pale or limp), she may be given oxygen. If her scores remain low after assistance, she will be taken to a special care ward for more intensive medical attention.

Your newborn

Many things about your newborn may be surprising to you. For example, most babies are born looking blotchy, wrinkly, and a little "blue" – this is all very normal and their appearance begins to change in just a few days as they grow and develop. Chances are that you and your partner will be completely in awe of your new baby and experiencing many new emotions.

Your baby's head

Unless he was delivered by Caesarean section, your baby's head is unlikely to be perfectly rounded. His skull is made up of soft bones that are designed to give under pressure in order to ease his passage through the birth

canal. This malleability can make his head look slightly misshapen or pointy immediately after birth, especially if he was delivered by ventouse or forceps. This will not have damaged him in any way, and, as he develops, his head will soon return to a more regular shape.

The soft patches on your baby's skull are the fontanelles. You may be able to see his pulse beating in this area. If he was born very quickly, he may have tiny blood vessels visible on his face, and his head may look slightly purple, owing to the pressure put on it.

Your baby's face

Your baby's face may have a slightly "squashed" appearance, and his eyes may be swollen or puffy from pressure during birth. Don't be surprised if he looks crumpled – he's been putting up with some pretty cramped conditions for a while. Over the next few weeks, he will lose this newborn "scrunched-up" look as his face grows into its new space.

Your baby's skin

At birth, your baby may be covered in a creamy, greasy substance called vernix. This acted as a protective barrier for his skin, preventing it from becoming waterlogged

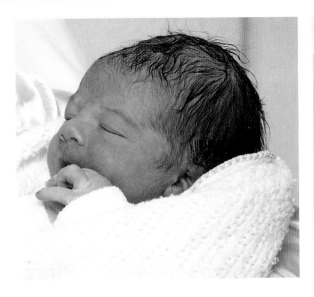

by amniotic fluid in the womb, but it is usually wiped off soon after birth.

His skin may be a little blue at first. It will gradually turn pink as his breathing becomes more regular and circulation improves. If his skin looks "loose" or wrinkly, it's because it hasn't had a chance to build up layers of fat. These will fill out gradually over the next few weeks.

In the first two or three weeks, newborn skin is often dry or flaky, and little white spots known as "milk spots", or milia, are quite common, too: these are enlarged, oily glands and will disappear by themselves.

Your baby's hair

When he was in your womb, your baby was covered with a fine layer of downy hair called lanugo. Some babies, especially those born prematurely, still have some of this hair when they are born. This is completely normal and rubs off during the first few weeks.

Any amount of hair on your baby's head, from none to thick and curly, is normal. Whatever its colour or texture now, it will gradually fall out during his first year or so and will be replaced by new hair, which may well look quite different.

What can he do?

Your newborn baby is born with an incredible number of skills, all of which equip him to survive in his new environment. Although he has limited voluntary control over his own body or movements, his powers of perception are sharp, and he is primed to take in all the information he needs.

★ **He can communicate by crying and by his behaviour.** This is his only way of telling you how he's feeling. He will cry to let you know he is hungry, uncomfortable, or lonely. You will soon learn to recognize and respond to his different cries.

★ **He can see.** Your baby will probably open his eyes almost immediately after birth, even if they don't remain open for long. Although his long-distance vision is blurred at this stage, he will be able to focus on objects that are around 20–25cm (8–10in) away from him, and will be particularly attracted to those objects that have lots of contrast of light and shade (such as your face) and objects that move.

★ **He can hear.** Your baby will also be alert to sounds – especially the sound of your voice, which until now has been muffled by amniotic fluid. Even at this stage, he will be sensitive to the inflections and rhythms of language. Of course, most interesting of all will be a very new sound – that of his own voice.

★ **He can smell.** Your baby's sense of smell is extremely well developed by the time of birth. Once he has learned your particular scent, he will use it to locate you by turning his head in your direction.

Other newborn characteristics

Other "surprises" at birth may include the size of your baby's genitals, which can look swollen because of the hormones that you've passed on to him via the placenta before birth. The swelling should subside within a few days. His cord stump, where the umbilical cord was cut, may also look strange to you. This quickly turns black, and will dry out and fall off in his first few weeks.

First health check–up

Now you have met your new baby, you will want to be reassured that she is in tip-top condition. Within the first hours after birth, a paediatrician, doctor, or midwife will give her a thorough examination.

The paediatrician will start by asking you about your baby's eating and sleeping patterns, how often you need to change her nappy, and what her behaviour is like. He will also ask how you are feeling and whether you have any concerns. Your baby will then be weighed and measured and the following tests carried out.

● Your baby's heart and lungs will be listened to with a stethoscope.

● The roof of her mouth will be checked to make sure there is no cleft in her palate.

● Her eyes will be examined.

● Her tummy will be felt to check that internal organs, such as liver and kidneys, are the right size and in the right place. The pulses in the groin will also be checked.

● Her genitals will be examined to make sure they are normal. If your baby is a boy, the doctor will check to see whether his testes have descended.

● Her spine will be examined to make sure all her vertebrae are in place. The doctor will turn her on her tummy to do this, and at the same time he will check that her back passage (anus) is open.

● Her limbs will be checked to make sure they match in length and that her feet are properly aligned, with no sign of club foot.

● Her hip joints will be examined to make sure they are not dislocated and that they are not "clicky", which can indicate instability.

Checking your baby's reflexes

The paediatrician will also test some of your baby's reflex responses. These will give a sound indication that she is generally in good shape, and that her central nervous system is functioning well.

Reflexes are instinctive responses, which help your baby to survive the first few weeks outside the womb. They will disappear when her physical and mental skills have developed and she is able to make more voluntary, conscious movements. There are more than 70 newborn

GRASPING REFLEX
The fingers of this baby's hand curl tightly around the midwife's finger as soon as it touches the baby's palm. Her grasping reflex is still very much intact.

reflexes, but only a selection will be tested. If your baby was premature, she won't respond in the same way as a full-term baby, and this will be taken into account.

The grasping reflex

The paediatrician will check your baby's grasp reflex by placing his fingers in the palms of her hands to see if she automatically clings on to them. For many babies, this reflex is so powerful that they can be lifted up by their fingers (although you should never try this). You may also notice your baby's toes curling when you stroke the soles of her feet, as if to grip on to something.

The grasping reflex is generally lost when your baby is around five months old, although the toe-curling may remain for up to a year.

Sucking, rooting, and gagging

Your baby's most basic reflexes include sucking, which ensures that she is able to feed. You may find that she sucks on her own fingers, or on yours, and that she turns automatically towards a nipple or teat if it is brushed against her cheek. This is known as the rooting reflex. Swallowing and gagging – which clear your baby's airways when necessary – are also reflexive.

The Moro reflex

This is also known as the "startle" reflex. Your baby will be undressed and the paediatrician will hold her, supporting the back of her head with his hand. He will then let her head suddenly drop back a little, which should cause her to throw out her arms and legs with her fingers extended, as though she's trying to find something to cling on to. Your baby will then slowly draw her arms into her body with her fingers clenched and knees bent up to her abdomen. Both sides of her body should respond simultaneously and equally. The Moro reflex disappears at around two months.

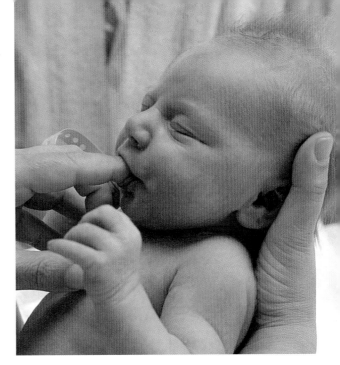

SUCKING REFLEX
This baby shows she will have no trouble sucking from her mother's breast or a teat – she sucks automatically on the finger of the midwife as soon as it is presented to her.

The walking reflex

The paediatrician may hold your baby under her shoulders so that she is in an upright position with her feet touching a firm surface, to see if she moves her legs in a "walking" action. This reflex disappears at around one month, and has nothing to do with learning to walk; the skill of standing and walking can only be accomplished when her muscles and joints, along with her sense of balance, is much more mature – usually at around 12 months.

The crawling reflex

When your baby is on her tummy, she will automatically assume what appears to be a crawling position, with her bottom high and her knees pulled up under her abdomen. When she kicks her legs, she will be able to shuffle in a vague crawling manner. This behaviour will disappear when she is able to lie flat, without curling her legs (usually at around two months).

Premature babies & twins

Around one in 18 babies in the UK is premature, or born before 37 weeks' gestation. If your baby is one of them, he will not yet be ready to cope easily outside the womb, so he will be taken to a special care unit where he will get the help he needs.

How your baby is affected

The earlier he arrives, the smaller your baby will be. If he was very premature, his skin may look almost transparent because it is so thin, and this means he will feel cold in normal room temperatures. For this reason, he will be placed immediately in an incubator, where the temperature can be adjusted to keep him warm. Your baby's cry may be very soft, and he may have difficulty breathing. This is because his respiratory system is still immature. If he is more than two months early, these

Bonding with your premature baby

Although special care is very important for your baby's survival, this can be a very tough time for you. On top of worrying about his health, you may miss the experience of holding, breast-feeding, and bonding with him right after delivery.

Research shows that the more contact a mother has with her premature baby, the more likely the baby is to thrive, so being there and being able to cuddle him, hold his hand, or soothe him with your voice even for short periods can make all the difference.

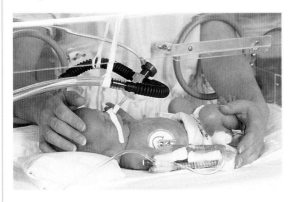

Although it may be difficult, effective bonding can still take place with your baby in an incubator.

★ Ask to see your baby as soon as possible after delivery, and try to be as active as you can in caring for him.

★ Spend as much time with him in the nursery as you can, and even if you cannot hold him, touch him through the holes of the incubator.

★ Breast-feed him if possible, or ask the nurses to help you express milk to feed him; this will stimulate your own milk production so you can nurse him later.

★ Try not to be intimidated by all the machinery.

★ Make sure you understand why your baby needs special treatment. This will help reduce your anxiety.

★ Get as much advice and support as you can. Talk to the nurses who are caring for your baby, your doctor, midwife, and health visitor. Ask them for information about support networks for parents of premature babies.

THE POWER OF TOUCH
This mother begins to bond with her premature baby by touching his head and legs through the specially designed armholes in the side of the incubator.

breathing difficulties can affect the other organs in his body, which may not get enough oxygen. To ensure this doesn't happen, he will be given extra oxygen, or special equipment may be used temporarily to help him breathe.

The impact on his development

A premature baby's development may be slow and erratic to begin with, but it shouldn't be compared with babies who are born at term. When thinking about his development, first correct his age by calculating how old he would be if he had been born at full term. For example, if he was born two months early, he is unlikely to reach the milestones of a "normal" three-month old baby until he is three months old plus up to two months. At his developmental checks, the paediatrician will take his "corrected" age into account. And by the time he is about nine months to a year old, he will have "caught up" with babies born at full term.

Twins and multiples

Because of advances in fertility treatments, twin and multiple births are on the increase. In the UK about one in 75 pregnancies are twins and one in 5,500 are triplets. They are frequently born early and therefore tend to be smaller and lighter than the average newborn, so they often need special care in the first few weeks of life.

Development of twins

Sometimes twins do not follow the same development pattern as other single babies of their age. Some twins seem to "share" the workload, with one excelling in motor skills, such as hand control, while the other perfects social or communication abilities.

Interaction with you is the key to their development, but because of the demands they make on your time it can be hard to make sure twin babies get enough stimulation through play and physical contact. As with all babies, try to take them out for a walk regularly: exposure to new people, sounds, and sights is stimulating in itself.

Do take up any offers of help you can to take the pressure off. Pick a set time for playing with your babies every day when you will be able to give each of them your full attention. Choose a time when someone else can be there too, so you can give your twins individual attention.

Bonding

Bonding is a very special process: a wonderful experience through which you and your baby learn to love each other. This relationship may begin to form as soon as you set eyes on your baby, or it may take many months to establish, strengthening every time you interact. Bonding is not only mutually rewarding on an emotional level; it is as crucial to your baby's long-term development as food and warmth.

How you bond with your baby

If your labour went well and your baby was handed to you immediately after delivery, she may respond to you straight away by looking at you and perhaps suckling at your breast, and you may feel a surge of love. Your baby will feel the closeness of your body, identify your scent, hear the sound of your voice, look into your eyes, and

perhaps get her first taste of your breast milk. All of these things will calm her and help her to feel secure.

Touching

One of the most powerful ways in which you bond with your baby is through physical closeness and skin-to-skin contact, which brings warmth and security to you both, instilling a sense of well-being. This closeness with your baby is also important for her emotional and physical development. Research has shown, for example, that premature babies thrive from the skin contact involved in "kangaroo care", when babies spend time lying against their mother or father's chest, instead of in an incubator.

Set aside some peaceful time when you can hold your baby against your skin, and enjoy the sense of closeness it brings. Bathe her gently in warm water, holding her securely, and afterwards massage her with baby oil.

Talking

Your baby will love you to talk to her. Even a newborn will respond to the sound of your voice, turning her head towards it and expressing her pleasure by wriggling or kicking. It doesn't matter what you say; she'll love the attention, and you'll enjoy watching her responses.

Look at her when you talk to her. Making eye contact is a great way of communicating, and it will really help to strengthen the level of understanding between you, as well as help her social skills.

Bonding takes time

Bonding is a process, and it may take weeks or even months before you begin to form a loving relationship with your baby, especially if you had a difficult labour or your baby needed special care. It's important not to take on any pressure about how you should or should not feel; go at your own pace, and remember that whether the bond is instant or gradual, sooner or later it will happen as you care for your baby.

Getting the right support

Up to 30 per cent of new mothers are reported to have some difficulty in bonding with their babies at first. If you feel like this, try to make sure there is someone – your partner, mother, or a close friend – who can support you and who will also interact with your baby, to take the pressure off you.

Having a new baby is exhausting, so try to cut back on activities around the home, and enlist the help of friends and family. And try to get some sleep when your baby

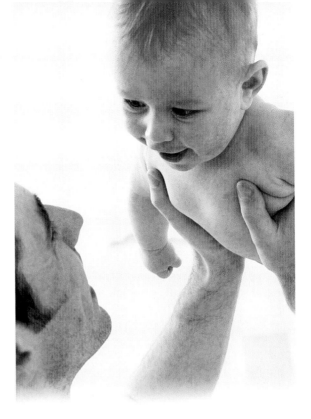

falls asleep during the daytime. Watch out, too, for the post-partum blues. This is the name given to a period of tearfulness that occurs in many mothers at around three to four days after the birth of the baby. These feelings of being completely unable to cope are due to hormonal changes and usually pass after a few days.

Postnatal depression

In some cases, mothers who have difficulty bonding are experiencing postnatal depression. Signs of this include lack of energy, irritability, loss of enthusiasm, and feeling overwhelmed and unable to cope for an extended period of time. If you suspect you may be suffering from postnatal depression, talk to your doctor or health visitor and ask for support from friends or family. This is absolutely crucial to your recovery.

One of the best ways to speed recovery from postnatal depression is to spend as much time as possible interacting with your baby. Physical contact stimulates "mothering" hormones, which can have a relaxing effect.

How do dads bond?

Many new fathers have very strong, even passionate, feelings for their offspring, while others may need a little time to adjust. Even though men don't have the same hormones, new fathers are increasingly embracing the role of being an active parent and look forward to "bonding" with the baby with the same enthusiasm as new mothers. Encourage your partner to feel happy in his new role: the more time he can spend with the baby, the stronger his bond will become.

Massaging your baby

Massage is a wonderful way to express your love for your baby – it helps the bonding process between you, calms your baby when he is unsettled, furthers development, and helps to instil a real sense of trust.

The benefits of massage

Loving, positive physical touch will make your baby feel safe and valued, increasing self-esteem and confidence. It has many other physical and emotional benefits, too.

● It will help you communicate with him, to read his body language and to learn his cues. This can be especially helpful if you and your baby got off to a slow start, perhaps because of early separation.

● It can help relieve pain, promote relaxation, aid digestion, and soothe your baby when he is distressed.

● It can improve circulation and boost his immune system. This is because it helps move lymph fluid around the body, clearing out harmful substances.

● It can tone your baby's muscles and help his joints become more flexible. For this reason it is especially beneficial for premature babies.

● It stimulates growth-promoting hormones. Research shows that babies who are touched a lot grow well – there seems to be a biological connection between stroking and massaging babies and their growth.

When to massage your baby

You can start to massage your baby from around two weeks – you may find it a very helpful way of getting to know him and increasing your confidence in handling him. Choose a time between feeds when he is not sleepy, and do it in a warm room with warm hands.

Getting started

Choose an oil or lotion made specially for babies that can be absorbed into his skin. Keep reapplying the oil to your hands regularly as you massage your baby, to ensure that your movements are soft and smooth.

Undress your baby, putting a towel underneath him to absorb any oil spills or accidents. If you like, just massage one part of his body to begin with. You can then gradually build it up as you gain confidence. In the first few weeks, many babies do not like to be

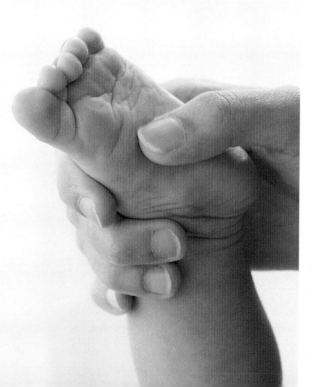

undressed. If this is the case with your baby, do bits of his body at a time so that he is never completely unclothed. For example, leave his vest on and concentrate on his legs, perhaps just after you have changed his nappy or when he's had a bath. Then, cover his legs and massage the top part of his body.

Massage technique

Start with your baby lying on his back, and massage the front of his body. Work from the head down, with light strokes, ensuring that both sides of the body are massaged symmetrically. Watch carefully and learn from his reactions. Always stop if he begins to show signs that he is not enjoying it – for example, by turning away from you.

Be very gentle at first, but increase the pressure of the strokes if you feel your baby likes it. Use sweeping movements, and do each part two or three times. When working on small areas, such as his toes, just use your fingertips. On other areas, such as his back, you may find it easier to use two hands.

Head
Lightly massage the crown of his head with circular stokes (avoiding his fontanelles), then stroke down the side of his cheeks. Gently massage his forehead, working from the centre out, moving over his eyebrows and ears.

Neck, shoulders, and arms
Stroke his neck in downward motions, then move to his shoulders, massaging from the neck outwards. You can then slowly move down his arms, gently "wringing" or squeezing them as you go. Then massage his wrists, hands, and fingers, stroking each finger with your fingertips and thumbs.

Chest and tummy
Gently stroke your baby's chest in downward motions, following the curves of his ribs. Rub his tummy in a circular motion, working clockwise and outwards from his tummy button with your fingertips.

Legs, feet, and toes
Work from his thighs to his knees, stroking in downward motions around the shins, gently squeezing or "wringing" them as you go. Rub your baby's ankles and feet, stroking from heel to toe, and then concentrate on each toe.

Back
Once you have massaged the front of your baby's body, turn him over and begin massaging his back, again working from the head down.

Your baby's personality

While all young babies have many characteristics and behaviours in common, there are also immense differences between them, even at the very beginning of life. Your baby is an individual who is genetically unique and has already had a particular set of experiences in the womb, during birth, and in the first few months of life. These experiences all play a part in how she settles and responds to the world and to you, and they go a great deal of the way towards defining her character or personality.

The influence of genetics

From the moment of conception, your baby's physical appearance – and many other characteristics – have already been set for life. She inherited half her genes from her mother (via the egg) and half from her father (from the sperm). But because each sperm and egg contains a different combination of genes, she has her own unique appearance, personality, and talents.

Babies vary greatly in the composition of their genes, unless they are identical twins. Many of your baby's physical traits are controlled by these genes, including her hair and eye colour, blood group, gender, height, and body shape, for example.

It is also thought that at least some of your baby's character or personality traits are determined by genes – shyness or intelligence, for example, may be inherited. But while genetic make-up can give the potential for your child to be extrovert or shy, academic or sporty, volatile or calm, the way in which she is brought up also has a powerful influence on her personality.

Gender differences

Most experts believe that gender differences, like personality traits, are attributable to a complex mixture of inherited characteristics (nature) and learned behaviours (nurture).

Social expectations have a great bearing on how babies are treated. No matter how "fair" and impartial a parent tries to be, subtle social influences tend to guide behaviour. One recent study found that when baby boys were dressed in girls' clothes, they were treated very differently by other parents who had never met the babies before. These baby boys, when dressed in their usual boys' clothes, were treated in a much more physical way than the girl babies and were offered "boys' toys" (noisy toys, cars and trains, for example). When they were dressed as girls, they were treated more delicately and given dolls or teddies to cuddle.

Differences in brain development

While outside influences play a major part in the development of your baby, some research suggests that the structure of the brain is responsible for many developmental differences between the sexes. For instance, the right side of the brain, which controls physical activities, is more developed in boys, while the earlier development of the left side of the brain in girls can mean that their fine motor skills and speech develops earlier than in boys.

But, although biological factors may be relevant, they should never be seen as a limitation on your baby's potential. Babies are individuals, and their capacity to learn is far stronger than any biological determinants.

Your baby's temperament

Many factors contribute to forming your baby's character and temperament. Genetics, gender, social environment, number of siblings, all play a large part. Of course, most of these factors are not within your control, and you will be well aware by now that you cannot choose your baby's personality.

But by far the most important of all influences on your baby during the first months – and years – of her life is her relationship with you. You may not be able to choose what "type" of baby you have, but the way you interact with her and respond to her now can have an incredible influence on her developing character.

Whatever personality she has, she will benefit from your love and attention. By following her cues, and being as nurturing as possible, tending to her needs and responding to her cries when she is tiny, you can help her establish a feeling of self-worth that will be invaluable throughout her life. Feeling confident and secure is not only a major asset in life, it is also fundamental to development.

Remember that your baby's personality at this age is constantly evolving. Try not to stick any labels on her, as this can affect the way you respond to her. Nobody can predict what sort of person she will eventually be, but you will undoubtedly delight in discovering all aspects of your baby's emerging personality.

Communication skills

Your baby is born with a strong drive to communicate, and quickly develops many different ways of "talking" to you. He has many different kinds of cry, which he uses to convey different needs, and uses eye contact and body language effectively. Before he is two months old, he will smile and coo to express pleasure or to engage you in interaction. He is already laying down the foundations of verbal communication.

Crying

Your baby's most effective way of communicating with you in the early months is through crying. He will probably do it a lot because it is the only way he has of letting you know what his needs and feelings are; in a sense, it's his first baby talk. Even your baby's first cry after birth has an important communicative role: it tells the doctor or midwife that his lungs have successfully filled with air for the first time and that he can breathe.

To begin with, you may think that every time your baby cries he makes the same sounds, but you will gradually learn that different noises convey different needs. While every baby's cry is unique, studies have

Body language

When your baby is awake, he is conveying his feelings to his caregivers all the time, in many subtle ways. Eye contact is a very powerful example of this: notice how he catches your eye to engage you in interaction with him, and watches you intently as you talk to him.

Body wriggles and kicks are another powerful means of communicating meaning: he may kick and squirm if he is frustrated or in need of attention, while at other times, these wriggles and jerks are carried out in pleasure and excitement – perhaps at the sound of your voice or to indicate that a particular toy has caught his interest.

He will express dislike or disinterest by turning away from something, point to something he wants (from around six months), and smile as a way of showing pleasure or recognition.

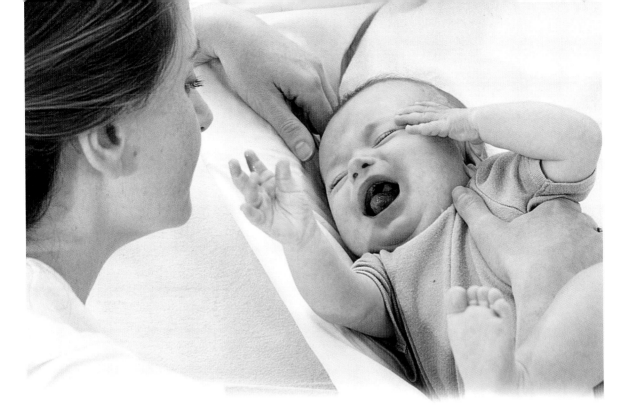

found that the hunger cry often follows a similar pattern of rhythmic noises, and is frequently accompanied by kicking, for example. In contrast, cries of boredom tend to be less regular or coordinated, and may have longer pauses in between as your baby awaits the desired response. Cries of pain are much more intense, and will probably send you running to him.

As you begin to understand the different tones, sounds, and rhythms of your baby's cries, you will be able to attend to his needs quickly and effectively – feeding him when he's hungry and comforting him when he is in pain, for example. This will lessen his need to cry to communicate as time goes on.

What you can do

Quiet babies are often described as well behaved; but a crying baby is not being difficult – he is just letting you know that he is not happy with something. The best thing you can do is respond to him by giving him the attention he needs. Research has shown that, on the whole, babies whose cries are answered quickly tend to be more secure and strongly attached to their parents than those who are left to "cry it out". They also learn at an earlier age to use more varied ways of communication that do not involve crying. By responding to your baby quickly, you are truly letting him know that he has successfully communicated with you, that you are tuned in to his needs, and that he can rely on you. Better still, learn to recognize his body language, so that whenever possible you can intervene before he starts to cry.

Holding him close, talking to him, and giving him lots of attention will give him a sense of security. If you let him know that you are always there when he needs you, he will feel nurtured and cared for.

When crying gets too much

A constantly crying baby can be hard to deal with, but try to remember that your baby is not crying deliberately to frustrate you. Ask friends and relatives to help out, so that you can take some time for yourself to restore your energy levels and give yourself a treat. Take your baby out for a walk and visit a friend. Above all, try not to blame yourself or your baby – it's natural for him to cry, just as it's natural to feel distressed when you cannot seem to do anything to console your baby.

Although it is normal for a baby to cry for long periods or to refuse to settle at times, if you are at all concerned about his health or well-being, you should always seek advice from a doctor.

Verbal communication

Your baby began to understand the power of language very early on, and started learning to talk from the day he was born. You will find it hard to resist his early

attempts at conversation, and it can be great fun to repeat his grunts and squeaks back to him. These intimate exchanges play an important role. They teach your baby the rudiments of language and conversation, and are vital to the bonding process.

Learning language

From the moment he sets eyes on you, your baby will watch your facial expressions intently and listen to the sounds you make when you talk to him. He will quickly learn to imitate them by moving his lips or muscles as if responding to your words. Listening and imitating are the two main ways in which he picks up language, and he is perfectly designed to do both.

By two or three months, his skills will have already developed to such an extent that he may even start to make his first sounds, cooing when you talk to him or to get your attention. When you coo back to him, imitating his sounds in a two-way "conversation", you are showing him the power of verbal communication, as well as how good it is to express himself.

By five or six months, his imitation skills mean he can babble whole "sentences". And by six months he may have learned to use consonants formed by putting his lips together. He may draw out these sounds to form "maa" and "daa" and will use tone as a means of communicating his mood – shouting out sounds or trilling when he's happy.

Helping him to learn to talk

The more you engage your baby in conversation, the more you will help him to use words to express himself. There are many ways of doing this (and you may find you do most of them automatically). Here are a few suggestions you might like to try.

● **Make lots of eye contact with him when you talk to him,** so that he knows your words are meant for him.

Being face to face also lets him watch how you make sounds with your mouth.

● **Include him and encourage him to participate in your conversations.** When you talk to him, leave time for him to "reply" to you. This may take a few seconds or even longer, so be patient.

● **Talk to him as often as possible.** Describe your actions as you go about your daily chores – say things like, "I'm putting you in the pram now," for example, to help him to match familiar objects with words.

● **Keep background noise to a minimum.** Switch off the television or radio so that you can give each other your full attention.

● **Repeat things to him as often as possible.** Babies love repetition, and need to hear a word many times before they can begin to understand what it means.

● **Sing nursery rhymes or simple poems over and over again.** This familiarizes him with the rhythms of language by making it fun.

● **Relax.** Learning to talk is a natural outcome of everyday interaction between you, so don't get too hung up about it!

The importance of reading

Up to three months

Reading books to your baby is a great way of interacting with your baby, while familiarizing him with everyday language. It's never too early to make this special time with your baby. Choose board books with big bold pictures in, and without too much background detail.

As his focus develops over the first eight weeks, he will be able to take in more and more. He will love looking at photos or drawings of other babies, and faces will really grab his attention, especially if they have big eyes and smiles. Point to the pictures and talk about them as you go. Encourage other family members to do the same.

Three to six months

Once his focus is perfected and he begins to understand and make more sounds, introduce books that have slightly more detail. Books with simple shapes, colours, and pictures of everyday objects, such as animals or flowers, will be of particular interest. Read him stories if you like – he'll love listening to the tones and rhythms of your voice, while sitting snugly in your lap.

Look for soft or textured books that have pages that feel different – he'll love to handle and explore them. You could also invest in a plastic book that he can enjoy looking at in the bath.

Feeding your baby

Feeding your baby will take up a lot of your time but it can be a great way for you and your baby to bond and enjoy each other. Your breast milk provides her with all her nutritional needs for healthy growth and development. Around four to six months she will have probably doubled her birth weight and will need more solid, nutrient-rich food to fuel her growing energy needs.

Breast-feeding

Breast milk is very easy for your baby to digest and absorb, and has very little "waste". It is much easier for your baby to absorb than formula. And the composition of breast milk adapts constantly to suit your baby's ever-changing needs: your breast milk is very different when your baby is newborn to when she is six months old.

The first "milk" your baby receives after birth is colostrum, a yellow, creamy substance that is high in antibodies, vitamins, and proteins.

After three or four days your breast milk will come in. At the beginning of each feed your baby will gulp down the thirst-quenching foremilk. This is high in lactose (milk sugar) but low in fat. Once her thirst has been met, her sucking will change to a slow, rhythmic action, as the fat-rich hindmilk comes in. A special enzyme in the milk enables the fat – essential for healthy growth – to be absorbed in your baby's system.

Health benefits

Breast milk far outstrips formula in its nutritional content – it contains more than 100 ingredients that are not found in cow's milk and which can't be made in a factory, for example. Because it is abundant in antibodies, it is extremely beneficial to your baby's immune system, and provides protection against a whole range of illnesses, including stomach, ear, and respiratory infections. It is also believed to protect against allergy-related conditions, such as asthma and eczema, and against childhood diabetes and some forms of cancer.

Getting started

Breast-feeding is a very rewarding experience. However, some mothers find it difficult to establish breast-feeding to begin with. Your baby may take time latching on, or she may want to feed all the time, giving you sore nipples and making you worry that you cannot satisfy her. Or your breasts may become "engorged" with milk. Try to get plenty of rest, drink more fluids than usual, and eat healthily. Most mothers do manage to overcome these early problems and go on to enjoy breastfeeding their baby for months.

If you have any concerns about breast-feeding, talk to your health visitor, doctor, or a breast-feeding counsellor. They will be able to offer you support, encouragement, and professional advice.

How your baby feeds

If you stroke your baby's lower lip or cheek with your nipple or a bottle teet, she will instinctively open her mouth wide and try to take it into her mouth and begin to suck. This is called "rooting". She has been practising sucking for some time – while she was in your womb she sucked on her hands and fingers. However, this does not mean that feeding her will necessarily be easy at first. Learning to feed – whether from the nipple or the bottle – can take time to perfect, and it may take several days or even weeks before you are both happy with your techniques.

The benefits of expressing

Expressing and storing your breast milk gives you flexibility without reducing your milk flow. It enables someone else to feed your baby sometimes, either simply because they would like to, or to give you a break once in a while. It also allows your baby to continue to enjoy the benefits of breast milk for a period after you have gone back to work.

Just because you're breast-feeding, it does not mean that your partner or other caregiver cannot feed your baby whenever it suits. There are a variety of pumps available to buy or rent, enabling you to express some of your milk into a bottle. You can then store the milk in the fridge (if you are planning to use it within 24 hours), or in the freezer for future use.

Bottle-feeding

If, for any reason, you cannot or choose not to breast-feed from the start or when you go back to work, years of scientific research have produced formula milks that meet your baby's requirements. Most of these are made

from cow's milk with modified protein, carbohydrate, fat, and added vitamins and minerals that contain a ratio of the proteins similar to those found in breast milk. Some also contain added long-chain fatty acids, although not in their natural form.

• Cow's milk alone is not recommended for babies under one year, as the high protein and salt levels are not easily digestible, and it is low in vitamin C and iron, which is necessary for healthy growth. However, it can be mixed with your baby's first food, such as baby rice, from six months.

• There are also soya-based formulas, which are made from soya plant protein modified with vitamins and minerals. These are often used as an alternative if your baby suffers from intolerance to cow's milk protein, which affects two per cent of infants.

If your baby is bottle-fed, one of the most obvious benefits is that you can share feeding with your partner or other family members and caregivers.

When to start solid food

Introducing solids is a major milestone in your baby's development. Your baby is not physically able to cope with solid food before she is four months old. Her digestive system is too immature to deal with breaking down food, and she doesn't have the muscular control in her jaws to move food from the front to the back of the mouth until this time. Her kidneys are not yet ready to process food, either.

Your baby is unique and will only be ready to move on to solids at her own pace, but you should offer her first food somewhere between four and six months. Look for signs that she is ready. If she is over four months old and seems to be hungrier than usual, wakes more often during the night, gets excited when she sees others eating or has food near her or tries to grab it, she may be trying to tell you something. Sometimes, babies who are ready to be weaned stop putting on weight too.

Taking it slowly

For the first two weeks just a teaspoon or two of runny fruit purée, such as apple or pear, and/or baby rice once a day will be all she needs. At this stage you are introducing her to new tastes and consistency, and getting her used to having something slightly more solid in her mouth. If she is too hungry, she won't have the inclination or patience to try solids, so choose a quiet time in between feeds. Don't force her to take the food – mealtimes should be fun, not a trial.

Gradually increase the amount of solid food until you are giving her solids three times a day. At the same time gradually increase the lumpiness of the purées. Avoid giving her wheat-based foods, milk (other than breast or formula), nuts, eggs, citrus fruits, fatty foods, or spices before she is six months old. These may upset your baby's stomach or trigger an allergy if given too early.

Although starting to introduce your baby to solids is exciting, it can be extremely frustrating. This is the first time that she will try food other than milk, experiencing new tastes and textures, and it may take a while for her to get used to solids. At first she will just learn to suck from a spoon, but as she gets on to more lumpy food,

Teething and feeding

Although most babies don't cut their first teeth until at least six months, a few babies begin earlier. Teething may make her irritable and her feeding will become erratic. She may appear to want to suck at the bottle or breast all the time, only to reject it soon afterwards because it is so uncomfortable. She may not express any interest in solid food, either.

Her appetite will pick up once the tooth has come through, but if your baby refuses all food (including her regular milk) for more than a day or so, call a doctor to make sure she is not ill.

she will soon start to use her gums to mash it up. Weaning takes a lot of time and patience and, in the beginning, more food will end up smeared around her face or on the floor than in her mouth. Don't worry about how little your baby gets into her mouth – her milk will be her main source of nutrition for some time to come yet.

Eating and social skills

Eating is a very social habit, and as she learns to sit up she can begin to join in family mealtimes. These will also provide a chance for her to develop her personality as she discovers and expresses her likes and dislikes.

Your baby is a keen copycat. She will watch you eat, and try to mimic you, picking up a spoon or rusk and guiding it to her mouth by herself. Although messy, allowing her to experiment like this is important, as it represents a leap forward on the road to independence. It also helps sharpen her hand–eye coordination.

Research shows that good eating habits start young. So, avoid giving your baby food with added sugar, as this is likely to give her a taste for sweet things, which may cause tooth decay later on.

Sleeping

Sleep is fundamental to your baby's development. His brain is incredibly active during the early months, growing and making new connections at an amazing rate. He is taking in new information about his world all the time, and while he sleeps this information is being processed and stored for future reference. His body also needs rest in order to store energy, gain strength, and grow.

How much sleep does your baby need?

Your new baby gets exactly the amount of sleep his body needs – he will "shut down" when his body needs to rest or when his brain has had enough stimulation, and he will wake up when he has had enough sleep. To begin with, there is nothing he – or you – can do to control this. He is physiologically designed to shut down and wake up as necessary.

During his first few weeks, he will feed and sleep at regular intervals throughout the day and night. Because he will sleep in relatively short stretches to begin with, you will probably feel quite exhausted – but bear in mind that as he grows he will be able to sleep for longer periods at a time.

It is very hard to predict when and for how long your baby will sleep. On average, a newborn will spend around 16 hours a day sleeping. As he develops, this will gradually decrease, so that at six months he will probably sleep for around 14 hours a day and spend much longer stretches of time awake.

Although newborn babies will drop off at any point of the day or night whenever they need to sleep, by the age of six months your baby will fight to keep himself awake if there is something amusing or stimulating him.

What happens while he is sleeping

It may not look like it, but your baby is doing a lot while he sleeps. His body will be storing the calories he's gained from your milk and converting them into energy for growth and warmth. All the cells in his body and brain are multiplying at a rapid rate, and he is also making white blood cells, which are essential for his immune system. This is also the time when he does most of his growing, as sleep stimulates his growth hormones. Your baby's brain is also very active during sleep.

Your baby's sleep cycle is much shorter than yours – 47 minutes for a newborn compared with 90 minutes for an adult. During this cycle he also spends more time (about 50 per cent) in the lighter REM (rapid eye movement) phase of sleep than adults. During these phases his body twitches and his eyelids flicker, indicating that he is dreaming. He is more likely to wake up during these periods. The rest of the time is spent in non-REM sleep – a more peaceful sleep that deepens in four stages, and from which it is difficult to wake.

Developing a sleep pattern

From around four to five weeks, with your help, your baby will start to develop a pattern of sleeping more at night than during the day, which becomes more established over the next few months. At the moment, he cannot differentiate between day and night, so you need to help him learn this.

You can help begin to establish a day/night pattern by putting him to sleep during the day in a room which is not too dark, and where he can hear normal daily sounds, such as the phone ringing, the vacuum cleaner, or people talking. Then, at night, put him to sleep in a different room, which is dark and quiet.

Once your baby is around two months old, you can begin to lay the foundations for a sleep routine. Put him down for his daytime naps at roughly the same time every day – probably during mid-morning and mid-afternoon – and put him to bed at the same time every night. This helps teach your baby that life has a rhythm to it, and instils a sense of security and confidence in

himself and his environment. By six months, he may be sleeping for around ten consecutive hours at night and five non-consecutive hours during his daytime naps.

Establishing a bedtime routine

As he becomes more aware of what's going on around him and his memory skills improve, your baby will learn to anticipate events and familiarize himself with the patterns of his days. He will probably respond very well to routine at this stage, and start to enjoy the rituals of preparing for his night-time sleep. Try to follow the same pattern at around the same time every evening. For example, you could start off with a warm bath, followed by a cuddle and gentle play. You could then feed him and put him into his cot, drowsy but awake, perhaps accompanied by a lullaby.

Putting your baby down to sleep while he is still awake means that he won't depend on your breast or the bottle in order to fall asleep. It also means that if he stirs he will know where he is and may feel secure enough to drop off again without disturbing you, unless he is hungry or uncomfortable.

If possible, involve your partner in your baby's bedtime routine. Perhaps he could bathe him or read a book with him. It will strengthen the bond between them, and help to build up trust, so that your baby won't rely solely on you for his sense of security and well-being.

Sleeping with your baby

Close proximity to your baby is important during the early months, not least because you will have to feed him frequently at night. Some studies have shown that co-sleeping is beneficial for your baby; it may help regulate his breathing and body temperature, and there is also evidence to suggest that it can be good for your baby's emotional development. The feeling of having him close to you can be wonderful, and may also decrease your anxiety about his well-being. However, a recent study has identified a link between Sudden Infant Death Syndrome (SIDS) and babies under eight weeks bedsharing with an adult (*see box*), so it's best to avoid co-sleeping until your infant is two months old.

Whether you sleep with your baby is a very personal choice. Parents in many cultures do so intuitively, but this does not mean that you will. It is important that both you and your baby have periods of restful sleep. If you try having your baby in bed with you, and find that you and your partner are uncomfortable, then placing the baby in a crib is probably the best option for your family.

Why does he keep waking up?

During your baby's first six months, his sleep patterns are bound to change. He may sleep for five hours at a time for a few weeks, and then suddenly start waking up every two hours. Sleep during the first six months is very much linked with his feeding requirements: he may be having a growth spurt, for example, and will need more milk than usual to be sustained. Erratic sleep patterns are normal, and sticking to a routine will help

Important safety tips

SIDS

All parents worry about the possibility of cot death, technically known as Sudden Infant Death Syndrome (SIDS). Although the chances of this happening to your baby are remote, it is sensible to take a few simple precautions that are known to reduce the risk.

★ Put your baby down to sleep on his back with his feet at the foot of the cot.

★ Use loose blankets and sheets (never duvets or quilts as your baby will get too hot).

★ Do not use cot bumpers.

★ Never use a hot-water bottle or an electric blanket.

★ Do not give him a pillow.

★ Use a firm mattress, and make sure there's no gap between the edges and the sides of the cot.

★ Never smoke around your baby, and keep him away from smoky atmospheres.

★ Make sure your baby's bedroom is the right temperature – around 18°C (65°F).

Overheating can be life-threatening – his body is not mature enough to deal with the excess heat by sweating. This is believed to be a primary cause of cot death.

Considerations when co-sleeping

An recent study by the London School of Hygiene and Tropical Medicine has led experts to recommend parents do not sleep with babies under eight weeks. After this time, there are several things you must keep in mind to ensure he is safe and comfortable while in bed with you.

You will want to ensure there is adequate space in the bed for the baby. If the bed is too cramped, he can become overheated or you might crowd or roll on him. Never give your baby a pillow for his head or cover him with a duvet. Use blankets instead.

It's also important that you and your partner are alert and attentive to the baby's needs. Therefore, you should avoid having the baby in bed with you if you are overly tired, taking a medication that makes you drowsy, or have recently consumed alcoholic beverages.

you both get through these difficult times. Many babies don't sleep through the night regularly until they are six months old or more.

Coping with broken nights is hard work, but your baby is waking up for a number of reasons. In the early days, his stomach is so small that it can only hold tiny amounts of milk that won't keep him going through the night, so hunger wakes him. Other factors can also affect his sleep: he may have tummy ache, a soiled nappy or teething pain. A blocked nose causes difficulties, as babies only learn to breathe through their mouths at two to three months old. Reaching a new developmental milestone can affect sleep patterns. For example, it is thought that mental stimulation from learning to sit up or crawl at five to six months may disturb a baby's sleep, although other theories say that this can actually make the baby sleep for longer periods.

Checks and charts

Regular development checks with your doctor or health visitor will reassure you that your baby is doing well and provide an opportunity to talk about practical aspects of parenting as well as any anxieties you may have about your baby's development.

Development reviews

Development reviews will take place at various intervals during the first few years of your baby's life. These informal check-ups are available to all babies and young children, and the results (along with a record of which immunizations your baby has had) are recorded in your

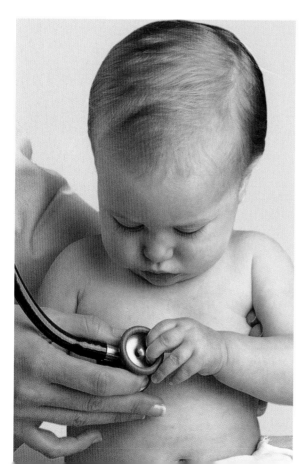

Child Health Development Book. You will be given this book to keep with you, so you will need to take it along with you every time you take your baby to visit your health visitor, doctor, or baby clinic.

The stage at which reviews are done varies, but, as a general guide, you can expect one at around six to eight weeks, and again between six and nine months.

The six-week development check

The six-week check is primarily concerned with your baby's physical health and how she is feeding, as well as her overall development.

This check is quite informal and will not be the same for every baby in every area. Normally, your baby's weight, head circumference, and sometimes her length will be noted. You will be asked to undress your baby to do these measurements, and her hips may be checked too, as occasionally dislocation is not picked up at the newborn check.

The health visitor may then listen to your baby's heart and lungs with a stethoscope and look into her eyes with a hand-held light (ophthalmoscope). She may also check your baby's ears and mouth for infection.

Many of the reflexes she was born with, such as the grasp reflex, should have disappeared by now, and your health visitor will probably test these. Your baby's growing head control will be assessed, too, because it is an important developmental pointer. Her motor

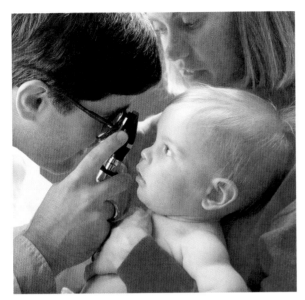

development begins at the head and travels down through her trunk, arms and legs (so, as unlikely as it sounds, being able to hold her head up is the first step to learning to walk).

Questions you may be asked

You may find that when your baby is being examined, the doctor or health visitor does not formally "test" your baby but instead asks you questions about her. These questions may include:

• how your baby is feeding
• whether you have any concerns about her hearing
• whether she watches your face or follows moving objects with her eyes
• whether she smiles at you
• whether she is startled by loud noises.

You may also be asked some questions about how you are coping, because the key to her healthy development is in her relationships with you and her immediate family. Your health visitor will also probably want to book you in for your baby's first immunizations, which occur at around two, three, and four months.

Growth and height charts

Recording how much your baby weighs and measures can provide a very useful guide to the general progress and development of your baby.

Weight gain varies considerably between babies, but on average they gain around 100–175g (4–6oz) per week for the first few weeks of life (although immediately after the birth, her weight will probably take a dip first). After this, the average baby gains between 450 and 900g (1 and 2lb) until she is around six months of age. Weight gain is usually quickest in the first six to nine months.

If you take your baby to be weighed every week, you will probably find that some weeks she has gained weight and others she hasn't. This is perfectly normal. What is important is her general weight gain over a period of weeks, which is plotted on a centile chart in your baby's development book. Some baby clinics will plot on a centile chart that is not only appropriate to the gender of the baby but also to her racial origins.

Your baby's centile chart

Every centile chart has a "middle line" plotted on it. This represents the national average (for white British babies). For example, if 100 babies were weighed at the same age, 50 will weigh more than the amount indicated by the line, and 50 will weigh less.

★ Most babies will fall somewhere in the shaded areas of the chart, although around four per cent may fall outside these centiles. Boys and girls have different charts because boys are on average heavier and taller, and their growth pattern is slightly different.

★ Whatever weight your baby is at birth, she should have a fairly steady growth, resulting in a line curving in roughly the same way. If it suddenly drops or climbs severely out of this range, it can occasionally indicate a problem – an illness or feeding difficulties, for example.

Developing good health

Your baby's health is intricately bound up with his emotional well-being and general development. By nurturing him and responding to his needs, you are ensuring that he will develop into a happy and a healthy baby. Touching and caressing your baby regularly helps everything from cell regeneration to digestion. Making sure that he is not distressed or uncomfortable will enable his body to get on with keeping healthy.

Boosting your baby's health

To maximize your baby's health, try to do the following:

• **Breast-feed him.** This gives him the healthiest possible start in life, as your breast milk contains antibodies that protect him from harmful diseases in the early months and boost his immune system.

• **Don't smoke around him.** By keeping him away from polluted atmospheres, you will reduce the chances of his getting respiratory diseases or allergies such as asthma.

• **Avoid weaning him too early.** Before he is four months old, his digestive system is not mature enough to cope with anything other than breast milk or formula. Weaning too early could damage his kidneys and may possibly leave him more at risk of developing allergies.

• **Take him to the baby clinic regularly,** and make sure you don't miss his reviews.

• Discuss when and how to get your baby **immunized** with your healthcare professional.

Immunization

When your baby is around two months old, you will probably be asked to take him for his first immunizations, which will protect him against many severe infectious diseases.

When your baby is immunized, he is given a vaccine that contains harmless amounts of the virus that causes the disease. The vaccine is too weak to cause the illness, but it makes your baby's body produce antibodies, which will protect him from developing it in the future.

Your baby may develop a mild fever afterwards, and may have a small, hard lump at the site of the injection. This will last a few weeks and is nothing to worry about. But if he develops any other symptoms, or if his crying sounds unusual or his temperature rises above 38° C (100.4° F), you should call your doctor immediately.

The following guide outlines the jabs your baby will be given during the first six months of his life.

★ At two, three, and four months, your baby will be immunized against:
  Diphtheria
  Meningitis (Hib)
  Tetanus
  Whooping cough
  Polio (given by mouth)

★ At some point during the first six months, your baby will also be offered a jab against Meningitis C.

How babies learn

The first six months of your baby's life will be an incredible learning experience for you both. You'll soon become the world's expert on your baby – and she'll get to know you pretty well, too! During this time, your newborn will develop into a confident person who has learned a lot about herself, her environment, and how to relate to the people around her.

How babies learn skills

Each time you pick him up, play with him, talk or sing to him, cuddle him, smile at him, or soothe him, you are giving your baby information about his world and what it means to be a human being. Above all, you are teaching him that he is loved. This security gives him confidence to explore his environment, developing new skills on the way, mainly by watching and copying you.

As the weeks and months pass, your baby will enthral and impress you with a dazzling array of new skills. He will gain control over his own body, and learn that he can control his environment (by picking up toys, or kicking at his mobile to make it move, for example). He will respond to you with real excitement, communicate his needs and desires, and know just how to make you laugh. He will become well attuned to the sounds, rhythms, and tones of language and will love to practise his own. He will be fascinated by his environment, and actively participate in everything going on around him. Best of all, your baby will become adept at expressing real pleasure in life – smiling, gurgling, cooing – and he will know just how to make you feel this pleasure, too.

How to help him learn

Being your baby's "teacher" doesn't mean you have to give him constant stimulation and surround him with bits of coloured plastic. "Playing" with your baby during these early months is about giving him your attention when he wants it. Research shows that parents tend to do this naturally, but here are some pointers on how to help him get the best out of his developing awareness.

- Stimulate his senses. Before he can move about independently, your baby explores the world with his five senses – sight, touch, taste, hearing, and smell.
- Face up to him. He needs lots of eye-to-eye contact to learn to communicate effectively and to feel secure.
- Get him involved. Point out things, describe them, and talk to him all the time. By doing this, you are helping him pick up language as well as stimulating his curiosity.
- Repeat yourself. Babies learn by repetition, and you'll help him by repeating words to promote recognition.
- Take his lead. Don't push your baby to play if he's not in the mood – learn to read his cues.

FASCINATION WITH HANDS
This two-month-old baby has discovered her hands, and spends a lot of time watching them. She is fascinated by the noises the brightly coloured wrist toy makes as she moves her hand.

- Act it out. Describe and demonstrate whatever you are saying or doing. Babies really respond to exaggerated expressions.
- Entertain him. Play new games, think of new songs, and give him new experiences when you can, so he doesn't get bored.
- Respond to him. If he cries, cuddle him. If he laughs, laugh with him. Acknowledge how he's feeling.
- Tell him he's fantastic. Just like adults, babies love to be encouraged and told how clever they are.

0 to 6 months: your baby's milestones

The following is a very rough guide to which skills your baby is likely to develop, and when. Remember that there is a wide variation of what's normal for each month.

The first month

- recognizes your voice and smell
- may try to lift his head when on his tummy
- sticks his tongue out in response to you doing it

The second month

- moves his head from side to side
- smiles for the first time
- coos in response to you
- loses some newborn reflexes
- makes smoother movements

- shows excitement when he knows you are near
- can see things further away
- opens and closes mouth in imitation of you when you talk to him

The third month

- becomes more interested in people around him
- starts to notice his hands
- can open and close his hands and play with his fingers
- may hold his head for a few seconds
- may push himself up on his arms briefly when lying on his tummy
- clasps a toy in his hand
- swipes at toys
- reaches out and grabs at things
- experiments with vowel sounds
- may gurgle

The fourth month

- head control becomes steady
- uses hands to explore his own face and objects of interest
- may make recognizable sounds
- can remember some things – for example, that a rattle makes a noise

The fifth month

- grabs his toes and puts them in his mouth

- may try to take his weight on his legs when held upright
- starts rolling over from front to back
- turns his head away when he doesn't want any more food
- reaches for toys he wants
- concentrates for short periods
- puts everything in his mouth
- raises his arms to be picked up
- wants to be included in everything
- becomes excited at the prospect of food

The sixth month

- holds head steady
- grasps objects
- enjoys sitting up with support
- starts to chuckle
- blows bubbles and raspberries
- changes tone of voice to express himself
- initiates interaction by getting your attention by making sounds and banging objects

Birth to 1 month

It may seem to you that all your newborn does is eat, sleep, and cry – but from the moment she is born, she is developing new skills with incredible speed. By the end of her first month, she will have become more alert and responsive, started to gain some bodily control and coordination, learned to recognize you when she sees or hears you, and has even begun to respond to you.

Physical development

During the early weeks, your baby will still be curled up, with her legs drawn in and her hands clenched, but it will not be long before her body begins to stretch out as her joints become less flexed. Make sure that you always support her head, and never shake her.

Movement

Even before she was born, your baby was exercising her muscles – and now she has a lot more space to do it in. When she is alert, she will punch the air and kick her legs vigorously, especially in response to stimulation or when she is agitated or crying. These movements are jerky, random, and uncontrolled at the moment, but they strengthen her muscles and stimulate her nervous system, paving the way for more controlled attempts later on.

If you lay your baby on her tummy or hold her in the air face down, she will probably try to lift her head. Letting her do this now and again will help strengthen her neck, chest, and spine muscles.

Learning skills

Your baby is learning all the time – and the main way she does this is through her relationship with you.

She is incredibly receptive to any kind of contact you have with her: notice how she goes still and concentrates when she hears your voice, or how she watches your moving lips with fascination as you talk to her. Watch her carefully and you may see her move her body in excitement when she knows you are near. She is deriving enormous pleasure from this relationship, and her brain is being stimulated, too.

Senses

Your baby's senses are exquisitely attuned to help her to take in all the information she needs for survival and development. For instance, she can recognize your unique smell just hours after birth, and she will quickly learn to associate it with the sound of your voice and the comforting feeling of being held in your arms.

Seeing clearly

At birth, your baby can only see the edges of things, because the centre of her visual field is still blurred. During the first month, however, she will gradually acquire the ability to focus better – although full "binocular" vision won't come until she's around three months old.

At the moment, your baby will focus best at around 20–35cm (8–15in) – just the right distance for

Head control

Before your baby can control her body, she needs to master the art of holding her head unsupported.

To begin with, her head will be very floppy because it is so heavy, but over the next few weeks her neck muscles and the muscles at the top of her spine will gradually strengthen, allowing her to support her head herself.

Until she has full head control – which may not come until she is four months old – you must always make sure you support her head when you are holding her.

scanning your face when you are feeding and holding her. At this distance, your baby will be able to follow your face as it moves.

Focusing on your face and those of your family is crucial to your baby. But it is also useful to suspend a mobile above her cot (slightly to one side), so that the images on the mobile are roughly this distance away from her face but not immediately above it.

Language

Even at this stage, your baby is tuning into the tones and rhythms of language all the time. Talk to your baby as much as you can, and try to use exaggerated modulation in your speech. It's OK to use "baby talk" at this stage of her development. You are beginning to teach her the building blocks of conversation.

It won't be long before she starts to respond to you, by making little noises or moving her mouth.

Emotional and social development

Your newborn is a little bundle of emotions. From the first few moments of life, she is very sensitive to the moods and feelings of the people she is close to – for example, she may become agitated if you are feeling upset or worried, and seem more calm and content when you are feeling relaxed. This emotional sensitivity is an important newborn characteristic.

In later stages of development, it will help her adjust her behaviour

Activities to develop skills

At this age your baby has all the toys she needs rolled into one – you! You are the most fascinating thing to her, and will be for some time yet. Your face is the most captivating thing of all. Let her enjoy you as you make different expressions, talk, and sing to her. Encourage your partner and other members of the family to interact with her, too, by making different facial expressions and sounds.

Copy cat!

Try sticking your tongue out at your baby every 20 seconds when she is looking into your eyes, and you may soon see a tiny tongue sticking back at you. Be patient – it may take a minute or two before she responds.

Tracking games

Sound and motion attract your baby's attention and will help stimulate her brain. To help sharpen her visual skills, get her to follow your face with her eyes. Move your head slowly from side to side as you hold her facing you, and see if she "tracks" you with her eyes.

Light and shade

Your baby's attention will be caught by objects with bold patterns of light and shade: your face, a Venetian

MY TURN
After watching his father stick out his tongue at him several times, this baby is delighted to find that he can do it, too.

blind, or a black-and-white picture, for example. This is because strong contrasts are easily picked out even with poor vision.

★ Draw some black-and-white patterns and faces and stick them on to the wall by her cot.

★ Lie her by a window where there is a play of light and shade, perhaps caused by foliage outside.

★ Place her pram under a tree with low branches and let her enjoy the changes in light and shade.

Sense of touch

Splash water in the bath with her feet while you hold her carefully supported in your arm. This will stimulate her sense of touch without making her feel insecure.

and respond appropriately to the people around her. In other words, her awareness of the moods and feelings of others is fundamental to her development into a "social" human being.

You will probably find that, to begin with, it is hard to fathom exactly how your baby is feeling or what it is she needs or wants. But as your relationship develops, she will become easier to read, and both you and your baby will find the time you spend together increasingly emotionally rewarding.

Crying

For now, your baby's physical requirements take priority over everything, and she will express herself accordingly. She will cry to express hunger, tiredness, or discomfort, and sometimes she will cry because she is bored and in need of stimulation, or feeling vulnerable and in need of a cuddle.

Respond to your baby's cries and give her all the reassurance she needs. Lots of attention and love now will teach her how to respond positively to you, and will help her develop into a secure and confident baby.

Happiness

You will be able to tell when your baby is feeling happy or content because she will lie peacefully,

Toy box

Mobiles

For newborns, a mobile with bold black-and-white faces or patterns on it is ideal. Simple, colourful shapes will also catch her interest, and musical mobiles that go round will fascinate her and help her develop her "tracking" skills.

Hang the mobile to one side of her crib rather than directly above her – newborns rarely look straight ahead; they spend most of their time looking to their right or left in the early weeks. Don't worry if she doesn't appear interested in it at first; many babies don't take any notice until later.

Mirrors

Put a baby-safe mirror in the crib so that she can see her own face. This will help her focus, and reinforce her inborn response to the human face.

Music tapes

Whether it's Chopin or "Hey Diddle Diddle", your baby will pick up the rhythms, melodies, and repetition.

Test her memory by playing the same music over several days. Then leave it for a day or two before repeating the same music, and see if she recognizes it. You'll know if she remembers it because she'll kick or suddenly become more alert.

looking intently into your eyes or at her surroundings. These moments may be short-lived to begin with, because most of her time will be spent feeding or sleeping, but they will be very pleasurable for you both when they do occur.

Quiet, content times are very important for your baby for many reasons. They give her the chance to let her physical needs take a back seat for a while, and her brain can take over. This means she can exercise her curiosity, practise focusing on things, and, most

important of all, give you some undivided attention. And just being with you will make her feel secure and happy. These periods when your baby is quiet yet alert are some of the special moments when you and your baby can really get to know one another.

Knowing that your baby is content can be incredibly emotionally fulfilling – it is a sign that you are meeting her needs. This will increase your confidence as a parent, and, at the same time, strengthen your bond with your baby.

1 to 2 months

By the end of the second month, your newborn will have developed into a baby with a keen interest in what's going on around him, as well as more control over his body. At about six weeks old, he will also start to reward your affection with spontaneous smiles, and his personality will really begin to shine through.

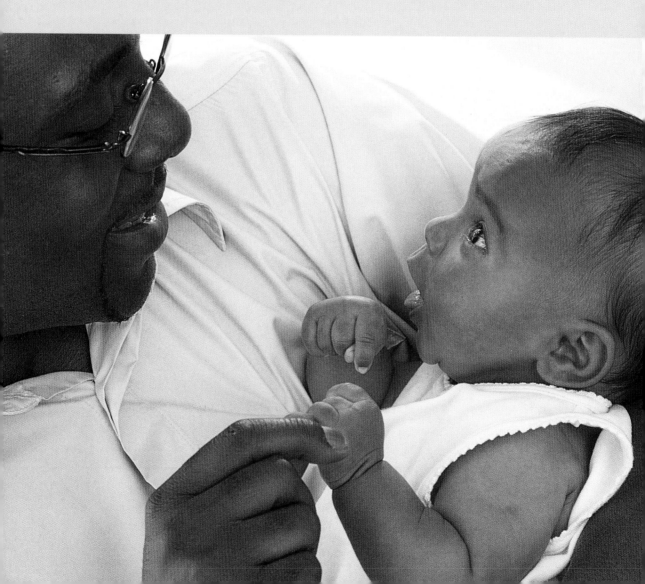

Physical development

Your baby is rapidly growing in size and strength. His muscles are getting stronger, his movements are becoming more definite, and, by eight weeks, he is already far less vulnerable than he was at birth. He will also lose many of his newborn reflexes at this stage.

Uncurling

Your baby will now begin to stretch out and uncurl from his foetal position. His knees and hips will be stronger, and they won't be as flexed as before. And the tightly clenched fingers of your newborn will unfold one by one into an open hand, ready for clasping objects.

By the end of this month, if you put a rattle into his palm, he will probably be able to grasp it automatically and to hold on to it for a little while.

Head control

He will now make more attempts to lift his head, and may be able to raise it to an angle of as much as 45 degrees for a second or two when lying on his tummy. This ability is a sign that his neck muscles are becoming stronger.

He will also turn his head when he wants to – for example, if his interest is attracted by a sudden or new

First smile

Your baby's first proper smile will probably appear at around six weeks. You can tell it's a real smile, because his eyes light up at the same time, and, as you respond by smiling back, it becomes stronger. Although he may have made previous practice runs during the early weeks of his life, you'll recognize the real thing because he'll use his whole face, especially his eyes.

This is a real breakthrough in his development. The more he smiles at you, the more you will smile back and talk to him. His happy face cannot help but engage you in interaction with him, and this is exactly what he needs to develop into a social human being.

Once he has learned to smile, there will be no stopping him. He will probably smile at anyone he sees to begin with, especially if someone is looking at him and talking to him. But within just a few weeks, you will notice that he is a lot more choosy about who he really smiles at; he will quickly learn to tell the difference between familiar faces and strange ones, saving his most meaningful smiles for the faces he loves most of all.

More than anything else, this is a thoroughly enjoyable stage in your baby's development. His smile is telling you that he is happy – so smile back at him and let him know you're happy, too!

RESPONDING TO YOU
Your baby's first smile will come in direct response to you or your partner's smiling at him.

sound or image, or simply when he hears the sound of your voice.

Movement

Those funny jerky kicks of the first few weeks will now become smoother, like pedalling actions. He will spend more time awake now, and a lot of his alert periods will be taken up by exercising his limbs and punching out with his arms, which are also gaining in strength. He will probably take more interest in his mobile. You could also try putting him under a baby gym on the floor, so that he has something to swipe at. He will miss most of the time to begin with, because, even though his arm movements are becoming more purposeful, his coordination and his ability to judge the distance between objects is still quite poor at this age.

Learning skills

Your baby will now take an interest in his surroundings. It will be very clear that he recognizes you. He will start to show his excitement when he sees you by jerking his whole body with pleasure, kicking and waving his legs and arms. You'll notice now that he looks in the direction of any sounds and movements, and he may also follow you with his eyes as you move around nearby.

Vision and sound

During this month, your baby will practise focusing both eyes on the same point at the same time. (This is known as binocular vision.) He will soon be able to scan faces more broadly than before, noticing the

Activities to develop skills

You are still your baby's number-one favourite play thing. Talk to him, rock him, sing to him, or put on some music or sing a lullabye and dance around the room with him – all these activities will bring him pleasure and stimulate him, with positive results. Sing to him as you bathe him: gently splash water over his toes and tummy as you support his body in the water.

Sensory stimulation

★ Prop him up in a car seat or a bouncy chair, so that he gets a good view of what's going on around him. Talk to him from different places in the room and watch how he tries to locate the sound. Games like this help him to coordinate sight and sound.

★ Play "Round and Round the Garden" or "This Little Piggy" to encourage his fingers and toes to relax. Open out his fingers or toes as you say the rhyme. This will also reinforce your baby's ideas about enjoyment and interaction.

★ Repeat the same song a few times, and see how long it takes before he learns to anticipate the tickle at the end.

★ Your baby will also love it if you tickle the palm of his hand and his fingertips with anything soft or furry in texture.

1 Supporting this baby carefully with his body, her father begins to play "This Little Piggy" with the toes of her right foot. She does not know what to expect yet, and looks slightly sceptical as a result!

2 The second time he goes through the sequence, she knows what is going to happen next. Her smiling face is alight with anticipation at the prospect of the tickling that ends this game.

details, such as eyes and nose, rather than the overall outlines and contrasts. Your baby will now also be able to see things that are further away, although he will still prefer to look at things that are close up.

His understanding of language has become more sophisticated, and he may open and close his mouth in imitation of speech when you talk to him. He will also adjust his behaviour to the sound of your voice, quietening when you speak soothingly and becoming distressed if he hears rough or loud tones.

Memory

Although your baby's memory is very short-term in the early weeks, his ability to remember is improving and becoming more sophisticated. To help stimulate his memory, let him experience things with more than one sense. For example, he is far more likely to remember a toy if he has been allowed to touch it as well as look at it, because his memory will include details about the toy's shape and texture as well as its outline and colour.

Emotional and social development

The lovely thing about this stage in your baby's development is that he is already learning to recognize and

Toy box

Baby gym

A baby gym or cradle gym (one that you hang over a pram or cot) has an array of interesting objects hanging from it and will keep your baby well entertained. Choose a gym with toys that make a noise as well as those that are colourful. He'll love things that squeak, rustle, or rattle.

A mobile will help his visual development and he will love to practise his swiping skills on it (see p.45). Move his position from time to time so that he can look at all the different toys hanging from it, and frequently change the toys that hang from it to prevent him from getting bored.

Books

It's never too early to introduce your baby to books. Choose board books designed for young babies that have clear, bold pictures of faces, babies, animals, or patterns. They will help your baby familiarize himself with everyday faces and objects. Stand the book up next to him so it's in line with his gaze, and change the pages occasionally. Better still, sit him on your lap and talk about the pictures, pointing things out as you go.

Rattles

He'll love to hold a rattle and enjoy the sound it makes when you shake it for him, even if he can't do much with it himself at the moment.

respond to you. The most rewarding response is the appearance at around six weeks' old of his first proper smile (see p.45).

He will still cry, but he is also discovering other ways to get your attention and communicate his feelings, using his whole face and body to get the response he wants.

Learning to be sociable

Your baby will look more intently at faces now because his vision is becoming less blurred, and he'll become more adept at imitating facial gestures. His awareness of what's going on around him means that he is taking in more, picking up more clues about how to interact with you, tuning into the nuances of language, tone, and expression and filing all this new information away for future reference.

Your baby will love any kind of interaction now, and he will adore physical affection, responding warmly to cuddles, rocking, and skin-to-skin contact.

2 to 3 months

Your baby is now stronger and more in control of her movements, and will become more responsive and communicative towards you, using gurgles, sounds, and smiles. By the end of this month, she will be able to hold her head steady, and she will have discovered a source of great pleasure – her hands.

Physical development

As your baby gains control over her body, she will begin to understand how she can use it to learn more about her world.

Pushing up

Her neck muscles will now be so strong that, when she lies on her back, she can lift her head and hold it up for several seconds. When you grasp her hands and pull her to a sitting position, her head may no longer flop back, but will lift up as her body is pulled upwards.

Sit her in a bouncy chair or a baby play nest, and she may be able to hold her head steady. Lie her on her stomach and she'll begin doing mini push-ups, trying to lift herself with her hands and arms, and turning her head to get a good look at what's around her.

She may not be able to hold these positions for long, but every time she does it her muscles are strengthening. This gives her much more opportunity to take in her surroundings, and she will become increasingly curious about them.

Happy hands

They may have been there all along, but your baby has only just noticed that her hands are there! Her hands will now become an ever-present source of fascination to her, and she will spend a lot of time lying still and intently examining her new-found fingers, watching as they interact with one another.

By the end of this month, she will be able to bring her hands together and play with her fingers, jamming them in her mouth, where she will enjoy sucking them. She will love to watch her hands as they clasp and unclasp, and will press her palms together in a clapping motion.

Learning skills

Your baby is already a keen thinker. She is now fascinated by her own body and is beginning to understand that she can make it move by herself when she wants to. This is an important first step in your baby's understanding of the concept of cause and effect. She is also beginning to connect seeing with doing, which is the first step in developing hand–eye coordination.

Memory

Your baby's memory will now have developed sufficiently for her to remember certain people and events. One study of babies of this age found that they quickly learn how to kick a mobile attached to their cot to make it move.

When the mobile was taken away for a week and then put back in place, the babies could still remember what to do.

Reaching and grabbing

Although she won't be able to reach for things by herself yet, if you hand her a toy she will clasp it for a short time, and may even try to bring it into her line of vision. When she is lying under her mobile or baby gym, she'll now take definite swipes at the toys hanging down, and may succeed in grabbing one.

Notice how she opens and shuts her hand as if to grab the object of her desire. Although she isn't yet coordinated enough to catch it, she will grab at anything that looks tempting and is within her reach.

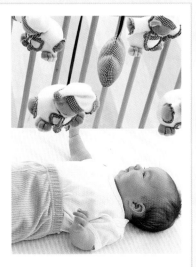

Language

Your baby will begin to experiment more with vowel sounds, and her vocabulary will range from brief, one-syllable squeaks and squeals to long "eh" and "oh" vowel sounds. She is beginning to discover which sounds are made by which combinations of throat, tongue, and mouth actions.

At first, these cooing, throaty gurgles will seem completely random, but you will gradually notice that the sounds your baby is making are directed at you when you talk to her. She is enjoying socializing with you, as well as the sound of her own voice.

Vision

Your baby's focus will really sharpen up now, although she may still work to focus with both eyes properly. She will be able to see more detail in patterns and faces, as well as differences between sharp and gradual changes in lighting. For example, if her room has a dimmer switch, you will be able to attract her attention by changing the lighting.

Emotional and social development

Your baby is learning that being friendly is rewarding because of the way you respond to her with cuddles, love, and soothing sounds. Now that she understands this, she will smile even more, knowing that you will smile back. She will also welcome you with definite waves and wriggles when she knows you are coming to her.

Recognition

One of the most significant developments that your baby's sharpened memory brings is that she now has a very detailed memory of the people closest to her, so she can recognize them as individuals. This starts to influence the way she interacts with you, your partner, her siblings, and anyone else she has a lot of contact with. For example, now that she knows you, she may have very distinct responses to your voice, which are quite different to her responses to your partner's voice: seeing or hearing you may calm her down, while hearing her father's voice may make her excited, for instance.

Happy talk

Your baby's different little noises are beginning to be recognizable now.

Toy box

Wrist toys

Now she has found her hands, your baby might enjoy having a wrist toy or bell bracelet Velcroed round her wrist. She'll begin to learn that by shaking it she's making the noise.

Rattles and mobiles

She will like to hold a rattle, and pull at toys hanging from her mobile with more confidence.

Noisy toys

Toys that make a noise, like a squeaky duck, will now be very entertaining. You'll need to help her squeak these for a while, as they may still be too hard for her to manipulate, but she will love the surprise sound they make.

Once she has learned how to make a toy squeak, she'll get even more pleasure from it – and, what is more, she'll be continuing to learn about cause and effect.

She is becoming more skilled at expressing herself. For example, she may show her feelings of pleasure by making attempts to "coo" to you. She may even shriek with pleasure, and even giggle to express her delight. She will also be learning that loud screeching will bring you running to her side – another lesson in cause and effect! Although your baby cannot repeat any words, she is listening to you and storing them all for the future, so the more you talk to your baby, the better for her.

Activities to develop skills

Now that your baby is responding to you and conversing with you more, you will have even more fun playing and interacting with her. She still needs all the cuddles and words of encouragement and reassurance, but you can expand your repertoire with more adventurous activities such as bouncing games and singalongs. Try lying her on her stomach from time to time. Roll a ball towards her and let her stretch towards it. As she plays, she is strengthening her neck, arm, and leg muscles.

Touching and kicking

★ Let your baby touch toys or objects of different textures, temperatures, and materials: fur, silk, velvet, water, warm skin. Let her lie on a play mat that has materials of different textures sewn carefully into it or Velcroed to it.

Singing games

★ Gently bounce your baby on your knee to the beat of many babies' favourite song: "Horsey, Horsey".

★ Sing splashing songs in the bath, counting songs when you play with her fingers, lullabies when it's time to go to sleep – she'll love them all!

★ Try patting out the rhythm of the songs on her tummy or hands as you sing to her. This will give your baby even more enjoyment.

FLEECY COMFORT
This baby is clearly delighted at the comforting, soft feel of this warm, fleecy rug on his legs as his mother sits him in the middle of it.

3 to 4 months

This month, your baby's increasing knowledge and understanding is transferred into action. He is really growing in strength and ability, with each new experience being stored in his memory. You will also notice that he has become far more responsive to the people around him, smiling, gurgling, and laughing to express himself and communicate with his favourite person – you.

Physical development

During this month your baby will take a real leap forward in the way he can control his movements. When he lies on his stomach, he will probably now easily lift his head and upper body off the ground, supporting himself quite well with his arms and hands, and turning his head to you or anything that interests him. He will be able to hold his head steady for a short while.

Movement

His developing neck control marks the beginning of a whole new adventure for your baby. His increased strength, confidence, and ability to manoeuvre himself up on to his hands means that sometime over the next three months, much to his surprise – and yours – he will suddenly find himself rolling over. Do not leave him unattended on a bed or changing mat, for example, as he might choose this moment to roll over for the first time, and fall off.

This is an important milestone, as he is gaining a sense of control over his whole body, paving the way for learning to crawl in later months.

Learning skills

Your baby's brain is growing at a tremendous rate, and this is reflected in his increased curiosity. He will now love being supported in a sitting position in a bouncy chair or play nest, and may complain if he is left for too long lying on his back. He is eager to take in everything around him – especially new faces, toys, and sounds.

Sound and vision

Your baby will be making even more effort to make his own sounds in response to you or your partner when you talk to him.

His eyesight will have greatly improved since those first hazy newborn days, and he can now use both eyes together to focus on something, whether it's close up or right on the other side of the room.

Increasing hand control

Your baby's hand control will be becoming far more refined, and by now he may be able to grab hold of a rattle or toy if you give it to him, although he will not be able to let go of it as yet.

★ He will be fascinated by what his hands can do. They, along with his mouth, are his tools for the exploration of his world. He will use his hands for searching out and exploring parts of his own face, such as his nose and his mouth, clutching at new and interesting objects. He will also use one hand simply to play with the other.

★ He will still enjoy swiping at toys within reach and will occasionally manage to grab hold of one. When this happens he won't quite know what to do with the toy – except, of course, to put it in his mouth to explore it with his tongue and mouth.

★ He will be intrigued by the sensation of holding different textured objects, such as a soft, squashy toy and a cool, smooth, plastic one.

FIRM GRASP
This baby successfully grabs hold of one of the hanging soft toys on her cradle gym and tries resolutely to pull it towards her.

This means that he is more able to judge the distance between himself and the things he is looking at, so his hand–eye coordination will be much better now.

This clarity of vision also means he can clearly focus even on something as small as a button, and follow a moving object, if held a few centimetres away. When the object disappears, you may notice him continuing to stare at the space where he last saw it.

Amazing memory

Your baby's memory is now really being put to use, and you will probably notice that he is learning quite quickly. For instance, the first time he shook a rattle was purely accidental. But he will have stored information about how the rattle feels, its colour, the way it sounded when his hand moved, and your reaction that he did something clever. After this, each time he holds a rattle, his behaviour will become more purposeful.

Emotional and social development

Your baby will not only smile when you smile now; he may even laugh out loud in delight when you do something that he enjoys. He is enjoying himself, and at the same time he's learning how to get you to laugh and respond warmly to him. In fact, he'll love to make you laugh – it's instant positive feedback. He will know that you're pleased with him and also that he's got your complete attention.

Getting a response

Your baby has now learned to expect a response when he does something – if he smiles he'll expect you to smile back, and if he wants your attention he may try to initiate a conversation himself by cooing or gurgling. This brings a whole new dimension of enjoyment to your

Toy box

Ball play

Your baby will be fascinated by objects that move – especially if he can control them. Try lying him on his tummy and rolling a brightly coloured ball in front of him across his line of vision, about 60cm (2ft) away from his body.

At first he will intently watch the ball as it moves from one side to the other, but he will soon come to anticipate this action and try to reach out to grab it on all the subsequent rolls.

Textured toys

Now that he is grabbing hold of things, it's worth giving your baby lots of different textures. Let him have a range of toys to explore: smooth plastic toys; toys that are squashy; beanie toys that change shape as you hold them; toys with bumpy surfaces. Make sure they are safe for a baby to play with before you buy them. His cradle gym and play mat may also become more fascinating now.

Glove and finger puppets

Glove puppets with fun faces can also be a great source of amusement – babies love looking at faces, as you've probably noticed by now! Make your own out of an old sock – he'll love it just as much as one from the toy shop. If you use buttons for eyes, do check that they are securely sewn on, as babies tend to put everything they can into their mouths, and if a button becomes detached in his mouth it could make him choke.

interaction with him. He is learning to take the lead, which is important to his sense of self-confidence, and, as you follow his lead, you will learn even more about his emerging character and sense of fun.

Encourage him to feel confident by making sure you always give him a response and acknowledging all the efforts he makes to interact with you.

Feeling secure

At this stage, your baby will probably be naturally outgoing and not at all shy or self-conscious. He will charm everyone with his smile, and, although he'll prefer you to anyone else, he will love to "talk" to people – other babies, complete strangers, even his own reflection.

By now, you may have decided to start a routine of regular nap times, walks outside, feeding, baths, and bedtime. This helps him learn to anticipate the events of the day, and teaches him that his life has a pattern to it. It helps him feel emotionally secure and increases his confidence. Establishing a routine also helps him to trust that you are near, even if he cannot see you.

Having a structure to your day and getting out and about with your baby will increase your pleasure, too. You may find that it boosts your confidence and helps you feel in control of your new job as a parent.

Activities to develop skills

As your baby gains better physical control and is more aware of objects and his surroundings, the range of toys and games he will enjoy increases. Interaction with you is still his number-one pastime, and he will show even more enjoyment of singing, clapping, and bouncing games. They will now be familiar to him, which will boost both his enjoyment and confidence.

Repetitive actions

Now that he can recognize familiar objects, your baby may love to play repeatedly with a toy that can make a sound if moved in a particular way.

By singing simple, repetitive rhymes, he will soon recognize the tune (even if he doesn't yet understand the words) and anticipate the actions that go with it. Try the action song "Row, Row, Row Your Boat".

Playing with finger puppets

Your baby will be fascinated by the distinctive and friendly faces of finger puppets. Bring them to life by moving your fingers, perhaps integrating the movement with a song or story.

Lie your baby on your partner's chest and get his dad to hold up the finger puppets. When he reaches out, he'll be strengthening his muscles.

1 *This baby is at first not sure what to make of these animal-face finger puppets, although he is clearly intrigued by their friendly faces.*

2 *After a few minutes of play with the puppets, the baby, feeling more secure, reaches out to grab one to find out more about it. What does it feel like?*

4 to 5 months

Your baby will now be making controlled movements and may be starting to use her limbs to manoeuvre herself by rolling from front to back. She's becoming more aware of new situations, can detect changes in atmosphere and mood, and is really expressing her feelings. Her new levels of coordination and understanding mean she will now begin to respond even more enthusiastically to new toys and games.

Physical development

Improved muscle control and understanding of what her body can do mean that your baby's movements are now quite deliberate – you will notice that she is much more effective in reaching and grabbing hold of what she wants or positioning herself on the floor to play, for example.

Keeping steady

She will now be able to hold her head steady when held upright, and will keep her head in line with her body without letting it lag behind when pulled from sitting – a major developmental milestone. Although she cannot support herself sitting up, she will definitely feel happiest propped up in a sitting position, so that she can keep an eye on what's going on around her and join in with everything. You may find she takes great delight in kicking the sides of her bath when she's in the water, or kicking out at any surface within reach of her toes.

Your baby will enjoy any activity that gives her a chance to push with her legs and feet – and doing this will help strengthen her muscles ready for crawling.

If you hold on to her hands she may try to bounce up and down, although she won't be able to hold a standing position for very long. Don't let go of her, as she does not yet have the muscle strength or physical coordination skills to take her own weight on her feet.

Learning skills

Your baby is increasing her non-verbal forms of communication, using her body to make her point: she will push you away if she wants to do something else; reach for something she wants to play with; or turn her head away to let you know she doesn't want something.

Talking to you

Your baby's ability to communicate with you through language is also becoming more sophisticated. She can deliberately change the tone or inflection of her sounds, showing you her discontent or frustration as well as her enjoyment and pleasure.

She is probably more vocal in letting you know what she wants by making particular babbling sounds, which mean "Pick me up" or "I want to play with that!"

Talking to her

Although she doesn't understand the meaning of your words yet, she will understand their tone. She will be very sensitive to the change of tone in your voice. A firm tone will stop

Coordination skills

Your baby's visual skills now mean that she is able to judge how far away a toy is and manoeuvre herself to reach out for it and grab it with one or both hands.

★ She will be able to hold a toy firmly in her grasp, with her fingers securely curled round it. If she holds a rattle, she may now know what to do with it (thanks to her improved memory!).

★ Her own body still holds great fascination for her, and she will love to grab hold of her foot and suck her toes when the mood takes her.

HAND–EYE COORDINATION
This baby is now able to work out how far away the ball is and reach out for it accurately.

her, but is also likely to make her cry. If overused, it will discourage her natural curiosity and learning later on. To help her grasp meaning, make lots of eye-to-eye contact, because it is through your facial expressions that she can assess situations and begin to understand what you are saying. By letting her watch you as you speak, you are continuing to lay important foundations that will later help her to form words through imitation. Reserve using "No!" for periods of danger.

Concentration skills

Your baby will really be able to concentrate now, and some toys, games, and activities will hold her interest for longer periods.

Not only will she hold a toy, she will examine it, manipulate it, and feel and taste it by putting it in her mouth. This is her most sensitive area, so it's a natural place for her to put things to find out more about them. Make sure that small objects are not within your baby's reach, as she could easily choke on them.

Emotional and social development

At this stage, your baby will really benefit from being part of everything that is going on. Encourage her, and acknowledge her when she makes her contributions – whether it's a gurgle or a hand lifted up with a toy in it to show you. Encourage everyone else to respond in this way, too. The more attention she gets from siblings, friends, and your partner, the better for her!

Activities to develop skills

Now that your baby is so keen on interacting with you rather than simply observing what you are doing, she will try to attract your attention to let you know when she wants to play. Keep her toys within easy reach for her, and respond when she guides you to what she wants by reaching for something. If she knows that you understand what she is communicating to you in this way, you will be giving her confidence a great boost.

Physical fun

Because your baby's upper body is so strong and her head control is complete, she will probably know how to roll over now from front to back. Try playing floor games with her that allow her show off her new skill to you and allow you to help her perfect it.

Action songs

There are plenty of songs you can sing to encourage your baby to use her limbs and improve her motor skills. Sing songs that have accompanying hand actions, such as "The Wheels on the Bus" and "Pat-a-cake, Pat-a-cake". Hold her hands or legs as you sing, so that she can join in the action.

Your baby's face is full of expression and she will show a wider range of emotions – frustration at not being able to grab something, distress if her favourite toy or bottle is taken away, gurgling with delight at seeing something that amuses her.

Security

Although she will probably be quite happy to be entertained by anyone, you are still her favourite person. She will raise her arms to be picked up when she sees you, and may start to become agitated if she sees you leaving the room. She'll feel most secure when she's in your arms and will react more readily to your voice.

Socializing

Although she will happily examine objects by herself and watch what is going on around her, she is getting more keen on social interaction, wanting to join in conversations that take place around her. She will also watch you intently while you show her how to play with a toy or play games together.

This interaction makes her feel part of the family, contributing to her emotional security and helping her develop her social skills. These extremely important skills fall into two categories: learning how others think and feel; and learning how to care about them.

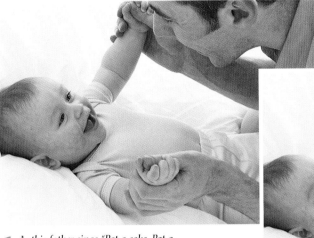

2 *In time with the beat of the song, the father pulls his son's hands out to the side and then brings them together again in a clapping motion.*

1 *As this father sings "Pat-a-cake, Pat-a-cake" to his son, he engages his attention fully by making eye-to-eye contact with him and helping him join in the action.*

Quick change

It can take only seconds for your happy, easy-going baby to dissolve into tears. A tickling game or splashing about in the bath can quickly turn from fun into floods of tears, as there is a fine line between enjoyment and too much stimulation or excitement.

Try to anticipate these changes – perhaps they happen when she is tired, for example – and respond to them quickly. Remember that your baby still needs quiet time, and may even want to be alone for a while. By recognizing her need for a break, you can build trust and give her time to calm down and refocus.

Toy box

Surprise

Your baby will love games with an element of surprise. A jack-in-the-box, or a toy that makes a noise if you press it in a certain place, will be great fun now. Encourage her to interact and use her hand and visual skills by helping her to push down on toys to make them pop up.

Squeak?

Put a different squeaky toy into each of your baby's hands. Make sure they are pliable enough to make a noise with just one hand. Watch as she tries to work out which hand the noise is coming from when she presses it.

Music and movement

Your baby will enjoy toys that she can manipulate easily. A baby tambourine will be great fun for her now, as will a clear plastic toy shaker with colourful beans inside that she can shake around. Both teach her about the power she has over things.

5 to 6 months

Six months is a developmental watershed for your baby as he grasps new concepts as well as physical skills. At around this time he will really be able to demonstrate his love for you and desire to be with you – he will want to touch your face, grab your hair, or hold out his arms to be picked up, for example.

Physical development

Your baby is coming on in leaps and bounds, and each week brings new physical developments that increase the range of activities he can enjoy.

Mighty muscles

During this month or the next, your baby might learn to sit unsupported, although, for a while yet, most babies will still need some support when sitting. When he's lying down, the improved control he has over his limbs means he can now easily roll over on to his back from his front.

Keeping focused

Your baby's eyesight and his hand-eye coordination have improved so much that it is almost as good as yours. He can now deliberately reach for an object and bring it straight to his mouth. Faces are still his favourite thing to look at, and he is getting better at distinguishing facial expressions now. He can tell a happy face from a sad face.

Learning skills

Your baby is very keen to experiment with whatever he can lay his hands on, feeling toys for their different textures (and tastes!) and trying to work out why it's more difficult to hold a large toy than a

Happy hands

Your baby's hands are still his key to exploring. Tasks that were beyond him just a couple of weeks back, such as rotating his wrist to inspect a toy, are now part of his physical repertoire. He can pick up small objects using his fist in a scooping action.

★ Your baby will start to pass an object from one hand to the other with his fist as he works out what he wants to do with it. If he accidentally drops the object, he may reach down to try to retrieve it if it is within sight.

small one. He will increasingly be trying out cause and effect, too, noticing that when he shakes a certain toy it will make a noise while another one is silent, or swiping at some bricks to watch them fall across the floor.

Understanding

Your baby's greater comprehension of what is going on around him means that he will now concentrate on subjects for longer, whether it's looking at a toy in his hands or watching you.

He will focus intently on one thing at a time, mainly using just one sense – listening to music, watching you, or examining a picture in a book, or scooping up a building

brick with his hands – before becoming distracted and moving on to a new activity.

Making conversation

Your baby is keen to communicate with you, and will try to make different sounds with his mouth.

He will practise using his tongue, poking it out and blowing raspberries with his lips to make different sounds. Listen to him carefully and you may notice that your baby is also becoming more adept at changing his tone of voice in the hope that you will turn and look at him as he realizes that people use different noises to communicate.

He is beginning to understand a little of what you say, too. He may turn his head towards you when he hears you use his name in conversation and will understand often-repeated words, such as "mummy" or "bedtime".

Emotional and social development

By now you will have a good idea of your baby's personality and his growing individual characteristics.

Social skills

Although he may still be quite happy to be held by strangers, he is now able to distinguish between people he knows and those he doesn't, and will show a definite preference for familiar faces – yours most of all!

He will get a lot of enjoyment from social situations, such as watching other children play, sitting in his highchair at family mealtimes, and being taken to the park. These events also help him to interact with other people, and feel comfortable in new situations when they occur.

Let him be a part of everything that is going on. Encourage him as he tries new things, and acknowledge him when he makes his own contributions – whether it's a gurgle or a hand lifted up with a toy in it to show you. Encourage everyone around him to respond to him in

this way, too. Siblings, friends, your partner – they will all be sources of endless fascination for your baby, and the more attention he gets from them, the better.

Getting emotional

As your baby is now emotionally more mature, he will show a wider range of emotions in different situations. He can show you that he is excited by bouncing up and down, that he has seen something

that gives him joy by gurgling with pleasure, remaining quiet and watching warily when he is unsure of a situation, or crying when his needs are not met.

Personality changes

Although genes play a part in determining your baby's personality, he will already have developed many of his own characteristics, likes and dislikes. However, many of the traits you see in him now will not

Activities to develop skills

Your baby will probably need only minimum support when sitting up now, and is keen to explore and examine everything around him. He'll still love all the singalongs, bouncing games, and clapping games, and you will be able to be a little more physically playful with him now that he's stronger. He'll enjoy being tickled – try blowing raspberries on his tummy and see his delight!

Hide the teddy

To help your baby learn the concept of something being there when it cannot be seen, try hiding his teddy

under a blanket. Pull away the blanket and watch your baby's interested and surprised face as he watches something he thought was gone suddenly appear.

SURPRISE
This baby expresses surprise and indignation when her mother appears from behind the curtain. She was there all along!

necessarily stay with him for the rest of his life. For example, he may be impatient for solids at every meal or frustrated by not yet being able to move around freely and reach the things he wants, but this does not mean that he will grow into an impatient or frustrated child.

Remember that your baby has a long way to go before he can understand, reason, or use language to communicate effectively what he is thinking or wants.

Toy box

Mat exploration

His play mat will now be more useful. Athough he is not crawling yet, your baby will be able to move himself around a little by rolling or using his arms. A brightly coloured activity mat with attached toys will keep him amused as he explores the different areas on it.

Cuddly toys

Your baby will love soft toys with faces now. Encourage him to be gentle with them – role-play by cuddling a favoured teddy or puppet and saying "Aah" (to teach your baby about sociability, gentleness, and kindness). It won't be long before he will start "looking after" his toys, too.

Cot contentment

Your baby will appreciate a range of toys attached to the bars of his cot to play with when he wakes up or before he falls asleep. These are useful for amusing your baby for short periods, but are no replacement for interaction with you, your partner, and siblings.

Your baby may already have a favourite soft toy or blanket, which gives him a sense of security.

Plastic blocks

Your baby will be delighted at his own skill at pressing buttons on simple toys to make a face pop up or a noise to sound, as well as knocking down a tower of plastic blocks, or swiping at a roly-poly doll that rights itself after it has been pushed over.

Not only is he mastering his hand–eye coordination, but also learning about cause and effect.

1 This baby watches with enormous interest as her mother builds a tower with her colourful bricks. What will happen next?

2 The baby cannot restrain herself from knocking the tower over with her fists. She will not be satisfied until the tower is entirely demolished.

The second six months

Your baby is now six months old – and he's bursting with life! Over the coming months he'll amaze you with his achievements and delight you with his love as he develops into his own unique little person.

Your baby's development

For the first six months of your baby's life, you were the centre of her world: she relied on you for all her physical and emotional needs. During her second six months, however, she'll begin to develop new skills to help her extend her horizons, explore her environment, assert her own will, and discover her independence.

The wider world

Reaching her natural milestones – such as discovering how to sit, crawl, and communicate – enables your baby to really start interacting with the wider world. She can see a favourite toy and move forwards to grab it. Her older brother may pull a funny face to make her laugh and she can pull one back! If she meets another baby she can reach out with interest towards him.

Developing independence

Watching your baby acquiring new skills is exciting, and will give you a sense of her developing independence. The fact that she can soon sit on her own, crawl happily around on the floor, amuse herself with a new toy, and feed herself at the table gives you a little taste of freedom: every now and then you may even have time to sit down with a cup of coffee. A daily outing in the buggy is another step in introducing your baby to the wider world, and gives you both important "out and about" time together.

New relationships

Your baby will also become more involved and responsive with other people, especially close family members. With their instinctive sociability, babies at six months and older can start to develop a close bond with people other than their parents, such as grandparents and caregivers. This is a good time to help your baby establish separate relationships with people who will become important in her life – especially as, in a few months' time, "stranger anxiety" (pp.70–71) may make new friendships a lot harder.

Part of the family

During these next six months your baby will also really begin to enjoy her siblings, or love to watch an older toddler or child bouncing around. And as she begins to move about herself and becomes capable of doing more things, many activities can be shared, such as singing songs together, playing clapping games, or having a game of chase (on all fours!) around the sitting room. Older children can also play the role of teacher for your baby. She'll love to imitate them and may try hard to look at a book or blow raspberries like her big brother or sister.

Making friends

Your friends' babies can offer similar benefits. If this is your first baby, her encounters with other babies and toddlers will probably be as a result of the friendships you have made during pregnancy and after birth. Over the next six months, your baby and your friends' babies may start to interact, gurgling at each other, touching, and trying to imitate each other's sounds and movements.

About this book

During these thrilling six months of change, your support, encouragement, and love can do more than anything else to help your baby blossom. Understanding how your baby develops is vital to helping you tune into her needs and give her what she wants.

Section 1

The first half of this book explains how your baby's development will affect both her physical and her emotional needs. For example, why does your eight-month-old keep waking at night when previously she slept through? How important is it that she moves on from purées to lumpier food at a certain age? Now she has begun crawling, how can you keep her safe?

Being one step ahead in terms of knowing what to expect from your baby will help you understand her so you can respond in the best and most effective way possible. And being able to meet her needs in this way will not only help her feel loved and valued but boost your confidence as a mother or father, too.

Section 2

The second half of this book contains a breakdown of each new milestone in your baby's life, and when she might be likely to reach the next stage.

Although this information is organized month by month, it's important to remember that the time-scale is flexible. All babies develop at different rates, and your baby will progress at the speed that's right for her. A certain amount of growth and development needs to take place before a new skill can be acquired by a child. So don't expect your baby to pull herself to standing, for example, before she's strong enough to support her own weight easily with her knees and hips.

Once you see your baby trying to do something new, there are lots of things you can do to try and encourage her along the way, and this section includes ideas for games and activities you can play with her. Giving your baby the right kind of stimulation at just the right time will build her confidence and self-esteem and help give her the best possible start in life.

Developing socially

As your baby enters the second half of his first year, you'll see him become more sociable and he'll reward everyone with big smiles and gurgles. Being exposed to lots of friendly faces will allow him to relax in other people's company, and help deal with the inevitable onset of separation and stranger anxiety in the next few months.

Separation and stranger anxiety

From around seven months onwards, and probably for some time to come, your sociable and outgoing baby may become more clingy and be wary of people he doesn't know well. He may be reluctant to be left with anyone other than you, and even new settings may upset him. While some are more affected than others, all babies go through separation and stranger anxiety. It's a major emotional milestone and shows that your baby is growing up. For the first time he can tell the difference between familiar and unfamiliar situations. He's also beginning to realize that you and he are different people.

Child care and what your baby needs

Introducing your baby to a new babysitter or caregiver can be especially difficult when your baby is experiencing separation and stranger anxiety. But with the right person, your baby will gradually accept the situation and even benefit from having another warm and loving relationship in his life. At this age, a good babysitter or caregiver should have the following qualities:

★ Be happy to go at your baby's pace. If she forces herself on your baby, she could easily upset him.

★ Be understanding and patient. If your baby cries when you leave him, you need to feel reassured that your babysitter or caregiver won't take it personally and begin to feel inadequate.

★ Be fun and imaginative. If she knows how to distract your baby so that you can slip away peacefully, it will help both you and your baby.

★ Enjoy cuddling and chatting to your baby. Your baby still needs lots of physical affection and attention to help him feel happy and secure.

Make sure that your baby feels really special. If he feels safe and well-loved, his confidence will be boosted and he will cope better when you leave.

How to help

When your baby wraps his arms tightly around you, you will melt. But when he refuses to be put down and cries as if his heart will break if you leave the room, you may feel overwhelmed by his intense feelings. Try to remember that this is a stage that will pass.

● **Take it in stages.** Gradually realizing that you always come back when you say you will can help your baby: if you need to pop into another room, tell him where you're going and that you won't be a minute – if he cries, call to let him know you're on your way back. Also allow your baby to crawl into other rooms to give him the confidence to explore places on his own, but always follow close behind him to make sure that he stays safe.

● **Meeting new people.** Don't force your baby to be friendly – let him make eye contact in his own time. Even family members whom your baby hasn't seen for a few days may upset him without intending to.

KEEPING YOU IN HER SIGHT
Your baby's desire to be near you is a positive sign. It shows that she has developed a deep attachment to you as a parent, and to others close to her. And the more secure she feels, the faster – and more smoothly – she'll pass through this phase.

● **Giving advance warning.** When you know you have to go out, always tell your baby a little while in advance (but never more than 10 or 15 minutes beforehand or he'll forget!). This way he'll know what to expect rather than worry that you might leave him any time.

● **Getting acquainted with a caregiver.** If you have arranged for your baby to be looked after by a caregiver or babysitter, give him time to become familiar with their face and begin to respond and form an attachment to them while you are still in the same room.

● **Act calmly.** When it's time to leave, give your baby a hug and a kiss goodbye and go without a fuss. If you look calm and happy, your baby will feel reassured. If your baby cries, tell him you know he'll miss you, and you'll miss him too, but you will be back shortly. Waving out of the window is a good distraction.

● **Try not to worry.** Chances are that even if your baby is in floods of tears when you leave him, within a few minutes of your departure he'll be engaged with the person caring for him. Rather than spending your time away worrying and feeling guilty, make a quick phone call home or peep back through the window to reassure yourself that your baby is fine.

Developing personalities

Your baby is a unique individual, with her own set of fingerprints and a distinctive personality that will develop in the months and years to follow. How does this happen? Some of her traits may be inherited, but much of the way she develops will depend on her daily experiences and her interaction with you and others close to her.

Recognizing character traits

Walk into a baby clinic and you can already see a whole range of identifiable personalities – from cheerful and adaptable, to fretful and demanding. Some babies love to be cuddled, others will only want physical affection when it suits them. Some are sociable and daring, others are cautious and reserved. And, of course, many babies are a mixture of some or all of these characteristics.

Understanding her requirements

Your baby's character traits will become more obvious to you as she grows. Watching them unfold is not only thrilling, it also helps you tune in to her needs so that you can nurture the positive sides of her personality and help her moderate other behaviour. For example:

• an easy-going, placid baby may be a dream to care for, but she still needs attention and stimulation even if she doesn't always demand it.

• a shy, reserved baby needs time to adapt to new situations and people. You need to be supportive and reassuring to help her cope with experiences she might otherwise find overwhelming.

• an unsettled or demanding baby needs you to be calm and consistent, with lots of patience, and a regular routine.

At this time, all babies can be more demanding of your attention. It is important to keep in mind that your baby won't always be this needy, and that her character is still forming. From the age of six months onwards, most babies are starting to settle down and become more responsive to you. The key is to try and focus on bringing out the best in your baby.

Helping her personality develop

Although your baby may be showing clear character traits at a young age, her personality is still emerging. And in the same way that her character traits affect the way you respond to her, so your responses will have an impact on her personality.

From six months old and beyond, as your baby becomes increasingly aware that she is a separate person to you, it is important to help her develop a strong sense of self. You can do this in a number of ways:

● **Show her how much you love her.** Giving your baby lots of smiles, hugs, and kisses will make her feel valued as a separate and unique individual.

● **Praise all her achievements.** Whether it's waving to you or banging two blocks together, her self-confidence will be boosted by your applause and encouragement.

● **Tune in to her needs.** Knowing when she's frightened, excited, or bored, and responding accordingly, will help her feel important and loved.

● **Give her time to discover things for herself.** Letting her work hard to reach for a toy, for example, will help her develop her sense of independence as well as improving her movement control.

Putting it into practice

As you tune in to her individual personality and start to encourage the positive characteristics she displays, within a few months you may begin to see your baby's developing sense of self in action as she starts to gleefully assert her will. Whether she's refusing to cooperate with you when you get her dressed or try to change her nappy, insisting that you play peekaboo again for the umpteenth time, or banging her spoon in fury because she wants to eat her food right now, you'll be left in no doubt about her likes and dislikes! But it is all these qualities – what makes her laugh and cry, her favourite foods, the games she loves – that combine together to help create her unique personality.

A question of gender

Although you may not consciously realize what you are doing, chances are that the way you care for and respond to your baby will also be affected by her sex.

Research has shown that parents of girls tend to:

★ talk gently, smile a lot, and hold them softly

★ avoid physical fun like flying them through the air

★ keep bath time quieter than with boys

★ encourage play with soft cuddly toys

★ allow them to cry when they hurt themselves and offer lots of sympathy.

On the other hand, parents of boys tend to:

★ speak loudly and hold them firmly

★ give them lots of physical stimulation – swinging them about, for example

★ encourage them to kick and splash about in the bath

★ admire their physical strength and sense of adventure

★ let them play with tough, durable toys

★ discourage any tears and sympathy when they hurt themselves.

While boys and girls are naturally different in lots of ways – for example, girls do tend to be more sociable and less adventurous than boys, and boys are usually more physical and inquisitive than girls – the way we adults respond to them also tends to reinforce these gender differences. Tempering your behaviour towards them – encouraging your boy's gentler side, or stimulating your girl's sense of independence – will begin to help eliminate any sexual stereotyping and allow your baby's own individuality to emerge.

Encouraging individuality

The way you bring your baby up will have a strong influence on his personality. And whatever genes and personality traits are passed down your family line and inherited by your baby, he will still develop his own characteristics. But how should you encourage identical twins, or triplets, who share the same genetic make-up and the same family and experiences, to develop their own identities?

A question of genes

Every baby inherits half his genes from his mother (via the ovum) and half from his father (via the sperm). Each sperm and ovum contains a different combination of genes, which is why every child has his own unique looks and personality.

   And while it is easy to see where certain individual physical characteristics come from – those dark-brown eyes are definitely his mother's, but that auburn hair must be his dad's! – what about your baby's personality? How can you tell which parts are inherited and which

parts have developed over the weeks and months? You can only guess. Trying to spot any family similarities is great fun – maybe he has inherited his mother's calmness or his father's sense of humour – but because your baby is influenced by his surroundings and experiences from the moment he is born, it is impossible to know precisely which characteristics he has inherited, and which have developed over time.

Being a twin

Nurturing babies as individuals is especially important if you have twins, or even triplets. This is even more important if they are identical twins.

   Identical twins develop from the same egg and are always the same sex. And because they appear so very much alike physically, it's easy to expect them to be alike emotionally and think in the same way. Treating twins as one unit rather than as two separate individuals can actually delay their physical and emotional growth, as well as slow their language and intellectual development. Thinking of your twin babies as different children and and treating them as such is vital. This will help them develop their own personalities and give them a firm emotional foundation from which to grow.

Influencing the genes

The way you react to your baby's temperament and behaviour has a big influence on his developing personality. While your baby's genes may suggest that he is going to be outgoing or shy, calm, or volatile, the way you interact with him and his day-to-day experiences may or may not mean he stays this way. If you are consistently calm with an easily agitated baby, he may gradually become more relaxed. If you are supportive and reassuring with a naturally shy baby, he may, with time, become more outgoing and sociable.

Seeing twins as individuals

There are lots of practical ways of encouraging your twins' individuality, including:

- choosing names that sound very different
- not calling them "the twins" but referring to them as "the girls" or "the children". Ask family and friends to do the same, too.
- making sure that you and everyone else can tell them apart from each other. You may like to paint a little fingernail on one hand each in a different colour, give them different hairstyles, or even different-coloured socks so that they don't get called by each other's name.
- avoiding dressing them in the same clothes
- letting them have their own selection of books, toys, and other personal items, even if it means duplicating some of them. You can identify whose is whose with their initials or name labels.

Encouraging a sense of self

There are also lots of ways of nurturing your twins' unique sense of self.

- **Spend time alone with each twin.** This can be hard, especially if you have another child or children, too. But regularly having some one-on-one time with each separate twin will make them feel loved and valued as individuals, not just as a unit.
- **Look for the unique in each twin.** Learn how to appreciate what is special about each individual child, even if it's just that one baby chuckles more when he's tickled while the other loves bouncing on your knee.
- **Try not to compare them.** General statements that tend to compare twin siblings can sometimes become permanent labels. As they get older and more aware, such labels may actually damage their individual self-esteem and even create an unhealthy competitiveness. Always find something positive to say about each individual baby.

INDIVIDUAL IDENTITIES
Twins may be reluctant to be separated, but as they get older it is important for them to feel happy about being apart if they are to grow up secure and well-balanced.

- **Introduce them to other babies.** Do this from an early age so that they feel happy in social groups. With their similarities and close physical proximity, twins often develop a special bond, which may occasionally lead them to prefer each other's company over everyone else's.

Developmental check-up for 6 to 9 months

During her first year your baby will have at least four main health checks with your GP or health visitor, including a developmental review when she is between six and nine months old. These checks are to ensure that your baby is progressing well. They are also a good chance for you to discuss any worries you may have *(see box)*.

The timing of your baby's six to nine month check, and who undertakes it, will vary depending on where you live. When you go to the clinic you'll need to take your baby's Child Health Development Book, or a similar record book, which you were given when your baby was born. This not only contains details of the check required but provides a place to have her progress recorded.

If your baby has been unwell recently, or was born premature, make sure that you let your GP or health visitor know. Illness could affect how your baby behaves at the check-up, while babies born early need this factor taken into account since it can affect their rate of progress.

Your baby's physical checks

Your baby will have changed a lot since her last main check. Now she'll be babbling, sitting up, and really aware of the world around her. For this reason, your baby's development will play a larger part in her six to nine month check-up.

● **Is she growing normally?** Your baby's length, weight, and head circumference will be compared to previous measurements to make sure her growth rate is normal.

● **Is her fontanele closing?** The fontanele, or soft spot, at the front of her head will be checked. By six months it should be getting smaller, and by nine months it may even have closed.

● **Are her hips and legs okay?** Although your child's hips and legs were checked at her six to eight week review, hip dislocation can still occur in older babies as well as in newborns.

● **Is her eyesight alright?** This will be assessed for a number of reasons, including: to make sure that she can focus clearly on an object held three metres (10 feet) away from her; and to check that she can follow a moving object at this distance.

● **Can she hear clearly?** In order to check your baby's hearing, your GP or health visitor will probably shake a rattle or whisper just behind your baby's head to see if she turns round to find out where the noise is coming from. Not all babies respond first time, especially if they are absorbed in something else, feeling sleepy, or have a cold. If this is the case, you will be asked back for another assessment at a later date to make sure that her hearing is fine.

- **Can she bear her own weight?** By nine months of age your baby should be strong enough to be able to take all her own weight on her feet if you hold both her hands to help her balance.
- **Can she feed herself finger food?** Your baby's hand–eye coordination and manipulation skills should be good enough at nine months for her to pick up small pieces of food and put them in her mouth.
- **Can she reach for and hold objects?**
- **Can she swap an object easily from one hand to the other?**
- **Does she look for dropped or hidden toys?**
- **Does she enjoy playing sociable games, such as peekaboo?**
- **Is she communicating with you?** You'll be asked whether your baby is babbling (making sounds such as "ba-ba", "da-da", etc.). Your GP or health visitor will also watch to see if she's interested in listening to you talk, and how she manages to get your attention.

Your baby's developmental checks

At this age, most GPs or health visitors check a baby's development simply by watching the way she behaves and interacts with you, and by asking you about how she's doing at home. Questions they will usually ask include the following:

- **Can she sit alone?** By nine months, your baby's balance should be good enough for her to manage sitting up unsupported.
- **Is she attempting to crawl?** Don't worry if your baby hasn't mastered crawling yet as long as she is trying to get mobile – for example, rolling over or shuffling on her bottom to get a toy she wants that's just out of reach.

Questions for you to ask

Your baby's developmental reviews are a great chance for you to raise any concerns you may have – whether they are about your baby's health, her development, or just general parenting issues. It's a good idea to make a written note of any questions you want to ask before you go to the clinic. These may include, for example:

★ how to wean your baby from the breast or bottle onto a beaker

★ how to stop night feeds

★ how to help your baby sleep though the night.

At the same time you may be given useful information by the health visitor about general health and safety issues, such as how to make sure your baby has a healthy diet, how to protect her against sunburn, and how to keep her safe in the car.

Keeping records

From the time he is born until he starts school, all aspects of your child's health development will be checked regularly. Keeping records is important to ensure that your baby is progressing well; it also provides a useful history of your baby's well-being. You, your health visitor, and your GP can record everything to do with your baby's health and development in his Child Health Development Book (*see pp.76–77*).

Growth charts

At every check, including the six to nine month review (*pp.76–77*), your GP or health visitor will note your baby's weight, height, and head circumference and record the results on a centile chart in his baby development book.

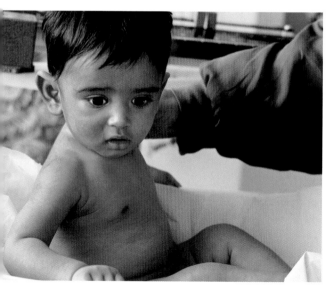

WEIGHING
During the second half of his first year your baby's weight gain will be slower than during the first half. This is perfectly normal, as are fluctuations – especially when he is unwell or going through a fussy period about eating his food.

These graphs, based on statistics, show the rate at which your baby is growing. There is a separate chart for girls and boys – usually pink for girls, and blue for boys! – and in each chart the middle line marks what is called the 50th percentile. This means that if you take 100 babies, 50 will be heavier and taller than the 50th line (above it) and 50 will be lighter and smaller (below it).

Plotting the measurements

Your baby's height will be plotted on one centile chart and his length on another; all you or your health visitor has to do is find the age of your baby in months at the bottom of the chart, and his length or weight in centimetres or inches on the left-hand side of the chart. The spot where the age and length or weight meet is marked with a cross. Each cross is then joined up to make a curve.

What to expect

As long as your baby's chart shows that he is growing steadily, there is nothing to worry about. Most babies are on the same percentile for both their weight and height, and stay roughly on the same percentile during their first year, although there will be small fluctuations. These fluctuations are nothing to worry about – babies can

Immunization schedules

Included in your baby's Child Health Development Book is a record of his immunizations. It's important that all immunizations are recorded here so that your GP or health visitor knows which ones your baby has already had, and whether he suffered any adverse reaction.

Your baby should already have had the immunizations listed in the table below during his first few months of life, although immunization schedules do vary greatly from one country to another. If, for any reason, your baby has missed any or all of these vaccinations, it is important that you contact your GP. As long as your baby is well and has not suffered any previous side-effects, he can still be immunized whatever his age.

It's largely down to successful immunization programmes that major childhood diseases such as diphtheria and polio are now rare. But we can't forget about them – all the diseases children are vaccinated against can be dangerous, and if immunization rates fall the diseases could become commonplace again. Some immunizations such as DTP and Hib are available in combined forms, which means your baby needs fewer injections. Ask your GP about this.

After being immunized, your baby may appear fussed and tired. He may also have a slight temperature, and the area where he had the injection may be red and sensitive. These are all normal reactions and can be treated with infant paracetamol.

Vaccine	To protect against	Age usually given	Method
DTP	Diphtheria, tetanus, pertussis (whooping cough)	Two, three, and four months	Injection
PV	Polio	Two, three, and four months	Injection or oral drops
Hib	Haemophilus influenza type B	Two, three, and four months	Injection

have periods of rapid growth and then slow down again for a while. Centile charts are just guidelines, and it is the general pattern over several months that is important.

Only significant changes are cause for concern – if, for example, your baby's weight starts to fall into the lower or climb into the higher percentiles, or if there is a wide discrepancy between length and weight.

Medical history

Keeping a record of your baby's illnesses and particular treatments is useful if your GP needs to know anything about his medical history. Faced with a sick baby, most parents feel anxious and may find it hard to rely purely on memory. Any notes you have to hand to give your GP will help him with important information, such as which childhood illnesses your baby has already had,

if he is prone to certain kinds of illnesses, and whether he has ever suffered an allergic reaction to a certain type of medication.

Details of illness

If there is no space in your baby's Child Health Development Book, keep your records in a separate notebook. Include:

- the date when your baby became unwell
- the date when he recovered
- what his symptoms were
- when you went to see or called your GP
- what the diagnosis was
- what instructions your GP gave you
- what medication was prescribed and for how long
- if there were any side-effects from the medication.

Teething

Spotting your baby's first tooth is an exciting moment. First teeth usually make an appearance between six and nine months, although some babies cut theirs as early as three months or as late as 12 months. Other babies are even born with a tooth already in place. Like lots of changes in your baby over the next few months, teething is affected by hereditary factors, and every child's circumstances are unique.

Changes in behaviour

When your baby begins to teethe, don't be surprised if you notice a change in her general behaviour. She may, for example, now refuse to drink from her beaker, having previously delighted in the independence it gave her, or insist on being held all the time when before she was quite happy to have periods sitting and playing by herself. Pain or discomfort from teeth can temporarily affect a baby's pace of development and there may be

some regression with previously acquired skills. Once she's feeling like her old self again, your baby will quickly pick up where she left off and continue to make progress.

How her teeth grow

Most babies first start to lose their gummy grins at about six months when the bottom front teeth, known as the lower central incisors (the cutting teeth), appear. The upper central incisors come next, at between six and eight months, and the four lateral incisors break through at around nine months. Next come the four front molars (the flat grinding teeth) between 10 and 14 months, followed by the canines (the pointed eye teeth) and the front molars at between 16 and 18 months. Your baby's back molars probably won't appear until she's nearing her second birthday. Most babies have all 20 milk teeth by the time they are two and a half.

Is she teething?

Many babies show no obvious signs of teething, and you may be taken by surprise when her first tooth pops up through her gum. Other babies, however, are fretful and irritable, sometimes for a couple of months before a new tooth appears. It can be difficult knowing whether this unhappiness is being caused by something else such as illness (*see below*). But common signs of teething may include one, or all, of the following:

- swollen, reddened gums
- excessive drooling
- an inflamed cheek
- mild cough
- low-grade fever
- biting down on anything she can get in her mouth.

Teething and illness

Complaints such as those listed below are often blamed on teething, but should be treated as separate illnesses.

- **High temperatures.** A fever of 38˚C (100.4˚F) or higher for more than 24 hours could be a sign of infection. Give your baby infant paracetamol, and if the fever continues for more than one day see your doctor.
- **Diarrhoea.** This is serious since babies can become dehydrated very quickly. Give her plenty of fluids, and if it continues for more than 24 hours call your doctor.
- **Earache.** If your baby is tugging at her ear, she may have an infection that could cause damage to her ear. It can also become painful very quickly. Call your doctor.
- **Chest infections.** A mild cough is common when teething, since the excessive saliva produces extra mucus. If your baby has a temperature and has difficulty breathing, she may have a chest infection. Call your doctor.

Caring for her teeth

As your baby's teeth appear, start cleaning them twice a day with a child's soft toothbrush and add a pea-sized blob of toothpaste when she's able to spit out. If she won't open her mouth for a toothbrush, use a clean finger. Encourage her to spit out, not swallow, the toothpaste. You should also avoid giving her sugary snacks, sweets, and drinks in between meals, and never give her sugared dummies, fruit juice, or honey drinks at bedtime.

Soothing your baby

If your baby is cranky, she'll need soothing. Check first that there isn't an underlying cause such as illness (*see below left*). Otherwise, the following suggestions may help:

★ Something cold to chew on – teething rings, any clean, age-appropriate toy such as a rattle, or even a frozen bagel may all help, but remember never to leave your baby alone with food in case she chokes.

★ A gum massage: pressing down on her gums with a clean finger may give her relief.

★ Teething gels. Available from your local pharmacist, these gels contain a mild local anaesthetic that can temporarily ease the pain, although they may quickly wash out of your baby's mouth.

★ Lots to drink, especially if your baby is drooling a lot and needs the extra fluids. Try cooled, boiled water or diluted fruit juice.

★ An occasional dose of sugar-free infant paracetamol for mild temperatures over 38˚C (100.4˚F).

Healthy eating

As your baby learns how to sit up properly, grip a spoon, and discover how to feed himself over the next few months, he will become an active participant in family meals. And he'll love it when you all eat together. Mealtimes will also become easier for you as he starts to enjoy the same food as everyone else.

The number of foods you can now give your baby is rapidly expanding. It's also a good time to set healthy eating patterns that will benefit him for the rest of his life. Advice on which foods are suitable can sometimes change, so check also with a health visitor or at your baby clinic.

Eating for healthy growth

As your baby enters the second half of his first year, he should have two or three meals a day in addition to breast or formula milk, which is still part of his main diet. He can try most family foods, as long as they do not contain added salt and are not too sweet. Introduce them one at a time to check he has no allergies or sensitivities.

Once your baby has been on solids for a couple of months, move on from purées to mashed or chopped foods with more texture. From nine to 10 months old, he should be happy to eat family meals such as chicken casserole or cauliflower cheese as long as there is no added salt, but remember that if three meals a day is not possible then eating little and often can be just as good.

Encouraging healthy eating for life

One of the best ways you can help your baby to grow up fit and healthy – and stay that way – is to encourage him to develop healthy eating habits now.

● **Introduce variety in the form of different tastes, colours, and textures.** This will keep him interested in

THE RIGHT DIET
The key to eating well at this age is to make sure that your baby has a wide variety of foods – cooked and uncooked – from each of the four main food groups (see box), and nutritious snacks to keep his energy levels up.

The right foods to give

Your baby should have at least one portion of fish, meat, egg, lentils, or beans every day, since these are the best sources of protein and iron. By the time your baby is six months old, the stores of iron with which he was born are used up, and milk alone will not provide all his daily requirements. Give your baby food from each of the four main food groups every day:

★ **Dairy products** such as cheese, yogurt, or full-fat fromage frais. Until he is 12 months old, your baby still needs about 500-600ml (17-20fl oz) of breast or formula milk a day. Although he can't have cow's milk as a drink until he is one year old, you can now start to add cow's milk in small quantities to a cheese sauce, for example, or to his breakfast cereal.

★ **Starchy foods** such as potatoes, bread, noodles, rice, pasta, couscous, and breakfast cereals. Foods containing gluten are now fine to try.

★ **Fruit and vegetables** – increase the variety.

★ **Meat and meat alternatives.** Start your baby off with some soft, white flaked fish such as cod or haddock, or some well-minced chicken or lamb. He will also enjoy small quantities of well-cooked lentils or beans. Eggs are okay if they are also well cooked: try a hard-boiled egg, or strips of cooled omelette. Start by giving him the yolk of the egg only, since it is less likely to cause an allergy. Many nutritionists recommend cooked egg white only after your baby is one year old.

his food; even small babies get bored with the same food every day. Don't worry if he leaves something new: babies' tastes are fickle and he may try it again tomorrow.

● **Praise him when he eats well.** If you want your baby to love natural, healthy foods, make sure he's offered plenty of it, and give him lots of praise when he eats it.

● **Avoid sugary "treats".** Sugar, which suppresses the appetite and is harmful to teeth, can easily be avoided altogether for your baby's first year. If your baby gets used to the idea that sugary foods are a special treat now, he'll quickly think they are a good thing – and studies show that babies who are exposed to sugar early on develop a stronger taste for it than those who haven't been offered it so early on.

● **Offer healthy snacks.** Babies use up lots of energy, and once they are on the move they can quickly become hungry again. Boost your baby's energy with nutritious snacks such as little pieces of fruit (fresh or dried), natural yogurt, rice cakes, and breadsticks.

● **Avoid fast food.** Take healthy foods with you for mealtimes when you are out and about with your child so that you don't have to rely on fast food restaurants; chips, hamburgers, sausages, and soft drinks are all high in fats, salt, and sugar and may contain lots of additives, which should be avoided.

Foods to avoid

At this age there are still certain foods that are not suitable for your baby to try. These include:

● **Salt, sugar, and honey** (sweeten desserts with mashed banana instead).

● **Fruit squashes and diet drinks.** If you want to offer your baby an alternative drink to milk at mealtimes, give him diluted, unsweetened fruit juice.

● **Foods that carry a high risk of food poisoning.** These include foods such as mould-ripened cheese, liver paté, and soft-boiled eggs.

● **Nuts.** Avoid all nuts and nut products containing peanuts, especially if your family is known to have a history of allergies.

● **Low-fat and high-fibre foods.** Babies need more calories and less bulk to give them the energy they need to grow.

● **Foods that present a choking hazard.** These include whole grapes, nuts, popcorn, large pieces of apple or raw carrot, uncooked peas, and celery. Even hamburgers and hot dogs are a risk unless they are well chopped up.

Learning to eat

At around six or seven months old, your baby's developmental progress means that mealtimes are becoming a very different affair. Now she can sit up unaided, you'll need to invest in a highchair. She'll enjoy watching you get her food ready, but if she can't wait try keeping her busy with a selection of toys on her tray attachment.

Learning to chew

You need to start introducing your baby to lumpier foods if you want her to develop chewing skills, but don't imagine she can cope with a steak just because her first teeth have appeared! She'll still use her gums to chew for a while yet and needs her food lightly mashed until she is around one year old – although softer food such as bread or pasta can be left whole if you wish.

Some babies don't take kindly to finding lumps in their previously puréed food, and may react by spitting them out. If your baby does this, don't rush her: learning how to chew is quite a difficult exercise, especially as she has only known how to suck until now. Instead, offer her finger foods (*see below*) as soon as she can hold them, to help her practise chewing and explore new textures.

Introducing finger foods

By seven months, your baby will probably be eager to start finger foods. Her hand–eye coordination has improved to such an extent that she can now pick up

CHEWING PRACTICE
Learning how to chew is important not only because it will increase the range of foods your baby can eat, but also because it helps him practise moving his mouth and tongue, ready to learn how to talk.

a piece of food and put it to her mouth, albeit none too tidily. For now she'll hold the food in her fist and work hard to push the last messy mouthful in with the flat of her hand. By nine months, however, she has better control of her thumb and forefinger, and with this pincer grip she can pick up tiny pieces of food such as raisins or peas.

First finger foods for your baby are those that can be gummed to a soft consistency for swallowing or that will dissolve in the mouth without chewing. Always cut food into manageable chunks and don't offer too much at a time: she'll either try to stuff it in all at once or sweep the lot onto the floor. Foods to try include:

- bread, rice cakes, toast
- tiny cubes of hard cheese
- chunks of soft fruit such as banana, peach, or melon
- small pieces of cooked carrot, broccoli and cauliflower (cut the stalks off), sweet potato
- well-cooked pasta – cut up as necessary
- scrambled egg.

Once your baby's front molars appear – from about 10 months onwards – you can offer her harder, firmer food such as pieces of apple or small pieces of chicken. And remember always to stay with your baby when she's eating, in case of choking.

Trying to self-feed

Babies like to try feeding themselves with a spoon from an early age. Until she's nine months or so, your baby will probably keep overturning the spoon before it reaches her mouth, so it is worth remembering these points.

- Self-feeding is an important step forwards and boosts your baby's confidence and independence.
- She needs lots of practice, which means it's important to ignore the mess! Rather than be tempted to take over, put a mat under her highchair to catch spillages and dropped food, and remind yourself that this phase passes.
- Make sure she's getting enough food in her mouth by

Weaning to a beaker

This is a good time to introduce a two-handled beaker in place of a bottle or breastfeed at lunchtime. You'll have to show your baby how to move it to her mouth and tip the liquid out, and it will be a while before she's happy to take all her daily milk quota this way. Be patient – moving off her bottle will help improve her speech development, and drinks from a beaker spend less time in contact with her teeth so it's better for her dental health. It's also beneficial to wean your baby off her bottle earlier rather than later so that she doesn't become attached to it as a security object.

slipping in mouthfuls of food with your own spoon in between her attempts. Later on you may only need to help with loading up her spoon.

When she won't eat

There will be times when your baby rejects her food. It may be that she just isn't hungry today, she's teething, or that there are distractions in the room. Never force-feed your child, and avoid making mealtimes a battle. She may play with her food, which is perfectly normal, but if she is bored and does not want any more, take it away and try again later. However, talk to your GP or health visitor if you are concerned about your baby's diet.

Sleeping

Sleep – or lack of it – is a major issue for most parents. But sleep is vital for babies, too, so that they can grow and develop properly: it is during sleep that growth hormones are released and new cells grow fastest. Not enough sleep can make an otherwise happy baby irritable, difficult, and maybe less responsive.

By the time your baby is six months old he should be able to sleep through the night. If he isn't sleeping through, there are steps you can take to help give you both a good night's rest. But that doesn't mean your baby will go through every night without a problem: as he experiences separation anxiety (pp.70–71), for example, he may start waking again and looking for you for comfort.

How much sleep does he need?

While newborn babies tend to sleep for as many as 18 hours out of 24, by the time they are six months old many babies need 12 to 14 hours of sleep in a 24-hour period, including a couple of one- or two-hour naps. This arrangement may not last long, however. Within a few months your baby may drop one daytime nap – usually the mid-morning rest – while a few babies decide to drop both naps and want to stay awake all day!

Are daytime naps important?

Daytime naps provide welcome and much-needed free time for you. The more rested your baby is, the happier he'll be during the day and easier to settle at night.

Some babies are naturally more wakeful than others, however. If your baby seems content without his regular morning or afternoon nap and settles easily at night, then the chances are he's found a balance that works well for him.

But if he seems tired and fussy, yet resists a daytime nap, it may be that he just finds life around him too exciting and doesn't want to leave it even for a second. As his daytime nap draws near, try not to overstimulate him. Keep him calm and quiet and try putting him down

SLEEPING PRACTICE
Encouraging your baby to drift off to sleep in her cot on her own helps her establish good sleeping patterns.

for a sleep before he becomes overtired. Make sure the room is dark and quiet with nothing to distract him. If he still resists, and you're faced with the prospect of dealing with a cranky baby for the rest of the day, you could try taking him out for a walk or a drive in the car. Lots of babies nod off when they are on the move, and even a 20-minute nap in his buggy or car seat will refresh him for the rest of the day.

When will he sleep through the night?

Every new parent is desperate for this moment to arrive! While, very occasionally, some newborn babies will give their parents an unbroken night after six to eight weeks, most won't sleep for more than five hours or so at a stretch until they are over three months old. But by the time babies are six months old – when they no longer need a night feed (*see box*) – they should be able to sleep through the night for anything up to 11 or 12 hours.

However, even though your baby may be physically ready to sleep through the night, he may still find it hard. This may be because he is ill or teething, or experiencing separation anxiety. But often babies wake in the night simply because of their sleep pattern. During a normal night your baby will alternate between periods of deep sleep and light sleep. During these lighter sleeps – which can occur five or six times in a night – it's not unusual for babies to wake up and open their eyes, and even cry out if they can't see or feel you.

Settling back to sleep

Babies who depend on being nursed, rocked, or cuddled to sleep at bedtime will find it especially hard to settle themselves back down again if they wake during these lighter sleeping patterns. However, if you have established a good bedtime routine for your baby (*pp.88–89*), and he is used to settling himself down, he should quickly fall back into a deep sleep pattern again.

Feeding at night

By the time your baby is six months old, he should be able to sleep happily through the night if he is thriving and is established in a good routine (*see left*). If he is still waking and demanding a feed, it's more likely to be out of habit or for comfort than because he's hungry, especially if you've recently started to wean him. At this age there is no physical reason for feeding your baby during the night.

Breastfed babies, however, find it particularly hard to give up a night-time cuddle. One solution is to ask your partner to try and settle your baby back to sleep when your baby wakes. If he can't smell your breast milk, he's more likely to drop off again. It may take a while but eventually he'll stop waking altogether.

Bedtime routines

You can avoid many sleep problems by helping your baby develop good sleeping habits. Even if it's been hard to get her into a good night-time routine when she was younger, six months is not too late to start. And although illness, or even a change of environment, may unsettle her, once she's recovered or you are back in familiar surroundings, your baby should soon settle back into her old routine.

There are several methods you can try to help your baby get to sleep, and encourage her to learn how to sleep through the night without needing attention from you.

Follow a bedtime routine

The first step to helping your baby sleep well at night is to make sure she has a regular bedtime routine. By the age of six months she has a greater understanding of the world, and is starting to recognize her daily rituals.

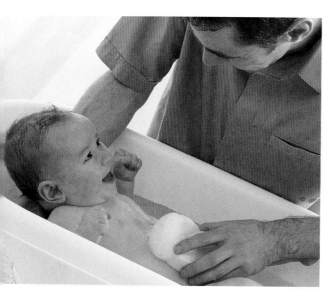

If you follow the same routine every night she'll quickly know what to expect and will soon understand that when it's night-time it's a time to sleep, not play. Lots of parents start the bedtime routine with a warm, relaxing bath followed by a bedtime story, final feed, teeth-brushing, and into bed. The key is to help your baby unwind, so avoid any stimulating activities.

Let her cuddle a comfort

Now your baby can roll over unaided, you may like to try putting her to sleep with a special comfort blanket, a muslin square, or a soft toy that meets all the required safety standards – but make sure that she can't be smothered by the toy. If a favourite teddy or something similar is waiting in bed for her every night, she'll quickly start to associate it with going to sleep. And after a while, if she wakes in the night, the teddy's comforting presence may help her drop off again. Try cuddling the teddy yourself so that it smells of you, then she'll feel like she has a little piece of you with her during the night.

BATH-TIME BONDING
Bath time is an important opportunity for a mum or dad to spend intimate time with their baby as they settle him down ready for bedtime.

Say goodnight while she's awake

Rocking, cuddling, or feeding a baby to sleep are major causes of sleep problems. Although it's tempting to let your baby fall asleep in your arms, this won't help her learn how to drop off to sleep again on her own when she wakes in the night. The key to developing a good sleeping pattern is to put her to bed when she's calm but still awake, give her a kiss goodnight, and leave the room.

Let her cry for a while

Most babies, especially those who are used to dropping off in a parent's arms, have trouble sleeping this way to begin with. If your baby cries out as you leave the room, try not to go back immediately. She needs a chance to cry, stop crying, and then lie there until sleep comes. When her crying sounds more desperate, go back, kiss her, tell her she's okay, and then leave again. You may have to do this repeatedly over several hours before your baby finally drops off. But it's worth persevering now, and for the next few nights. By the sixth or seventh night, most babies will learn that they are fine without you and discover that they can get themselves to sleep.

If she wakes in the night...

It can be much harder to stay calm if your baby wakes in the night. Sometimes rocking or feeding her back to sleep will seem like the fastest and easiest option, but this will prolong – not solve – the problem of night-time waking. Instead, resolve to follow the same technique as before: go to her, check she's safe, kiss her, and reassure her that she's okay before leaving the room again. At six months old your baby should be secure enough in your love for her to accept being left on her own. Although you'll find it emotionally and physically exhausting initially, remember that it is worth persevering! For most babies, it doesn't take more than a few nights to break the night-waking habit.

Into a separate room

Most parents like having their baby sleep in the same room as themselves – a practice that is commonplace around the world – and some medical experts agree that this is a good idea.

Once a baby is in the second half of her first year, she can make the move into a separate room if you wish. At this age babies can be easily disturbed while they sleep and may actually wake up when you come to bed or if you cough or turn over during the night. At this age a baby will also be able to keep herself awake if she's disturbed; something she couldn't do when she was younger.

If you do want to move your baby into another room, choose a time when she isn't having to cope with many other changes, such getting used to a new childminder. Also, if she's experiencing separation anxiety it would be a good option to keep her with you in your room until she's settled again.

Communication

From the day your baby is born, he is communicating with you. Initially this is just by crying; later by smiling, too, and from six months old onwards he'll use a whole range of signs and gestures. It will be many months yet before your baby can actually say his first words, but that isn't going to stop him expressing himself!

It is also the case that your baby doesn't need to know how to talk in order to understand what you say to him. In fact, a baby's understanding of language naturally develops faster than his ability to use it.

Understanding first

Babies learn how to talk at such different rates that their receptive language – how well a baby understands what is said to them – is a much better sign of the progress they are really making.

You can see this in lots of different ways. First you may notice your child turn to you when he hears his name. Then by around nine months, for example, you'll notice that he is beginning to recognize lots of words that name familiar people or objects, such as "beaker" or "teddy". He'll laugh in the right places when you sing certain songs, look for his beaker when you ask him where it is, and follow simple commands such as "Kiss mummy".

Some babies do say their first words before their first birthday (and these are usually recognizable only by their family!), but many children don't utter any

PREPARING TO TALK
By the end of his first year, your baby will be getting ready to talk – and the more you respond to him as though he is speaking, the more you'll stimulate his desire to communicate.

understandable words until they are around 13 months old. Some children are still making themselves understood with signs and gestures well into their second year. As long as your baby seems to understand what you are saying, the chances are his speech will develop normally.

Using signs and gestures

As your baby's understanding of language is developing, so, too, is his ability to express himself with signs and gestures – another important stage in language development. He loves communicating with you, and is very creative in finding ways of letting you know what he wants. For example:

● from around seven months he may open and shut his hand when he wants something, and shake his head or push you away if you are doing something he doesn't like. Watch his face, too: his expressions will let you know if he's cross, happy, or frightened.

● from around nine months old he may start pointing at what he wants, wave goodbye to you, and lift his arms in the air to show he wants to be picked up.

● from around 10 months he may be able to follow simple questions such as "Do you want a drink?" and respond by shaking or nodding his head.

Though these signs and gestures are a stop-gap until your baby learns how to talk, it's important to try and decipher them and show that you understand. Seeing you respond correctly fills him with confidence, develops his trust in you, and encourages his desire to communicate.

From first sounds to first words

As with all milestones, babies develop language skills at different rates, but their steps on the language ladder will usually progress in the same order:

● babbling is one of the first major steps, and usually starts at around six months old when babies gain control of their tongue, lips, and the palate of their mouth. Your

The importance of hearing

Being able to hear properly is vital for a baby's speech development since it encourages imitation, which in turn stimulates language skills. You'll notice that your baby's hearing is fine if the following occur:

★ by six or seven months he babbles, tries to imitate sounds, and turns to hear your voice across a room

★ by nine months he listens carefully to familiar everyday sounds such as a dog barking or the doorbell ringing

★ by one year he is responding when you say "No" or "Bye-bye".

Even partial hearing loss – caused, for example, by repeated ear infections – can interfere with speech development. If you are at all concerned about your baby's hearing, speak to your GP or health visitor who will be monitoring his reflexes and hearing ability.

baby will discover his consonants first, and usually utter sounds such as "ba" or "da".

● once your baby can control his sounds well enough he'll have great fun repeating them over and over again, for example, "ba-ba-ba" or "da-da-da".

● at around eight months old he'll be producing double consonants that sound like real words – such as "ba-ba" or "da-da" (much to his father's delight!).

● between 10 and 12 months old, your baby will be stringing sounds together and using intonation in a way that sounds like real speech.

Eventually your baby's experiments with sounds will help him utter his first words – usually around his first birthday. But don't be surprised if he is only understood by you and other close family members who are familiar with the routines of his life and the words associated with them. These often aren't real words, but if you recognize what he wants and repeat the correct word back to him he will eventually begin to say the word properly.

Learning to talk

Hearing your baby's coos and gurgles turn into real words is a major thrill for you and a huge milestone for her. Learning to talk helps her discover more about the world around her, as well as bringing her closer to you. And while language learning is inbuilt – babies are natural communicators – the part you can play is crucial. With your help your baby discovers that, not only is talking important, it's fun too.

What to expect

From six months onwards your baby will start to make an incredible range of sounds and over the following months her happy babbling will start to resemble more and more the pattern, tone, and pitch of adult speech.

By the end of this year some babies may even be saying their first "words", such as "gog" for dog, or "dat" for cat. However, most children won't master all their spoken consonants until they are three or four years old, and some not until later.

Don't be surprised if, after getting off to a flying start, your baby doesn't learn any more new words for a while. It can take up to three or four months after their first few spoken words for babies to acquire many more words. This may be especially true if, at the same time as learning to talk, your baby is busy trying to master other skills such as walking.

Developing at different rates

If your baby has older brothers or sisters, you may find that she learns to talk later than your other children did. First children often do best since they have lots of one-to-one attention: mum and dad have more time to encourage and listen to them. And although second or third children might hear lots of chat going on around them, they may have little chance to practise their own talking – especially if their siblings try to translate for them! For this reason it is important to make special time alone for you and your baby.

Ways to help

Every time you talk to your baby she'll be soaking up new information about language, and if you talk in a way that makes it easier for her to listen and learn then you'll make the most of your time together.

● **Chat away.** Whatever you are doing with your baby, one of the best ways of helping her speech improve is by talking to her about your activity. Whether it is cooking her meal or changing her nappy, describe and show her what you are doing.

● **Give her a chance to respond.** Conversation is a two-way process and your baby will love taking turns with you, so remember to pause and wait for her "reply" when you are talking to her.

● **Keep it simple**. Use short, simple sentences and try not to speak too fast. Your baby needs time to understand what you are saying and will miss anything that you say at speed.

At this age she's fascinated by lots of everyday objects such as the kettle or washing machine.

- **Repeat correctly.** If she has begun to say sounds such as "wa-wa" for water or "nana" for banana, build her confidence by using the correct word ("Would you like some water?" or "Here's your banana") to show her that you know what she's saying. Eventually she'll learn from you how to say the word correctly.
- **Play games together.** Action songs, peekaboo, and clapping games are great fun for your baby – she'll also love anticipating what comes next and the repetition will help her learn familiar words.

First books

Your baby may be too young to concentrate on proper stories but looking at books together is invaluable for helping her communication skills. Try to find time every day for sitting and reading quietly together. Point at the pictures to encourage your baby to look too. Use lots of emphasis and exclamation to hold her attention.

- **Use lots of expression and emphasis.** This will add interest for your baby, especially if you exaggerate your expression sometimes for fun and use humour.
- **Be consistent.** Try to use the same words for the same objects – using "beaker" one day and "cup" the next will only confuse her.
- **Help her listen.** Your baby learns to listen better if she has no distractions, so cut out any background noise.
- **Follow her lead.** When you see your baby looking with interest at something or pointing, tell her what it is.

Choosing books

When choosing books, look for:

★ sturdy board books that will survive chewing, throwing, and tearing; vinyl books are particularly good for bath time

★ large illustrations or photographs that are bright and bold

★ realistic, recognizable pictures of animals and objects

★ books that will help your baby learn to make animal noises

★ simple rhymes or one-word-per-page books

★ activity books such as "touch and feel" books to help your baby learn about texture, or books that encourage games such as peekaboo.

Safety

As your baby becomes more active, you'll need to be increasingly aware of his safety. As soon as he can roll himself over, for example, he risks falling off the changing table. Then once he gets moving he can reach dangerous places, open forbidden cupboards, even touch and taste things that could harm him.

Young babies are naturally driven to explore the world around them, yet they have no sense of the potential dangers of their environment. And although your baby will start to recognize the word "no" at this age, you can't rely on him remembering what it is he can and can't do.

Your baby needs space and a sense of freedom to stimulate his development – so being overprotective in order to avoid accidents isn't the answer. Instead:

● provide a safe environment for him to explore
● be aware of potential problems to prevent accidents before they happen

● supervise him all the time; babies should never be left alone unless they are asleep in a cot or safe in a playpen
● get down on your tummy to play with your baby – this will give you the best chance of seeing what's safe, and what isn't, in your home.

Around the home

● fit stair gates when your baby shows signs of crawling
● use anti-slam devices on doors to avoid crushed fingers
● avoid using a baby walker – your child could tip over
● fit window locks
● use a five-point harness to keep him in his highchair
● keep any furniture he could climb on right away from windows
● fit corner guards to any sharp corners on cupboards and table edges
● check that there is no furniture your baby could pull over on top of himself
● check banisters and railings on landings or balconies to make sure he can't fall through, over, or under them
● check floors regularly for dangerously small items such as buttons, batteries, loose coins, or safety pins
● keep matches and lighters out of reach and out of sight
● cover electric sockets with heavy furniture or with safety socket covers
● fit smoke detectors and check batteries every week.

Hygiene

⭐ replace or rinse any toy, food, or beaker that your baby has dropped in the street

⭐ don't let your baby eat food that he's dropped in the bathroom, puddles, or other damp or wet surfaces

⭐ don't let him eat something he mouthed and then left lying around for more than an hour or so

⭐ keep rubbish bins and pet food well out of your baby's reach.

In the kitchen

- store sharp implements well out of reach
- never leave hot drinks on tables or on the floor, and don't use tablecloths – your baby could tug on it and pull hot objects on to himself
- never hold a hot drink if you are carrying your baby, and watch for him crawling if you walk with a hot drink
- always supervise your baby when he is eating or drinking, to prevent him choking
- use back burners on the cooker and turn pan handles inwards and out of reach – or use a pan guard
- avoid trailing flexes
- be aware that oven doors and radiators get very hot
- use safety catches on cupboards and keep cupboards that contain household cleaners and cleaning fluids locked
- cover refrigerated, cooked food, and do not reheat it.

In the bathroom

- never leave your baby unsupervised in the bath since young children can drown in only a few centimetres of water
- use a non-slip mat in the bath
- turn the cold tap on first when running the bath and test the water before putting your child in
- keep your baby away from the hot tap in the bath or wrap a flannel around it and turn it off tightly

- turn the thermostat on your hot water heater to 48°C (120°F) to avoid scalding water
- lock medicines and razors out of reach in a cupboard
- keep the toilet seat down and remove the toilet brush.

In the bedroom

- once your baby can stand, check there are no toys in his cot he could use to climb out
- keep his cot well away from the window
- once he can get on all fours, remove hanging mobiles
- never leave him alone on a changing table.

In the sitting room

- always use fireguards around fires and heaters and make sure the guard is firmly fixed to the wall
- clear away left-over alcoholic drinks.

Out and about

- keep garden tools and chemicals safely locked away
- always use a harness in the pram/buggy
- remove any poisonous plants from your garden
- never leave your baby alone with or near water.

SAFETY COMES FIRST
Your baby will find all sorts of ways to investigate the world around him. Ensure that you don't leave anything dangerous on low surfaces, such as cups of hot coffee, that could spill and hurt him.

Massaging your baby

When your baby is born, the first thing you instinctively do is lovingly touch her. Physical contact, whether it's cuddling, stroking, kissing, or rocking, comes naturally and helps you develop a close relationship with your baby. It's also vital for her emotional well-being, showing that you love her and building her sense of self-worth.

Lots of mothers and fathers use baby massage to enhance their relationship with their baby. It is a wonderful way of expressing your feelings while fulfilling your baby's emotional need for skin-to-skin contact. But massage has physical benefits too, and can be used to ease lots of minor baby niggles.

Good for your baby

Massage has lots of emotional and physical benefits for your baby, including:

★ helping develop a close and trusting relationship with you

★ calming her when she's fretful – massage reduces the circulation of the stress hormone cortisol in the bloodstream

★ increasing her sense of well-being – massage also stimulates endorphins, which can lift your baby's mood

★ easing wind and constipation – stroking her tummy can help disperse trapped air

★ releasing tension caused by, for example, teething

★ relaxing arm and leg muscles and helping your baby become more mobile.

Baby massage can also be calming and relaxing for you, and knowing that your touch is comforting your baby can make you feel happy and confident as a parent.

When to do it

The best times for a massage include:

● **between meals** – if your baby has just eaten she'll feel uncomfortable during a massage, and if she is hungry she won't feel settled

● **last thing at night after her bath** – she'll be naturally relaxed and responsive

● **when there are no other distractions** – if the house is quiet and you are not expecting visitors, you'll be able to focus on your baby without interruption.

Don't massage your baby if she is unwell, she obviously doesn't want to be massaged, or if she's just been immunized – the area of the injection may still be sore.

How to begin

● **Make sure the room is warm,** with no distractions

● **Wash your hands** and dry them thoroughly, and take off any jewellery.

● **Make sure your hands are warm;** rub them together first if they feel cold to the touch.

● **Use a specially formulated baby oil or lotion** that is labelled as 100 per cent safe. Don't use products containing arachis oil since this contains peanut oil and may cause a reaction.

● **Undress your baby** and lie her down on a soft, warm towel on your lap or on the floor.

Head and face

2 Gently massage
her forehead,
working from the centre
out and moving over
the eyebrows and cheeks
towards her ears.

1 Stroking and kissing your baby's face
helps release tension. Try using your
thumbs to make smiles on her upper and
lower lips. Use a circular motion on her
crown and then stroke down the sides
of her face.

Arms and hands

2 Open one of her hands gently and rub
it between your palms, then massage
her palm and the back of her hand with
your thumb and index fingers.

3 Spread her
fingers and
thumb, and one
by one pull each
finger gently
through your
thumb and
forefinger. Then
repeat with her
other hand.

1 Massage one arm at a time. Stroke
down her arm to her fingertips, then
using your finger and thumb gently squeeze
all along her arm, starting at the top.

Tummy

1 Place both hands in the centre of your baby's chest and push gently out towards the sides, following your baby's rib cage. Without lifting your hands, bring them back round in a heart-shaped motion to the centre.

2 Gently stroke her tummy using one hand in a circular clockwise motion, then walk your fingertips along her tummy from left to right.

Legs

1 As with your baby's arms, massage one leg at a time. Work from the thigh down, gently squeezing as you go.

2 Finish by gently pulling her whole leg and foot through your hands.

Feet

1 Gently knead and rub the top of each foot and roll each toe between your forefinger and thumb, separating her toes.

2 Use your thumb to rub the sole of her foot. Finish by gently pulling each toe with your fingers.

How babies learn

Over the next few months your baby is going to learn an astonishing amount. She will discover how to sit, crawl, and maybe walk, how to pick up a small object, how to recognize her family, point to what she needs, or make you laugh – and that's just for starters!

How babies learn skills

Your baby's mastery of her physical and mental skills is staggering, especially when you think how she started life – as a tiny bundle only just starting to gain a sense of herself and the world around her. So how do these incredible changes take place?

Genetics will play a part in how your baby develops, but much of her progress will also depend on the kind of stimulation and attention she receives from you. From the moment of her birth she is absorbing information from the world around her, and in particular from the people closest to her. In a way, you are your baby's first teacher. This isn't as overwhelming as it sounds since your baby's natural way of learning is through play and exploration: if she shakes a rattle and discovers that it makes a fantastic noise, she's learning about cause and effect; when she tries to crawl over a mountain of cushions you've built for her she's finding out how to balance and coordinate her limbs; and when she listens to you sing a nursery rhyme she's starting to understand the basis of language development.

Encouraging your baby

How is your baby motivated? Again, it's partly an inbuilt drive to discover and learn. But your encouragement and support is also incredibly important. When, for example, she eventually manages to wave goodbye as a friend leaves, it's your delight and praise that boosts her sense of achievement, and convinces her that learning is fun.

Taking your lead from your baby is key to motivating her. When she's ready to try a new challenge, you'll see the signs. Understanding how and when your baby develops can help you prepare for each stage and be ready with the right kind of games and activities to stretch her and fulfil her needs. In fact, making sure her family environment is fun and stimulating is one of the most valuable things you can do for her.

Playing with your baby also brings you closer together and helps develop your baby's self-esteem and sense of security, proving that you love her unconditionally for who she is, not just what she can do.

6 to 12 months: your baby's milestones

Your baby will master lots of new skills and reach many important milestones over the next few months. It's important to remember, however, that while each baby will reach all of the following milestones, the time it takes to reach them will vary from baby to baby. After all, every child develops differently.

If you ever become concerned about your baby's development, speak to your GP or health visitor – although, chances are, your baby will be progressing perfectly normally.

Movement milestones

By 12 months she will probably:
- sit unsupported
- crawl, or similar
- pull herself up to standing
- cruise, holding onto furniture
- stand momentarily without support
- maybe walk two or three steps on her own.

Hand and finger milestones

By 12 months she will probably:
- bang two blocks together
- feed herself finger foods
- put objects in a container and take them out again
- let go of objects in her hand when she wants to

- point with her finger
- use the pincer grip (hold a tiny object with her forefinger and thumb).

Social and emotional milestones

By 12 months she will probably:
- cry when you leave her
- cling to you if strangers directly approach her
- understand the meaning of "no"
- play jokes
- enjoy imitating people.

Language milestones

By 12 months she will probably:
- babble
- listen carefully to you when you talk to her
- respond to simple commands
- recognize her name and other familiar words
- use gestures such as shaking her head for "no"
- try to imitate words.

Intellectual milestones

By 12 months she will probably:
- find hidden objects easily
- explore objects in different ways (e.g. banging, throwing, dropping)
- understand cause and effect (when she shakes her rattle, it makes a noise)
- start to understand how objects are used (drink from a cup, brush her hair, listen into a telephone).

Some babies may also be able to stack blocks, for example, or say "mama" or "dada" with meaning. But these milestones aren't just about achievements, they are also about helping to ensure your baby's healthy emotional and social development.

6 to 7 months

Over halfway through her first year of life, and your baby is beginning to take a greater interest in the world around her. Now that she can sit upright she has a new perspective on her environment; she is also more sociable and remembers day-to-day routines, developing a true sense of herself as a unique person.

Physical development

Constantly exercising her body over the last few months has helped your baby develop her muscles, balance, and control.

Grabbing toys

Once she learns how to sit upright (*see box, right*) and no longer needs her arms to keep herself supported, your baby will be working hard to grab anything nearby that excites her, twisting round and stretching forwards. Make sure there are always some toys, safe household objects, or baby books nearby to keep her interested – but don't expect too much. Her concentration skills are still developing and even something she has never seen before will only hold her attention for a few minutes.

Hand–eye coordination

As her grip develops, your baby will be able to hold objects more firmly and steadily, turn them over to have a good look at them and then put them in her mouth, pass them from one hand to the other, and even bang two objects together.

As her hand–eye coordination improves she'll be grabbing a spoon as soon as it's in sight, and probably overturning it before it reaches her mouth. You may like to try offering her a two-handled cup to drink

from. Before too long, she may be drinking from it herself. You may also want to start offering her finger foods, such as a piece of bread or rice cake. To begin with she'll hold it in her fist, working hard to push the last mouthful in with the flat of her hand. In time, she'll learn how to hold food and other things between her thumb and forefinger. Never leave her alone with finger food in case she chokes.

Growing stronger

Your baby is growing stronger by the day and will be keen to flex her muscles and show off her skills. Some babies may even try to pull themselves up to a standing position from sitting by holding a parent's hands or piece of furniture. All of this is great practice for the next important milestones – learning to crawl, stand, and walk.

Social and emotional skills

Up until now your baby's main interests in life have been food, sleep, and you. Now her personality will begin to shine through.

Becoming sociable

You'll notice that your baby is becoming more sociable, turning to listen to voices around her. She'll also try and join in conversations,

Learning to sit

Thanks to all the wriggling, twisting, kicking, and stretching she has been practising in her first six months, your baby can now sit up on her own – at least for a few minutes, and probably longer. Sitting up enables her to look around more easily, watch family members coming and going, and reach out for toys to keep herself entertained – if only for a little while.

SITTING UP
As a precaution, keep cushions around your baby to break her fall. At first she may use her arms for support, but she won't need them for long.

responding to your chat not just with baby babble but also with a range of gestures and facial expressions. Watch her look at herself in a mirror, too. She doesn't realize that she is looking at herself but she is interested in the baby she sees, and will gurgle away in the hope of a response.

Loving you

Now that she can sit up on her own, your baby is much happier with her own company, but, as always, you are her favourite play thing. Has she dropped that toy again – and is she yelling for you to come and help? Maybe it's not the toy she's after, but a chance to smile and laugh with you.

The pleasure your baby takes in your company is a sign that she is forming a deep and genuine bond with you, her main carer. You may find towards the end of this month that if you vanish from sight for a moment, her bottom lip may begin to wobble as she fears you've gone forever. Return before the tears are in full flow, and she'll beam and bounce with happiness.

A sense of self

Part of this deepening attachment comes from her realization that she is a separate person to you. This is a huge and important milestone. Over the next few months she may be increasingly anxious when separated from you. This can be upsetting, but it is perfectly normal and often continues through toddlerhood.

Meanwhile she will also start to develop attachments to other important people in her life – her siblings, granny, or caregiver, for example. Gently encouraging these relationships will help her adapt to being without you when she needs to be cared for by someone else.

Activities to develop skills

There are several activities you can now enjoy playing with your baby to build up her physical coordination and social skills. Always remember to keep encouraging and praising her as she plays.

★ All babies love bubbles – and being able to pop them with their hands allows them to develop their hand–eye coordination as well as progress their understanding of cause and effect. Catch a bubble for your baby on the plastic wand and hold it right in front of her so she can reach out and pop it herself. Remember to clean her hands afterwards so she doesn't get soapy water in her eyes.

★ Encourage your baby's sense of fun by playing lots of bouncing games – hold her on your lap or on the bed and let her practise bouncing up and down, bearing as much weight as she can on her legs.

BOUNCING GAMES
Your baby will delight in the fun and movement of being swept up in the air and then bounced down again on your knees or a bed.

Language and intellectual skills

Your baby's everyday routines are now very familiar and she can also remember things that have happened before: she may start laughing even before you tickle her or say "Boo!"

Is it still there?

Your baby is also starting to learn about "object permanence". Up until now, when something disappears,

Toy box

Pop-up toys

Pop-up toys will give your baby much fun. If you buy toys with pop-up animal characters, you can make appropriate animal noises and play guessing games with her.

Bubbles

Bottles of bubble mixture and a plastic wand are cheap to buy and give great pleasure. Never let your baby grab hold of the wand or bottle.

Finger puppets

Use soft finger puppets with simply drawn faces that meet the right safety standards. Since your baby won't be able to hold them herself yet, they should also fit an adult's hands.

POP-UP TOYS
At this stage your baby will only be able to push the characters back down on the toy, but she will enjoy the satisfaction of making something disappear herself.

★ By now your baby will love to play with pop-up toys that burst out when a button is pushed or a dial turned. Let her push them back down herself, and she'll develop strength and coordination in her hands and arms.

★ Encourage you baby's social skills with a group of ready-made pretend friends – make finger puppets from cut-off gloves and give them eyes, ears, and a mouth – and show her how they can sing, dance, tickle, kiss, and chat to her.

Safety first!

Since most babies explore objects by putting them in their mouths, make sure all toys meet safety standards and ensure nothing can come off and choke a baby, especially any toys you make.

your baby thinks it no longer exists. By the end of this month, she may be beginning to realize that just because she can't see something it doesn't mean it isn't there. You can see this in action by partially hiding a toy under a towel so that only part of it is showing. Chances are she'll try to lift the towel to find the toy – and in a month or so she'll look for it even when it's fully hidden.

Making conversation

By now your baby will be able to recognize her name and turn her head when she hears you calling. When she responds with her own babbles and gurgles, you'll begin to notice how much the tune and rhythm of her chatter sounds like real speech, and how she loves to repeat strings of familiar sounds such as "bababab" or "mamama".

7 to 8 months

Your baby is very attached to you and is becoming demonstrably more affectionate.

He is never happier and more secure than when you are together, and so he may

become more clingy in unfamiliar surroundings or with people he doesn't recognize.

Physical development

Your baby may now roll from side to side with ease, flipping himself onto his back and over again. He may also sit for quite long periods and lean forward without falling over. However, he still can't twist sideways or swivel at the waist, and may often topple over when trying to reach for a toy. Comfort him if there are tears, but always let him try again.

Towards crawling

Although many babies learn how to crawl between eight and 10 months old, there will be some babies who don't begin to move until they are a few weeks older. To crawl properly, your baby needs to be strong enough to push himself up on all fours and then discover that by pushing down with his knees he can move forwards. First crawls are often backwards, and it may be a week or so before your baby learns how to move forwards. Give him lots of praise whichever way he chooses to move around.

On his own feet

Pretty soon just sitting won't be exciting enough for your baby. Always looking for a new challenge, he will be keen to try standing, and may make his first attempt by, for example, hauling himself up in his cot while hanging onto the rails. To begin with he'll collapse in a heap or remain stranded and yell for help – he hasn't yet developed the balance or coordination to lower himself down gently. When you come to his rescue, take his weight and gently allow him to relax so that he can slide into a sitting position.

Social and emotional skills

Your baby is very affectionate – he'll kiss you when encouraged, hold his arms out to be lifted up, pet his toys. He'll love older children and will reach out towards them. But while he's sociable and outgoing one moment, he may be fearful and shy the next.

Meeting new people

When you meet people your baby doesn't know well, you may find he buries his head in your shoulders, clings to you, and cries. Becoming anxious if strangers directly approach him is one of his first emotional milestones. "Stranger anxiety" is normal, and can last for up to two years or so. Forcing your baby to be friendly or telling him he's being silly will undermine his confidence – instead, praise him when he does smile back. It is also worth encouraging newcomers to interact gently and slowly with your baby.

Separation anxiety

Around this age your baby may also become much more clingy and start crying when you leave him, even for a moment. This, too, is a normal stage of healthy emotional development. Reassure him with lots of physical affection and with time he'll learn that parents always come back!

Finger coordination

Your baby will now start to be able to pick up objects using his fingers and thumb, rather than just using the palm of his hand. His grip has developed, too, and it's now controlled and strong enough for him to be able to tear paper, for example. He'll also love banging anything he can get hold of, and enjoy the noise it makes. He will still want to put objects in his mouth, so be careful what you allow him to have within his reach.

DEXTROUS FINGERS
Let your child practise picking up a number of differently shaped objects.

Language and intellectual skills

Your baby can communicate well with gestures and facial expressions. His attention span is still short but it hasn't stopped his mission to explore everything he can put his hands on.

Gestures and expressions

You'll notice your baby's understanding of language is developing faster than his ability to talk. He is starting to respond to the names of familiar objects and people, glancing over at a favourite toy you've just mentioned, for example, or looking at his sister when you call her name.

Real speech is still some way off, but your baby has lots of ways of letting you know what he's thinking. Gestures, for example, are now a regular part of his repertoire – see him open and shut his hand if he wants something, shake his head or push you away if you're doing something he doesn't like, or try to wave when you say "Bye-bye". Watch his face, too – his facial expressions will convey a variety of emotions.

First words?

At this stage your baby recognizes his name and probably understands the meaning of a few other words and responds to them. And as he practises his babbling, his sing-song "conversations" may sound increasingly like proper words, such as "dada" or "mama", so give him lots of encouragement and he will soon learn how to say them correctly.

Comparing sounds

The covering of a nerve that connects the ear to the brain – allowing your baby to pinpoint where a sound is coming from – is complete at about this age. Now he can compare his sounds with yours, and over the next few months he will increasingly attempt to imitate your sounds.

Discovery zone

As soon as your baby can propel himself in a chosen direction, he'll be into everything: cupboards, drawers, and wastepaper baskets. He has an overwhelming sense of curiosity to discover more about its shape, size, and texture. Does it taste good? Does it do anything exciting? Although he can use his hands to great effect, your baby will still put things in his mouth so take steps to child-proof your home (*pp.94–95*).

I know you're there!

Your baby's understanding of objects is growing every day. He may now be beginning to see how things relate to each other – how a small box fits inside a big box, for example. More importantly, he's learning that something can still exist even if he can no longer see it. If you try the same experiment as last month (partially hiding a toy under a towel; *see p.105*), but this time completely cover the toy, he may now pick up the towel to find it.

Toy box

Plastic stacking cups
Try to buy differently sized cups in bright, contrasting colours that fit together well.

Squeaky, noisy, and musical toys
Babies love the sounds and noises of squeaky toys. They will also enjoy the repetition of hearing a particular little tune over and over again. Buy toys that they can grasp easily and operate themselves.

Nursery rhymes cassette
If your baby enjoys listening to you sing familiar tunes to him, record a few songs on tape, or play a cassette of nursery rhymes while he has a quiet time. Encourage other family members such as grandparents to record stories and songs as well.

Activities to develop skills

Your baby is fast learning that he has a growing curiosity he needs to satisfy, and an urge to explore everything. Give him a selection of activities to keep him busy for a short while, or help him discover how to crawl towards the toys he is showing interest in.

★ Satisfy your baby's desire to discover new things by allocating him a kitchen drawer or cupboard that you have filled with safe but interesting household objects (*see below*). This will give him a chance to explore them in his own time, and will teach him more about the shape, size, and texture of different things. If he begins to tire of them, make a few small changes such as putting a ball in the bowl to rekindle his curiosity in it.

DOMESTIC DISCOVERY
Let your baby play with safe objects such as tea towels, plastic bowls and containers, measuring cups, a cake tin or colander, and plastic spoons.

Safety first!
Check that your baby's toys have approved safety standards, and never give him small objects that he can pop in his mouth and choke on. See also pp.94-95 for ways of ensuring a safe environment for him.

★ Help your baby learn more about the relationship between objects by giving him some plastic stacking cups in different colours, shapes, and sizes. It will be many months before he can fit them into each other the right way – or even stack them himself – but he'll enjoy trying. And when he needs a change you can build a tower and encourage him to try knocking it down, a game he'll love to play!

★ Singing his favourite rhymes together and giving your baby musical or noisy toys will help him practise his listening skills. Giving him age-appropriate toys that squeak when they are squeezed will help to develop his improving manipulation skills as well.

★ There are lots of ways you can encourage your baby to crawl: make sure he has plenty of opportunities by putting him down on the floor whenever you can; keep his knees well-covered so that crawling isn't painful or uncomfortable; and place a toy or something interesting just out of his reach to encourage him to try moving forwards to grasp it.

BECOMING MOBILE
Place a favourite toy just beyond the reach of your baby and you'll soon find him using all of his ability to try to move along the floor to grab it.

8 to 9 months

Your baby's personality is really beginning to shine through, and as her physical skills continue to develop and she becomes more confident she'll start to show you that she really has a mind of her own when she wants something!

Physical development

Your baby may now be able to sit by herself for quite a while, as well as lean forwards for a toy without toppling over. Don't expect her to play like this for too long, though: the physical effort of maintaining her balance is tiring, so after 10 minutes or so she'll be ready for a change.

Fast mover

Once your baby discovers how to move herself around – whether she's crawling or shuffling – she'll move faster very quickly. It'll be a question of now you see her, now you don't, so you'll need to keep a constant eye on her and check there is no danger.

Hand control

As she now begins to spend less time putting things into her mouth and more time exploring them with her hands, her hand movements are becoming agile and controlled. You may notice, for example, that she turns the pages of her books herself, even though it's usually several at a time. And she can delicately guide small pieces of food accurately into her mouth with her fingers, making mealtimes slightly less messy than before. She can also bang two objects together by holding one in each hand, and watch her have fun with a plastic bowl and wooden spoon.

Standing tall

If she's managed it once, your baby will be keen to practise pulling herself to standing using either you or a nearby item of furniture for support. Initially she will cling tightly with both hands until she feels confident about putting all her weight on her feet, and may even stand on tiptoes. Don't worry, this is normal; with time she will put all her weight on her feet.

SAFETY CHECKS
Check that there are no unsteady pieces of furniture your baby might pull over as he moves. Too many accidents, and he may lose his confidence.

Pointing

Your baby may be starting to point, which is an important milestone. Controlling the index finger is the first step to mastering a pincer grip – being able to close the thumb and forefinger together to pick up tiny objects. It also helps her communicate with you as she may be able to point out things she wants. Encourage her by looking at books together and pointing at things as you name them. And let her practise picking up tiny things such as raisins or cooked kernels of sweetcorn.

Social and emotional skills

Your baby is quite a character now, with her own likes and dislikes. She may object if you take a toy away, or want to play the same game again.

Asserting her will

As her self-awareness develops, your baby will become more assertive and turn lots of everyday activities into a battle of wills! You may find she is beginning to arch her back when she doesn't want to be put in her car seat, or shake her head if you try to feed her something she doesn't like.

As frustrating as this behaviour can be, don't forget how easily your little bundle of energy can be distracted! Her memory is short, and a fun toy or some fast thinking can refocus her attention: if she hates being dressed, sing her a funny song to help her forget why she made a fuss – or try redirecting your child's thoughts to what she can, rather than can't, do.

Shows of frustration

Your baby may become frustrated if she can't reach a toy she wants, for example. While it's hard not to rush in and hand the toy to her just to make her happy again, giving her extra time and encouragement may give her motivation to figure out how to get it herself.

Good behaviour

Your baby will now recognize the word "no" and associate it with a cross or unhappy look from you.

This doesn't mean she'll stop what she's doing, but now is the time for her to start learning – if she's heading into danger, for example, or hurting a friend or sibling. At this age her memory is still very short, so be prepared to say the same thing over and over again.

However, your baby loves to see you smile. Giving her lots of praise if she behaves well, or hugs and kisses for something positive, will encourage her to do things that please you, and also help nurture good behaviour.

Language and intellectual skills

By describing and showing your baby everything you do, you can help her understanding of language.

Word recognition

By the end of this month your baby may be able to recognize up to 20 familiar words, such as "beaker" or "teddy". She'll also laugh in the right places when you sing her favourite songs, look for her beaker if you ask

Activities to develop skills

Around this age your baby can start to show off her problem-solving skills – as long as you can resist helping her when she faces a difficulty! Facing everyday challenges will help her work things out for herself.

★ If your baby is becoming mobile, build a miniature mountain of cushions for her to help develop her crawling skills. Peep out from behind the cushions or use a toy to encourage her to climb over them. Her success will give her a real sense of satisfaction, help develop her sense of body strength, balance, and coordination, and prepare her for climbing real stairs.

Safety first!
Don't leave your baby alone since she may lose her balance and hurt herself. Never leave her alone in or around water.

OBSTACLE COURSE
Encouraging crawling babies to climb over cushions or even pillows is a fun and practical way of playing together. Stay at ground level so that you can encourage her.

★ Satisfy your baby's urge to explore, and her growing ability to problem-solve, with an activity board. Choose a board with cylinders that can whirl, dials that spin, and buttons that squeak. Show her how it works to begin with, and then let her have a go and investigate it in her own time. At first she may only be able to do the simple activities, like sticking her finger in a dial, but during the following months she'll soon figure out how to work the other activities.

★ Playing peekaboo and hide-and-seek with your baby at this age helps teach her about object permanence, and there are lots of variations: cover your head with a towel and let her pull it off, then let her try; hide behind the door with just a hand or toe showing, before popping out and gently surprising her.

her where it is, and associate actions with certain words, such as saying "bye-bye" and waving your hand.

Her own babbling is developing all the time, and she may add new sounds to her vocabulary, such as "t" and "w". She may also try to imitate you coughing, for example.

Look what I can do!

She is also learning about cause and effect: every time she drops a toy from her highchair you appear to pick it up again – a favourite game!

Toy box

Push–down toys

If your baby has a pop-up toy or a toy with buttons to push, encourage her to practise pushing down and releasing the buttons.

Household objects

When you are busy in the kitchen, your baby may love to play with some simple, safe kitchen utensils. Let her have fun with a few unused items such as a saucepan, plastic bowl, tea towel, and wooden spoon.

Toy piano

A toy piano or xylophone is a toy that your baby can grow into. For now, she will enjoy the random sounds she can make while developing her listening skills.

★ Fill a basin with water and, using different spoons, cups, and containers, show your baby how she can fill and pour. Emptying and filling games such as this are good for helping your baby practise her hand movements and develop dexterity and hand–eye coordination. Water games are great for bath-time play, too.

★ Learning how to hear different sounds will help develop your baby's listening skills – and eventually progress her speech. If you play a familiar tune that she'll recognize on a xylophone or a toy piano, it will spark her interest and may encourage her to try creating some wonderful sounds herself.

WATER GAMES
Playing with water is a great form of supervised entertainment. Always keep a gentle but firm hold on your baby as she plays near water.

CURIOUS NOISES
Don't worry if your baby's coordination skills have not developed enough to play this toy – this new curiosity is the start of listening to noises she makes herself.

9 to 10 months

Your baby may now be gaining immense pleasure from all his activities, as well as enjoying having lots of fun with you and other members of the family. His ability to understand language is coming on in leaps and bounds and he's beginning to make a real effort to communicate with you.

Physical development

As your baby is now spending more time upright, playtime becomes more fun for him since he is able to see and handle his toys more easily.

Climbing stairs

If your baby is now an experienced crawler, he may be trying to attempt more challenging manoeuvres such as crawling upstairs. While stair-climbing may help him learn how to judge height and depth and develop his sense of balance, for safety reasons it is important to install stair gates so he can't attempt them without you on hand to help. Going up is easier than coming down, and it will be a while before he's ready to learn the skills needed to make a safe descent.

Cruising

Very mobile babies may now be attempting a few steps while holding onto a piece of furniture. If your baby is becoming more confident, he'll soon discover how to move across a room using pieces of furniture as balancing aids. Learning how to "cruise" like this is the last physical skill your baby needs to master before he begins walking without assistance. If he reaches a favourite toy by manoeuvring himself across the room like this, remember to give him lots of praise.

Attention span

Your baby's sense of his environment is growing rapidly. He now notices and is interested in people and things up to three metres (10 feet) away. At the same time, his attention span is increasing: he is becoming more absorbed in activities he enjoys, and you'll find it harder to distract him when, for example, you need to take something away from him.

ABSORBED PLAYTIME
Your baby's concentration skills are improving all the time, enabling him to play with toys for a little longer.

Fingers and hands

By now your baby has mastered the pincer grip and is able to grasp things accurately between his thumb and forefinger. Self-feeding, for example, is now much easier, and his finely tuned hand–eye coordination enables him to pick up anything he comes across. This manual dexterity means he can now use toys as they were intended – putting blocks in and out of a box, for example. And he still loves dropping and picking up games – he drops, you pick up!

Visual skills

Since his birth, your baby has been refining his visual skills and now he can judge the size of an object up to one metre (two feet) away. He'll know,

for example, that a ball rolled from this distance will get larger as it comes towards him. Watch how he holds out his arms to catch it. Ask him to roll it back, and initially he may swing at it with no effect, but eventually he'll be able to return it in your direction.

Social and emotional development

Your baby is probably familiar now with his routines and really enjoys being included in family activities such as mealtimes. He's also becoming great company, and this month he may play his first jokes on you. However, expect him also to develop some new fears.

Activities to develop skills

Now that your baby is becoming more alert and aware of what is going on around him, introduce some indoor equipment such as a large plastic ball and an expanding tunnel. And help him improve his fine motor skills by giving him harmless objects to handle and explore.

★ Your baby may be starting to become aware of the noises animals make, so now is the time to introduce some animal songs into your repertoire. Look at animal books together and let him hear you mimic all the different sounds they make. Once your baby learns to imitate lots of animal noises, his success will encourage him to copy other sounds too.

★ If your baby loves moving objects from one container to another, why not make a surprise box full of interesting and harmless objects for him to handle, explore, put back in and take out again. To make the game more interesting you could wrap some items in paper – he'll love ripping them open to see what's hidden inside. Never leave your baby alone if you give him paper to play with as he may put it in his mouth and choke on it.

★ Satisfy your baby's need to explore with his hands – and encourage his sense of touch – with a "touch-and-feel" activity book that contains pictures and shapes made out of different textures.

TIME TOGETHER
A shared activity is valuable time for parents and babies to interact, and all the more enjoyable if a parent can explain things and encourage their baby.

★ Babies at this age are intrigued by space – they love crawling behind sofas or around the back of chairs. Your baby will probably also love to crawl through a play tunnel. Roll a ball towards him inside the tunnel so that he can see how it works. As he becomes confident, he'll soon love being chased through the tunnel or hiding from you inside.

★ A daily trip out to the park or local playground is a good chance to spend time together. It also means you can encourage your baby's sense of spatial awareness, and improve his visual skills as you point things out to him.

EXPANDING TUNNEL
If you buy an expanding tunnel, check to see that any wire used in the frame is covered and sealed. These tunnels are often very lightweight and made of bright material.

His sense of humour

Your baby's first laughs were probably prompted by physical games such as being bounced on your knee or lifted high up in the air, and later by visual jokes such as you shaking your hair about or putting his bib on your head like a hat. Now he is more mobile, he'll enjoy teasing you by doing things you don't like – heading out through a forbidden door and then looking back to see if you're watching, or pushing the off button on the TV. He may also enjoy showing off to you by putting his plate on his head, for example.

Developing fears

At the other extreme, this is the time when your baby may develop fears about things that have never upset him before – the noise of a vacuum cleaner, perhaps. If he seems unduly scared of something, stay relaxed and comfort him and reassure him that he won't come to any harm. Slowly familiarizing your baby with the object of his fear can help conquer this tendency. For example, let him examine the vacuum cleaner once it has been switched off. Take things one step at a time and in time he will manage his fears.

Language and intellectual skills

By now your baby is beginning to communicate more and letting you know that he is an important family member with something to say.

Making conversation

Your baby loves interacting with people, and will enjoy social get-togethers such as mealtimes. He will try to join in conversations and may even initiate conversation. Now his strings of babble clearly follow the rise and fall of an adult conversation. And, although on the whole it still sounds like nonsense, it is important for you to listen and respond, since this encourages him to keep trying.

New sounds

Your baby may also be starting to use the beginning of words that sound as if they relate to specific things, such as "ca" for cat or "ba" for bath, for example. Complete words won't emerge for another few months, but trying to understand your baby's words – or invented words – and repeating what he might mean back to him will help him learn how to say these words properly over time. Seeing and hearing you trying to understand the sounds he makes will probably also give your baby immense pleasure.

Understanding language

Your baby's understanding of language is continuing to increase faster than his ability to use it to speak. In the meantime he may use gestures as well as sound to get your attention – perhaps waving at you or pulling at your clothes – and will even repeat himself if you don't understand what he is trying to say.

Toy box

Household objects

The simplest objects provide fun for a baby. He may like to pick up an orange from a small cardboard box and pop it back in again, or take dry clothes out of a plastic laundry basket and put his toys or a doll in it.

Touch–and–feel books

A selection of different activity books will give your baby a new perspective on the world. Choose strong, brightly illustrated books with clear images and interesting textures.

10 to 11 months

Your baby may be starting to behave more like a toddler if she is beginning to spend more of her time standing on her feet. And she feels more grown-up, too – she loves trying to help you around the house, and is a happy companion for you.

Physical development

At this age babies vary enormously in their physical achievement. Some are crawling; others have just started to sit. Don't worry if your baby is taking things slowly; she'll do them in her own time.

Leaning and twisting

Your baby's balance has improved tremendously. She can lean sideways while sitting without toppling over, and twist round to reach something behind her, enabling her to reach for things herself.

Standing alone

By now, early crawlers are likely to be spending a lot of time up on their feet and cruising confidently. Your baby may even attempt to take her hands away from her support and try standing alone for a few seconds. Be prepared for bumps and bruises, and give her reassurance if she falls. Her first solo step will happen soon and, meanwhile, she's working hard to perfect her balance and coordination.

Social and emotional skills

Your baby is keen to get involved in household chores, loves being with other babies, and may now become more attached to a comfort object.

Copying and helping

Your baby is understanding the world around her more clearly than ever before, and she wants to be involved in whatever is going on around her. If she sees you busy wiping her highchair after a meal or sweeping the floor, she'll want to join in and she may try to copy you brushing your hair or washing your face, too.

She may also try to help speed your progress when you dress her by slipping her arm into her sleeve, or getting her padders for you to put on her feet. Make sure you always tell her what you're doing and why. Give her a chance to have a go, too, although don't expect her always to get it right: many a baby has tried to brush her hair with her toothbrush, for example!

Making friends

By now, your baby will enjoy seeing other babies her own age – and may get excited when you invite friends around with babies of their own. She will happily play alongside another baby if they are put on the floor together, but don't expect too much interaction between them. For now, just sitting alongside another child is good for your baby. She can learn a lot just by watching them – and feeling at ease in company will help her take her first steps towards learning how to make friends.

Comforting objects

Around this time, lots of babies become attached to a special object such as a blanket or soft toy, which they insist on taking everywhere with them. Known as a "transitional object", this item will have a special place in your baby's life, helping her sleep when she's tired, and reassuring

Hand control

By now your baby has excellent hand control and can do lots of things for herself. For example, she can turn the pages of a board book one at a time, learn how to put blocks into shaped holes, or accurately roll a ball in your direction if you encourage her. And she can not only give you an object such as a block when you ask for it, but also release it at will into your hand.

THE ART OF LETTING GO
Mastering the art of letting go is an important step, since your baby can now place objects where she wants to.

her if she's unhappy, especially if you are not around to comfort her. This is especially true for babies still dealing with separation anxiety.

Your baby will probably rely on her comforter for some time to come. Only when she finds other ways to deal with upsets will she gradually give it up. Meanwhile, if you are concerned about cleanliness, try and have two identical comforters to hand in case one is mislaid or needs to be washed.

Language and intellectual skills

You and your baby may be able to communicate together well, and now that she is nearly a year old her understanding of what makes the world go round is developing fast.

Reacting to questions

Your baby may still not be saying very much, but her understanding of language and communication is coming on in leaps and bounds. She can now follow simple questions such as, "Where is your beaker?" and will probably reply by pointing or looking in the direction of the cup. If you ask a simple question such as, "Do you want a drink?", she may respond with a smile and move towards the beaker.

If your baby has older brothers or sisters, they will find this a rewarding time, since they, too, can begin to interpret what she is trying to express.

Activities to develop skills

Now she is in her eleventh month, your baby is becoming more interested in how her toys move, fit together, or make noise. With her improved hand skills she can put objects where she chooses, so give her activities that will help improve these skills.

★ Now she can easily let go of objects when she wants to, your baby will probably enjoy playing with a simple posting box.

Start with your own version made out of a shoe box, with a round hole cut in the top and a ping-pong ball for posting into it.

If she enjoys playing this simple game, you could then try cutting a square hole in a box and this time giving her a block for posting through the hole. This exercise will be harder than posting the ball.

When she needs a new challenge, buy her a more complicated shape sorter to play with.

LETTING GO
Your baby's improved hand coordination will now enable her to place objects where she wants them. Putting plastic rings back on a ring post is a good exercise for her to try.

Understanding concepts

As your baby's intellectual skills develop you'll be able to watch her making more sense of her immediate world.

Now, when she sees a picture of a dog in her book, she'll perhaps relate it to her grandfather's dog or the dog she saw in the park, and begin to realize that, even though every dog she sees looks different, they are all in fact dogs. She can now also grasp the idea of opposites.

Toy box

Posting box

Posting boxes should be durable and incorporate a selection of simple, recognizable shapes. Make sure the shapes are not so small that they fit easily into your baby's mouth.

Board books

A selection of different activity books gives your baby a new perspective on the world. Choose strong, brightly illustrated books with clear images.

Toy telephone

Your baby will enjoy pretend toys such as telephones, especially those that make noises. Buy a safe, well-made version.

★ As your baby learns to turn the pages of a book, make sure she has plenty of them to look at, especially board books. Encourage some regular quiet time together so that books become part of her everyday life.

★ Establish her interest in the adult world with toys that mimic real objects, such as a toy telephone. Copying you is your baby's first step towards fantasy, or imaginative, play and, by naming the objects she is playing with, you are helping her language skills too.

★ Show your baby how you can build a tower using blocks, books, plastic bowls, or even plastic cups. She may not be able to build a tower with objects yet, but being able to knock them all down herself will give her such a great sense of power — and a real understanding of cause and effect.

BOOKS FOR LIFE
Books are a valuable source of interest and learning for a child, even at this early age. You will both derive great pleasure from this activity if you make a point of doing it together.

With the help of your explanations, she will understand the difference between wet and dry, hot and cold, big and little, and in and out.

Linking objects to events

Your baby's understanding of cause and effect is now well developed – she knows exactly what will happen when she bangs her drum (it makes a noise) or drops her block (you will probably pick it up!).

She's also beginning to match objects to their intended purpose. For example, she'll put a toy telephone to her ear just as you do with a real telephone, or pick up the flannel in the bathroom and wash her face with it. This is an important step forward, since she will use this understanding to help her when she starts to match what she says to the objects she wants to talk about.

11 to 12 months

As your precious baby approaches his first birthday, you will look back in amazement at the incredible changes that have taken place. He is now a little individual with a unique personality, a wide range of emotions, and a strong sense of his place in the family and his daily routines. He is bursting with life and energy, full of love and affection for those closest to him, and a real joy to be with.

Physical development

This month your baby may attempt to stand alone and even take his first steps unsupported. But don't forget that the speed of your baby's physical progress depends on his individual development and he should not be compared to other children.

First steps

Towards the end of this month your baby may take his first steps – a really exciting development. If he's perfected his balance while cruising around your furniture, he may start to occasionally let go, grabbing hold of something only if he totters. Once he reaches this stage, encourage him to walk towards you, or widen the gaps between the furniture.

Initially, he may manage only one or two steps before falling; encourage him to try again, and before long he'll manage more and more steps on his own. Moving the furniture slightly further apart will also help him gain confidence. But be prepared for your baby to go at his own pace – lots of babies don't walk until they are 13 or 14 months old, and some not before 18 months.

Self-feeding

Now your baby has much more control over his hand movements, he is more accurate in everything he does with them, including feeding himself with finger foods with no difficulty. Using a spoon isn't as easy to master, since it involves difficult hand–eye coordination in addition to good muscle control. But now he can rotate his hand he is much better at getting food into his mouth, although it will still be a messy business.

It is worth encouraging your baby to feed himself, since sometimes he may refuse someone else feeding him, and he shouldn't rely on you entirely for all his food. On the other hand, it's still too early to leave it all up to him. Although he may start each meal enthusiastically, he'll soon get distracted and you may have to intervene to ensure he eats enough.

Throwing

Exploring different objects is still one of your baby's favourite activities but now he will probably have stopped putting everything that he picks up into his mouth. How an object feels in his hands is now more important to him, and he will experiment more and more with his hands. For example, he will try to hold more than one item – such as two building blocks – in his hand at a time, although for a while he will drop one, and maybe both. And having discovered last month how to let go of something purposefully, he is now having great fun throwing things deliberately!

Social and emotional skills

As the person or people closest to him, you are still your baby's first love and the most important focus in his life, but at this age he also enjoys being with other people, especially other children and his siblings.

Your growing relationship

Your baby is very loving towards you and showers you with hugs and responds to kisses when he chooses to. He can also be self-focused, believing that he should come first when it comes to getting attention from you. At the same time, his sense of independence is increasing and his desire to explore means that he won't sit contentedly in your arms for long.

Mixing with other babies

Now is a good time to introduce him to other babies and children, particularly if he doesn't have sisters and brothers at home. He'll still want to stay close to you, but he will be fascinated to watch and imitate the other babies and toddlers around him. At this age, however, don't expect him to mix actively, join in or share with the others. Your baby still thinks the world revolves around him and, while he'll be very happy playing alongside other children, he'll naturally assume that every toy is there just for him. He won't be able to understand the reasons for sharing for another year or more.

Copying good manners

Although at this age your baby doesn't understand how, or why, he needs to have good manners, he loves imitating you and his siblings. Learning the way you behave will help him get on with other people as he gets older. Even before he can talk, your baby can learn social rituals like how to wave bye-bye. And if he hears you using polite words, he is more likely to use those words himself once he can talk.

Language and intellectual skills

Your baby has been preparing for talking in lots of different ways, and his increased ability to concentrate will help him with his first words. His memory is also getting much better.

Preparing to talk

Most babies are still experimenting with sounds as they get ready to talk. By now they can use most vowels and many consonants. If your baby has stopped dribbling, this could be a sign that he's getting better at controlling his tongue, mouth, and lips. He may also be trying to imitate the last thing he heard you or someone else say. You may catch the odd recognizable word in amongst the gibberish!

First words

Some babies may be able to say two or three words by their first birthday, although usually only you and the rest of his family who are in tune with his routine may understand them. There may then be some weeks before your baby uses more words, which is quite normal.

Concentration and memory

You may notice your baby can listen to very short stories right through. This is partly because he can now understand you, and because he can give you all his attention for longer.

Your baby's developing memory and past experiences now affect a lot of his actions and behaviour. You may notice this in the way he loves to cause chaos to his routine – for example, crawling away at top speed when you are trying to get him ready for a bath or put his coat on. Knowing what's going to happen next gives him a great opportunity to play a joke – at your expense!

Toy box

Pull-along toy

If your baby is becoming actively mobile, he will probably enjoy playing with a pull-along toy on wheels that he can trail behind him. These are often available in the form of animals or trains.

Soft toys

Soft toys can become treasured possessions. Choose dolls that have expressive or appealing faces to attract his attention to them.

Nursery rhymes

Nursery rhyme books and songs will give your baby huge pleasure and are excellent for helping his language development.

Activities to develop skills

Help your baby expand his understanding, and particularly his knowledge of the names of objects, with familiar songs and books. Try also to encourage him to share well-loved toys, and develop his coordination and rhythm by playing clapping games with him.

★ Your baby may now be able to hold his hands flat when he claps his hands together; if not, let him hold your hands as you clap them together. Let him sit on your lap, or on the floor facing you, so he can watch and join in clapping games and songs. Putting words, gestures, and music together will help with first words as well as giving him the chance to play with and imitate you.

CLAPPING GAMES
Action games will become more and more enjoyable for both of you as your baby anticipates the next step in a sequence or song.

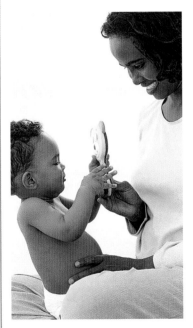

SHARING POSSESSIONS
Although your baby is still too young to learn how to share properly, a simple game such as giving and taking will gradually reinforce the idea for him.

★ Play give and take with your baby by offering him something new to look at, then asking for it back when he's finished exploring it. If he gives it to you, praise him. If not, take it gently, thanking him and praising him.

★ Soft toys such as teddy bears and clowns and dolls will give him lots of play opportunities for many years to come. Use them now to help him learn social rituals – encourage him to kiss his favourites goodnight, or say good-bye when he goes out for the day.

★ Your baby will love listening to song tapes and looking at books

again and again. This repetition will help encourage his first words and improve his memory.

★ If your baby is beginning to walk, he may be ready for his first push-along trolley. At first you may need to help him along, but he'll soon enjoy pushing the trolley himself.

Safety first!

Make sure that all soft toys and dolls have passed approved safety standards and do not have loose items such as buttons or beads.

The second year

The beginning of your child's second year is the beginning of a more independent phase, as your baby becomes a toddler. Learning to walk and talk opens up his world, and with you as his guide there is much to explore and discover about his surroundings, his family and friends, and himself. Every day there will be many new experiences to share and enjoy.

Your child's development

You have spent the first year learning to understand and meet your baby's physical and emotional needs, and it's been a very hands-on process. Now the focus changes. This second year is much more about helping your toddler become a self-sufficient individual, branching out into the wider world, with you as a guide.

Your toddler continues to need your active encouragement to explore her capabilities and her surroundings. She will also need you to return to as a safe emotional base because, for all her apparent independence, she needs your love and reassurance.

Developmentally the physical change is enormous. Once your child learns to walk, her horizons expand.

And learning to talk opens up her world to you, and the whole world to her, in a new and exciting way. Your toddler will constantly attempt to move ahead of her immediate capabilities, which may lead to enormous frustration for her. Learning about limits, her own and those set by you, is new for both of you. With patient teaching and encouragement, she can learn to follow basic safety rules and cooperate with your expectations.

Establishing a safe environment

As a baby, your toddler explored things with her hands and this continues, except now the exploration isn't limited to those toys given to her. She can move around her home, and everything is worth investigating, whether it's the dog's bowl, the kitchen cupboards, or the CD player. How can she tell the difference between those buttons she can press and those she can't? It's not possible without your help, so remove items that can be damaged and direct her attention to activities that take advantage of her natural curiosity and pleasure of exploration.

Setting the pace for your toddler

Toddlers cannot self-limit their activity. They tend to move straight from one activity to another without pause and to put every ounce of their energy into each. Your toddler will rely on you to help set the pace, so that she can manage to enjoy activities without overdoing them to the point of exhaustion, which is sometimes where the flash point of frustration ignites into a tantrum.

Toddlers still need lots of rest, and most will probably continue to need at least one daytime nap for this year. Well-slept and rested toddlers will manage life better than those who are tired. And if your toddler is a poor sleeper at night, don't be tempted to keep her going all day in the hope that she will sleep continuously through the night. The more tired she is, the less easy she will find it to relax into a good sleep pattern.

Ultimately, this is a wonderfully exciting time for you and your toddler, full of new experiences. Understanding what makes your toddler tick, and what her needs are, will help you create those opportunities that bring out the best in her.

About this book

During this thrilling year of change, your support, encouragement, and love can do more than anything else to help your toddler blossom. Understanding how your toddler develops is vital to helping you tune into her needs and give her what she wants.

Section 1
The first half of this book tells you about how your toddler's development will affect both her physical and her emotional needs. For example, why does your 20-month-old keep having tantrums in public places when previously she was well behaved? How important is it that she talks in simple sentences at a certain age? Now she has begun walking, how can you keep her safe?

Being one step ahead in terms of knowing what to expect from your toddler will help you understand her so you can respond in the most effective way possible. And being able to meet her needs in this way will not only help her feel loved and valued but boost your confidence as a parent, too.

At this age safety is so important. This book helps you to prepare a safe environment for your child's continuing development. It discusses how to balance safety issues with allowing your toddler the freedom to explore.

Section 2
The second half of this book contains what you need to know about how and when your toddler is likely to reach each new milestone. Although the information is organized month by month, it's important to remember that the time-scale is flexible. All toddlers develop at different rates, and your toddler will progress at the speed that's right for her.

Once you see your toddler trying to do something new, there are lots of things you can do to try to encourage her along the way, and this section includes ideas for games and activities you can play with her. Giving your toddler the right kind of stimulation at just the right time will build her confidence and self-esteem and help give her the best possible start in life.

Family life

The commitment and unconditional love provided by a family will ensure that a toddler has the best possible start in life. Now, a year after he was born, your toddler may still be the newest member of the family, but he is also very much a personality in his own right, beginning to forge his own independent relationships with other family members.

Sibling relationships

During this second year of your toddler's life you may be having another baby, and this will be a major but positive change in your toddler's life. Your toddler may feel hardly more than a baby himself to you, and you may wonder how he will cope with a new addition. He will take his lead from you, but keep it simple. Don't overplay the benefits of having a brother or sister because it will be some time before they will be able to play together. What he is likely to be most aware of after the new baby arrives is that he won't always be the only one who needs attention. Given that developmentally he is naturally very self-focused, this will take some adjustment on his part. His routine will also be changed. Give him time to adjust, and make sure he still gets some one-to-one time; otherwise his sense of fairness will be

offended too! "Role conflict" may also be a problem for a while, as your toddler gets used to no longer being the "baby" of the family.

If you already have older children, or stepchildren, then the relationship between them and their younger sibling will become even stronger, even if there are squabbles along the way. Many children seem to fight endlessly, but they are, in fact, forming deep emotional attachments and will probably be great friends and allies as adults. In some ways, children get into a habit of communicating by squabbling, so you will need to set some ground rules so they play together harmoniously.

Often an older child will be too "helpful" to his younger sibling. It is frustrating for a toddler who is trying to do something by himself to have someone more competent keep taking his game over. In such a case you may need to point out gently to the older child that the younger child needs more time. However, try not to be too interventionist – your children sometimes need to sort things out between them in their own way.

Position in the family

Numerous studies have been undertaken to understand if birth order has an impact on personality. If your toddler is your first child, you will probably have had more time to spend with him than is ever going to be likely with any subsequent children. However, with first children there is so much for parents to learn about their care and development, which becomes second nature with later children. First-born children tend to be more achievement-orientated, and are often more strong-willed than later children. They have had the unique experience of never having to share their parents' attention, at least for a while, and often have a strong sense of responsibility.

Second and subsequent children often have better social skills because they have always had to share time and attention with another child, and have sometimes had to take a back seat. They also have to learn to manage living with an older child who will always be more competent than they are. While this may be very frustrating, it may allow them to develop other ways to survive unequal competition.

Only children are often very successful in later life because they have had their parents' undivided attention, and been able to focus on their achievements without having to share with siblings.

Twins or more

It is important in the case of multiples to try to spend time individually with each baby. This may be a challenge at first, when the physical care of more than one baby takes up so much time. Enlist the help of another family member, or a childminder, to allow you the time and opportunity to do this.

There are two types of twins: identical and non-identical. The incidence of non-identical multiples has increased in frequency with the use of new fertility treatments. Those children born as a twin or triplet will always have to share. Non-identical or fraternal twins are no more alike than non-twin siblings, but identical twins – who have identical genetic material – will be very similar, although their developing personalities will differ.

Emotional development

Family life is an important arena for emotional development. You will already be familiar with the development of your baby's emotions over the first year. From a very early age your baby learned to express pleasure by smiling. Faced with a surprise or completely unknown situation, she may have shown fear by crying. Secure in your arms, she will have settled calmly and happily, expressing contentment.

Some children are emotionally very responsive, and others less so. Something that one child finds frightening, is merely of interest to another. During the first year of your child's life, you will have learned a lot about how she approaches the world and you will have been able to help create a balance for her between what she can cope with on her own and with what she needs help. Some babies are easily overstimulated and become fretful, needing more calm and soothing tactics than others. Others are more reticent and will need more encouragement to interact or respond to stimuli.

Expressing emotions in security

Your child's love for you is easily expressed. She may return your cuddles and kisses with great pleasure, but will also use you to demonstrate stronger emotions like anger. Often for children the development of a full range of emotions can be almost overwhelming, and can only be expressed within a secure environment. You are that secure environment, and in order to experience strong emotions she will need you to help her manage them because she isn't yet able to do so for herself.

You will learn what is best for your child, and it is your role to learn from her cues. Sometimes when children are angry, it may be beneficial to hold them in order to help them contain their feelings, talking calmly all the while. Some children respond better to being left alone until they feel better. But, after any emotional outburst, all toddlers need to be reassured with a loving cuddle.

The role of imaginative play

Apart from the immediate expression of emotions such as happiness, fear, and anger, which are relatively straightforward and easy to recognize in your child, she will begin to imitate expressions of love and concern for others. Being encouraged to demonstrate expressions of affection or sympathy for others, even if she doesn't actually feel it yet, helps with the development of these feelings of empathy. She may also act out different emotions with her teddies or dolls, practising them through her play. This is very important because it means she can experience difficult feelings in a safe place through her imaginative play and begin to understand what it is like to consider other people's feelings.

Relating to others

What you will notice during the course of this year is that your toddler's pleasure and appreciation of events will begin to include other people. Her excitement at going to a parent and toddler group, for example, will start to reflect her enjoyment and enthusiasm for spending time with particular friends. She may enjoy going to Granny's or visiting another family member because she is developing a close and loving relationship, independent of you, with that person.

All these experiences are helping her to develop a full and satisfying emotional life, where she can express her feelings in the safe context of knowing that she is loved and that they are validated. You can make her feel secure no matter what emotions she is expressing.

ACTING OUT EMOTIONS
This toddler is pretending her much-loved soft toy monkey, Timmy, is tired and needs to have a nap. She puts him to sleep on his back, and makes soothing noises to quieten him ready for sleep.

Managing separation

Allowing your child to develop other relationships – with relatives or childminders – independently of you is very beneficial and will help her manage separation from you. Many toddlers are still showing separation anxiety at this age, and every child will experience it at some point. So take it slowly. Start by playing simple games, such as peekaboo, to help her to understand that things that go away will come back.

You can help your toddler believe that she can manage without you for a while by providing her with the experience of doing so. Encourage her to spend time with other loved adults away from home as well as at home. Suggest that she take along a favourite toy or security object for extra reassurance. Even if she finds it hard at first, it will help her self-confidence in the long run. Above all, try not to convey to her that she is totally dependent on you or to impose on her your own anxiety about being separated from her.

Social development

During this second year, your toddler is inclined to see life with himself right at its centre. This egocentricity is essential to establishing the secure self-image that will eventually enable him to extend his consideration to other children and adults. Help him build on his self-image and become more sensitive to other people's needs by ensuring that you meet his needs.

A lot of social development happens at home quite naturally within the context of family and friends. And when there are siblings, there will probably be less need for your intervention. It's sometimes helpful to allow siblings to sort out their differences between themselves.

This day-to-day social interaction with other children at home is not available to first-born or only children, and needs to be sought elsewhere. Initially, this will be through children of parental friends, visits to the park, and parent and toddler groups. In a group of children

where most are older, some of the problems that arise between toddlers won't come up, and this can be an easier environment in some ways to begin social acclimatization. However, he will begin to work out ways of interacting socially with his peer group when he reaches a pre-school environment next year.

Teaching your toddler to share

Alongside your toddler's self-focus comes a strong streak of possessiveness, all of which makes social interaction a bit of a minefield amongst similar-aged children!

The concept of sharing is difficult for toddlers to grasp, so don't expect them to be able to do it willingly at first. Remember that the ability to share comes from feeling secure inside. So, instead of focusing too closely on the issue of sharing, try the following: remove toys "for later" that are being squabbled over; ignore bad reactions as far as possible; and look out for opportunities to reward and reinforce occasions when one child willingly relinquishes a toy to another. It may not happen out of any inclination to share at first, but it gives you a chance to praise this sort of behaviour, and toddlers respond better to praise than to anger and irritation on your part.

IT'S MY TOY!
This little boy doesn't want anyone else to have his toy, even though he doesn't want to use it himself at the moment. He fears that he will never get the toy back if he lets someone else have it. Learning to share requires careful management by his carers.

Considering child care

Being looked after by someone other than a parent, or close family member, can be positively beneficial for your child once you have found the right person or facility. However, it is important to consider what your child's needs are, and how best these can be met, bearing in mind that toddlers need lots of one-to-one attention, particularly to encourage language development.

There are several child care options to choose from. A nanny who comes to your home or a childminder who lives close by may be one option to explore. Interview any possible candidates thoroughly and check their references. Family members who live nearby may also be an option. You will need to find someone who is warm and attentive to your child, and has ideas and values similar to your own. Do not expect someone to care for your child exactly as you would: the relationship will inevitably be different.

A workplace creche or nursery may suit your requirements. Ask your local authority for a list of registered child care services. Visit several to gain an understanding of each one's approach to child care, and ensure that the manager and staff are properly qualified.

Discipline

Discipline is not the same as punishment. Discipline is about teaching your toddler what is expected of her, both within the family and in wider society. It is about setting consistent limits and understanding that your toddler's constant testing of these is part of how she will learn to accept them. It should always be done with love and respect for your toddler.

Don't expect too much obedience of your toddler. Remember that she still has lots to learn about good behaviour and consideration of others. Her learning will be gradual as she has a very short memory span and does not recall "lessons" except through repeated experience. At the moment she is very self-centred, and a lot of her behaviour, which you may consider naughty, is just an extension of exploring some of the new things she can do, and seeing how far your limits extend.

What also has to be respected is that a young child cannot always make herself understood, especially when it comes to explaining how she is feeling. Sometimes a child will test the limits when feeling anxious, in which case your toddler will need attention and reassurance, not punishment. Thinking about the world from a toddler's point of view, and being sensitive to situations that might be stressful for your child, helps you to see their behaviour in perspective.

A positive approach

Discipline requires a positive approach, using lots of praise and encouragement, and setting a good example through adult behaviour. You cannot expect a child to learn that hitting is not okay if you smack her. That is not

consistent behaviour and will only give mixed messages. If you want your toddler to behave well, it is important to notice when she does, and to praise her for it. Don't wait until she annoys you and then get cross, or she will learn that the only way to get your attention is to behave badly rather than well. Noticing good behaviour and commenting specifically about it is important. Your toddler wants to please you for the same reason she

Avoiding confrontation

You can help prevent some unnecessary daily confrontations by doing a few simple things. For example, you could move precious objects, and the plant that she enjoys pulling the leaves off, out of her reach. And you could get a security cover to prevent her posting her toys inside the video player that is so similar to her postbox toy. Your aim should be to provide your toddler (and her friends) with a safe environment in which to play, where she can do little damage to valued possessions.

cannot be expected of your child yet. Self-discipline comes from learning to manage and control your feelings and impulses, and is linked to self-motivation and self-esteem. If, through positive discipline, you can help your toddler learn that it is a particular sort of behaviour that gets attention and praise, what we would describe as good behaviour, you are sowing the seeds for her ability to manage her behaviour well in the future.

Remember that your toddler's behaviour is simply the way she learns. Allow her plenty of time, and offer her understanding and guidance.

smiled back at you when she was a baby: she loves you, and pleasing you makes her feel good. Praising her efforts shows your respect and validation of her efforts, which will also help develop her self-esteem.

Effective intervention

Distraction is often a successful technique to use when your toddler will not cooperate. For example, if your toddler refuses to put on a coat, distract her with a toy, and then put the coat on her while she's looking at it.

Giving your toddler a choice is also very effective. For example, when she refuses to put on the coat, try asking her, "Do you want to put this arm in first or this arm?"

You should ignore some of your toddler's unwanted behaviour to avoid it becoming attention-seeking. If your toddler deliberately throws a toy car, which may hit another child, explain that such behaviour is unacceptable and that you must intervene.

Combining the techniques

All of these strategies take time and patience, but be reassured that by using them you are helping your toddler learn some very positive lessons for life. Learning about discipline is also the beginning of learning about self-discipline, although this takes years to develop and

Tantrums

Tantrums are an expression of the overwhelming frustration felt by a young child, who doesn't yet have the emotional maturity to deal with such strong feelings. With all his new physical skills, it is right that he should want to explore his capabilities, but when he discovers there is something he can't manage, or isn't allowed, then the frustration can become too much to cope with.

Most tantrums occur around the age of 20 months. They often happen when there is a clash of interests – his desire for more independence, and your desire to keep him safe, for example. At this age, children can understand but not express themselves well. Tantrums can be very difficult to deal with, especially as the physical expression of anger can be difficult to watch.

To be overwhelmed by his feelings is also a surprising experience for your toddler, and he will need you to help him feel comforted and secure after it is over, even if you pay him minimal attention while it's happening (especially the first time it occurs).

Your toddler is more likely to have a tantrum away from home; for example, when you're in a shop or at

a friend's house. This is because he's feeling insecure. He may be feeling less secure when away from home because your attention is less closely focused on him, and this makes his frustrations overwhelming. It's difficult enough to make yourself understood when you aren't yet proficient at talking, but doubly so if your parent is distracted. At least when he is at home he feels secure, and probably has better access to your attention, so a tantrum may be less likely to happen there.

Minimizing the incidence of tantrums

It is also worth thinking about those situations that you know your child finds difficult at the moment. These can lead to the sorts of frustrations that can result in a tantrum.
• For example, does he find it difficult to deal with groups of people when he is tired? If so, either schedule events that involve others after a nap, or make sure he isn't overwhelmed in such a situation.

• Does he find it impossible to deal with the supermarket shop at the end of a day? Then try taking him in the morning instead and keeping the visit brief, or leaving him with a minder while you go shopping.

It isn't fair to ask him to manage situations that are beyond his emotional capabilities without some consideration of his needs, and it's easier for you, too, in the long run. Remember that tantrums are linked to this developmental phase and will pass.

Being reasonable

Try not to get yourself locked into a situation of saying "No" every time a request comes up. Be firm and consistent but also be reasonable.

The trick is to set the sort of limits that allow your child to develop greater independence from you, without also letting tantrums become an attention-seeking habit. Like many parenting skills, this takes thought and practice as you learn to "read" this next stage of your toddler's development, which is the beginning of a change from dependence to independence.

Dealing with tantrums

If a full-blown tantrum occurs, it may help to just sit it out, as long as your child is not in danger. Some children will need to be held tight and talked to in a reassuring voice. Losing control yourself doesn't help at all, and may just prolong the unwanted behaviour. Shouting at and smacking your child isn't appropriate, and is about as effective in dealing with the problem as having a tantrum yourself.

Thinking about how it feels from his point of view sometimes helps take the heat out of the situation. Diversionary tactics can sometimes head off a tantrum, either by walking away and ignoring a situation that you know could escalate, or distracting him with an alternative suggestion, keeping the mood calm and light.

Developmental check

Between 18 and 24 months you should take your child for a developmental and health check, which provides you with a good opportunity to ensure that all is going well, and to raise any concerns you might have. This check-up may be carried out by your health visitor, but it is more likely to be done by a community paediatrician, who has specialist training in child development.

Assessing physical development

Your child will be weighed and measured, and this will be checked against a standard chart and your child's previous measurements, to ensure that growth is appropriate for her. You may be asked about what

sorts of foods she enjoys eating now, and the doctor may make suggestions that are helpful to you. Her teeth will probably be checked to see how they are coming through, and you may be asked about taking your child to visit the dentist.

Her eyes and ears will be checked, and possibly her heart. Hearing is important for learning to talk, and if your child is too shy to talk to the doctor you will probably be asked about her speech. At this age, her social interaction and understanding is more important than what she is actually saying.

Assessing your child's skills

You will probably be asked various routine questions about what your child is capable of doing now. The doctor will assess her physical skills by watching her walk, and asking her to do simple play tasks like balancing a block one on top of another. These activities demonstrate her gross and fine motor skills (control of large-scale and more precise movements). The doctor may also show her pictures of different objects and ask her, "Which one is the cat?", for example, to test her comprehension. She may also be asked other simple questions about other pictures or items.

WORD RECOGNITION
The health visitor holds up a picture of a cat and another of a dog and asks the toddler to point to the picture of the cat. She identifies the cat without hesitation: her comprehension is good.

DEVELOPING FINE MOTOR SKILLS
The toddler is then given three bricks and asked to build them into a tower. She concentrates as she picks up each brick in turn and carefully and precisely positions one on top of the other.

A chance for discussion

This routine check-up will also be an opportunity to talk through any worries you may have about your child's development, eating habits, sleeping patterns, potty training, behaviour, and general health.

As toddlers are in more social settings with other children, they tend to get more colds or minor health problems as their immune system starts to get to grips with common infections. If your toddler seems to continually suffer from coughs and colds, you may want advice about how you can help boost her general health. In addition, such illnesses, if left untreated, could lead to hearing problems. If you have concerns about hearing or language development, talk to your doctor about them.

Behavioural development

If your child is consistently under the weather, or gets very tired, it can affect her behaviour. A toddler who hasn't had enough sleep over a consistent period will find it difficult to focus on behaving well, and will become frustrated and overwhelmed. Consider what your toddler needs physically, in order to develop emotionally. If you have reduced her daytime naps, for example, bring bedtime forward. Tired toddlers also have less interest in eating, so try to organize mealtimes for when your child is more alert, to avoid possible behavioural problems.

Immunization

There are a number of immunizations that are recommended during the second year, including the measles, mumps, and rubella vaccination (MMR). In the US, this is mandatory for school entry. Also in the US, the Varicella vaccination that immunizes against chickenpox is recommended.

In addition, there are recommendations for booster doses of those immunizations given during the first year. These include DTP (diphtheria, tetanus, and pertussis), polio, Hib (against the virus that can cause meningitis), and in the US this recommendation also includes a booster vaccination against hepatitis B. If you have any reservations about immunization, then take this opportunity to talk them through with your doctor.

Potty training

You cannot train a child to use his potty until his nervous system is developed enough to control the bowel and bladder sphincter muscles. This generally happens between 18 and 36 months, with girls tending to be ready before boys.

In the past babies were regularly sat on potties, until they had passed water, which avoided at least one wet nappy while giving the impression that they were being "trained". Predicting a time when you know your child is likely to have a bowel movement, for example after eating, and sitting him on his potty then until he does so may teach him that this is what his potty is for, but it won't teach him to control his bowel movements. That will only happen when he is developmentally ready.

In addition, it won't be possible to potty train your child until he is aware of the sensation of wanting to go, is physically able to control the urge until he reaches the potty, and can sit down safely on it. All these skills have to be mastered before you can expect your child to manage without nappies.

Beginning training

Look out for signs of training readiness, which suggest that it might be worth introducing the idea. These include being aware of having a wet nappy or of doing a bowel movement, or sometimes having a dry nappy for a long period, which indicates that your child's bladder is able to store urine in larger quantities. Your child may also show an inclination to copy you by volunteering to use a potty.

In summer months, allow your child to play outside without his nappy on. Without a nappy on, doing a wee is much more obvious! And this will help him to

Introducing the potty

Your first step, at around 18 months, will be to introduce your child to the idea of what will be expected of him in future months.

★ You can do this by having a potty around, close to the family toilet so the association is made, and letting him sit on it perhaps before his bath in the evening, after you have taken off his nappy. Don't expect him to use it, but just to get used to the idea of sitting on it. If something happens while he's sitting on it, great.

★ In a family that is quite relaxed about using the toilet, in which your child has seen you using it, it's easier for him to make the connection. Place the potty next to the toilet and encourage him to sit on it when you go to the toilet.

★ Choose a potty that won't tip up when being sat on, or when your child stands up. For boys, it is helpful to get one designed with a higher splashguard at the front; this will help ensure that his penis is pointing down into the bowl of the potty. Boys will probably want to stand up to wee in the toilet in time, but because a bowel movement is usually accompanied by passing water, starting off with a potty is probably easier for him at first.

★ Avoid a heavy emphasis on success and failure, as it will be counterproductive. Remind yourself that this is about introducing the idea of using the potty, not producing a toilet-trained child. Give praise when deserved, and be patient.

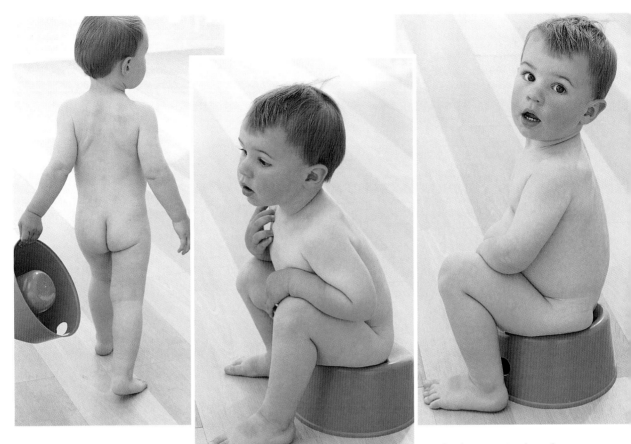

understand what it is you are referring to when you ask him if he wants to do a wee. For boys, imitation is important, so let him watch his father or older brother use the toilet.

Make sure you don't give mixed messages about your child's bowel movements. It's confusing to him if you praise his efforts, then say they are nasty or dirty. Be positive about any successes, but deliberately ignore accidents when they occur. Your child really cannot help himself and, because children focus so exclusively on one thing at a time, even when he is trained there are still bound to be accidents sometimes.

Above all, don't get emotionally fraught about the process, which can become all too common if you start trying to potty-train your child before he is ready. If your child is having repeated accidents then stop, and go back to nappies for a few weeks. Don't attempt to move from nappies to pants at any time of stress. It's not fair to ask your child to deal with too much at once – wait for a more settled time.

Controlling the bowels

You may find that even when your child is happy to use the potty for passing water, having a bowel movement is a different proposition, and he may want to continue doing this in a nappy. From his point of view, it is quite a different sensation doing this on the potty or toilet to doing it in a nappy, and some children find it a bit strange. Often, they will wait until they have had their night-time nappy put on before evacuating their bowels. Although this can be rather frustrating, try to stay calm. Your child's anxiety will pass in time. Do not hurry him.

Toddlers in action

The toddler years are often years of great physical activity. Now that she is mobile, and curious, your toddler will want to find out about what she is capable of and the world about her. She may seem to have a "Go" button but no "Stop" button. Help your toddler learn to manage her energy as constructively as possible, because this is an important step in her development.

Toddlers have lots of energy and masses of curiosity. They love practising their newly mastered walking and running skills, and enjoy exploring their environment fully. So, it is important to allow your toddler plenty of time to run around in a safe space, such as a park, playground, or indoor soft-play area. Take a ball with you to kick and chase.

The importance of physical activity

Channel your child's energy constructively as well as allowing for free play in the park or with other children. At this age, learning how to swim provides a good opportunity to become physically competent in water. Music and movement is also popular: it develops concentration, coordination, rhythm, and imagination if you devise different games for the music. There are also toddler gym classes and indoor soft-play facilities that allow toddlers to improve their balance and motor skills as they develop muscle strength and have fun.

The difference between boys and girls

Numerous studies have shown that boys need more physical activity than girls. Boys tend to become more restless more often and concentrate for shorter periods on quieter activities (such as playing with blocks or toy animals) than girls. If your toddler is a boy, when he becomes restless or frustrated instigate a short period of physical activity, such as a walk round the block with his

Calming activities

★ Sitting together and reading a book to your child is one excellent way of using a peaceful activity to promote closeness, while providing an opportunity for your child to practise her listening and concentration skills.

★ Drawing and scribbling with crayons, or painting with a brush, is another absorbing activity that requires you to stay peacefully in one place.

★ Listening to soft, gentle music while being cuddled is another way of helping your toddler to relax.

★ A warm bath, a familiar activity since birth, can be physically relaxing, which helps calm things down.

★ Gentle massage helps a lot of children. It helps them regain a sense of their physical selves. You can gently massage the feet, with or without baby oil, moving up the legs. A gentle head massage while she rests in your lap can feel wonderful as it releases tension in the neck and scalp muscles, while circular clockwise stroking of the abdomen can reduce stress in the stomach.

push-along trolley or a game of being chased by you in the garden or park. Once he has let off steam, he will be happy to sit down with his crayons or toy cars again.

Recharging the batteries

Try to balance periods where your toddler expends physical energy with quieter times that allow her to relax and recharge her batteries. A toddler who knows how to relax will also find settling down to sleep easier than one who does not. Children who consistently do not get enough sleep are often overactive because they become physically reliant on excess "awake" hormones to compensate for lack of sleep.

Small children have immature nervous systems and are easily overstimulated. An overstimulated toddler becomes frustrated when playing, requiring more intervention than usual. When this happens, involve your toddler in a quiet, soothing activity, such as reading a book. If she is consistently tired by lunchtime or early afternoon, try putting her in her cot for a daytime nap, to improve her energy levels for the rest of the day.

You may find that your child's energy levels are revitalized after eating. Small children easily flag without regular refuelling. Concentrate on giving her healthy snacks, and limit highly processed foods and those that contain a lot of chemical additives.

Sleeping

During the second year, toddlers need about 12 to 14 hours sleep within a 24-hour period. Sleep is very important to babies, and deep sleep is necessary for all children, as it is restorative and helps to promote growth.

Getting enough sleep

Ideally toddlers need a long period of uninterrupted sleep at night and one or two naps during the day. However, it is worth bearing in mind that, without adequate sleep, your toddler may find it hard to do all the growing and developing that this busy second year demands. A well-slept toddler is more able to make use of the time spent awake than a toddler who is cranky.

We are all too well aware of how we feel when we don't get enough sleep, and it's the same for your child. If you are concerned that your toddler is not getting enough sleep, especially on a regular basis, look for the signs in his behaviour. Is his hand–eye coordination less efficient that usual, making him misjudge movements slightly? Does he have tantrums more frequently? Is he more withdrawn and less sociable? Do games always seem to end in tears? Does he have little enthusiasm for going to the park, where formerly he was always keen? If the answer to several of these questions is "Yes", then he probably isn't getting enough sleep, and you should speak to your healthcare professional. Remember that toddlers can recharge their batteries during quiet periods – they do not always have to be asleep to do this.

Establishing a sleeping pattern

It is through the regular occurrence of different daily activities – getting up, mealtimes, nap times, and bedtime – that your child learns about the difference between day and night. As children's brains mature, their internal circadian rhythms adapt to the patterns of life they experience. So, if you want them to adapt to a pattern that suits you – sleeping through the night, for example – they have to experience how.

Your toddler's bedtime and waking patterns will have some influence on what times suit you and him for naps. You may find your toddler can keep going during the morning, have an early lunch, and then a good two-hour sleep in the early afternoon, before bed at seven in the evening. Alternatively, if your child wakes very early, a long morning nap and a short one in the middle of the afternoon works best. Although your routine will probably change over this year, as your child's sleep at night improves and the daytime sleep needs drop, a routine is helpful to your child. However, there may be days when you need to be more flexible.

Introducing a bedtime routine

One of the ways in which you can help your child learn about sleeping well through the night is by having a bedtime routine. If this isn't already a feature of your family life, it will be as well to introduce it now, because you want your child to get a good night's sleep and to learn that going to bed is in itself a good and pleasurable activity at the end of a busy day.

★ Don't wait until your child is overtired before you start the bedtime routine: it should be a calm and relaxed period of the day, leading gently towards the inevitability of bed and sleep.

★ If you have bathed your baby in the morning during the first year, try moving this wonderfully relaxing activity to the end of the day. A bath before bedtime will not only help your child to wind down, it will also – if it becomes a part of his daily routine – mean that your child will begin to associate having a bath with bedtime. It will thus become a gentle preparation for sleep.

★ Your routine might follow a pattern like this: About an hour after your toddler has his last meal of the day, you give him a bath, allowing him time to play. After the bath, you sit down quietly together and you read him a bedtime story, before gently putting him to bed.

★ It is consistency in the daily bedtime routine that is important, so if some elements of the routine need to be done by a caregiver, make sure she knows what they are. Routine helps create the security that allows your toddler to get into his bed happily, and fall asleep by himself.

If your child wakes very early, or is wakeful at night, don't be tempted to drop the day-time naps in order to try to increase night-time tiredness. Overtired children find sleep more of a problem than those who are generally well slept. When children don't get enough sleep for long periods of time, they come to rely on stress hormones to keep them going. This can make them cranky and overactive. If your child finds sleep difficult, he needs help to learn to sleep better, not less sleep.

If the bedtime routine seems a little difficult to you, it may be because you are starting it too late. Start it a little earlier when, being less tired, it may make it possible to manage the idea of bedtime more easily. And, if he has missed or had a shorter daytime nap for any reason,

aim to put him to bed a little earlier to compensate. The idea is that your child will be so calm and contented that he will be able to go to sleep in his own bed and by himself. All of which may take consistency and patience.

Dealing with night waking

When children of around a year old wake at night, many of them will not simply turn over and go back to sleep but will wake their parents up as well! Children generally will compensate for losing sleep at night by sleeping for longer during daytime naps. However, this will probably not be an option for you and you may well prefer to enjoy the day with your baby and for all the family to sleep well at night.

Habitual waking

If your child has got into the habit of night waking – because this is what it is, a habit – you can help him change it. There is seldom any other reason for night waking, other than during periods of ill-health, that isn't caused by not having learned to be self-sufficient, so that he is unable to get himself back off to sleep without your assistance. For example, if you have got into the habit of feeding your baby until he falls asleep, or holding or rocking him, he will be unable to fall asleep by himself if he wakes in the night. Given that a baby is on a 50-minute sleep cycle, compared to an adult's 90-minute one, this can mean regular wakings during the night, when you are needed to help your child get back to sleep.

What you need to do is give your child the opportunity of learning how to be self-sufficient, and allow him to learn how to go to sleep by himself. If he has learned how to sleep with you cuddling him, he can learn a new routine with your patience and commitment. This means that when, during his 50-minute sleep cycle, he hits a patch of light sleep and half-wakes or wakes, he will go back to sleep by himself. This is what we all do, every night. He may be disinclined to learn this new skill, because he is familiar with what he knows, but everyone in the family benefits if you help him make this change.

Making a new habit

As well as making sure that the bedtime routine is now a feature, which should help him adjust to this new idea of sleeping throughout the night, you will also have to reduce all stimulation at night when he does wake. This includes breast-feeding him or giving him any sort of bottle at night. He may ask for a bottle or a feed because he associates this with going to sleep, but, unlike the first year, you don't need to give him a bottle during the night as he gets all the calories he needs during the day. Feeding now will only stimulate his digestive system and disrupt his sleep pattern further.

In order for your toddler to learn how to get to sleep by himself, you may have to tolerate his protests and tears for a short period. Many parents find it helpful to

SECURITY TOYS OR BLANKETS
This little girl always takes her two much-loved dolls to bed with her. Their familiarity is comforting and gives her enough security to let you go. Many toddlers use a piece of blanket as their comforter.

Bad dreams

Bad dreams are thought to be unusual before the age of two, but if your toddler wakes during the night and is very distressed, it is possible that he may have been frightened by a bad dream. His developing imagination, combined with an inability to distinguish between imagined and real events, may cause him to panic as he remembers his bad dream on waking. Go and comfort him, and reassure him that he is in no real danger.

Dreaming occurs during REM (rapid eye movement) sleep, which occurs after the first four hours of sleep. If your toddler cries out in fright before then, he may be experiencing a night terror. Night terrors are very rare, and occur during deep, non-dreaming sleep. Your toddler may appear to be awake but actually he is still asleep and will have no memory of the event later.

bring about change gradually. What is important is that you are consistent. So, next time he wakes and asks for milk, say "No" gently but firmly, tuck him in again, and leave the room. If he cries, as is likely, wait for five minutes before going back into his room. Reassure him, but again say "No" to his request, and do not get him up. Tuck him in again, and leave the room. Increase the time you stay away by five minutes after each visit, up to 20 minutes, until he has fallen asleep.

Leaving your child to cry for 10 minutes or so will do him no lasting harm if it is within the context of your loving care. He won't be able to learn what is expected of him unless you are consistent, so don't give in halfway through. It sometimes helps to start by leaving him to go to sleep on his own during his daytime nap, as you will be less tired during the day.

Feeding

By the end of the first year, your child should be eating mainly family meals, although prepared with less salt or sugar than for an adult. She will bite and chew with her gums a long time before teeth appear, using the copious saliva she also produces to help soften foods. In fact, chewing and biting with the gums helps to promote the proper alignment of teeth as they come through.

By now you will be offering your toddler food that needs to be chewed, even if it is often chopped up in small, bite-sized pieces. In addition, offer soft foods from which she can take a bite; for example, pieces of banana.
• Introduce new foods one by one to make certain your toddler is not allergic to them.

• Certain food items are best avoided, as they run the risk of choking – peanuts, whole grapes, boiled sweets, large pieces of raw carrot, for example.
• Never leave a toddler who is eating unattended, and never allow her to eat while on the move.

Feeding herself

You can probably expect your toddler to feed herself with finger foods pretty well by now, and this will improve dramatically over the year as her hand–eye skills and her coordination and dexterity improve. She may be quite slow, especially to start with, and is unlikely to sit down and just eat – sometimes preferring to play with her food! – but, even if haphazard, using a spoon competently is possible at this age. You may need to help her finish off what's in her bowl, or feed her the occasional spoonful as she feeds herself, but by and large she should be able to manage by herself.

Providing foods that can be eaten by hand – pieces of fruit, or little sandwiches, for example – also helps her feel that she is becoming more independent and that should please her and make her want to eat, too.

Balancing liquids and solids

In addition to being able to feed herself, your child should be drinking regularly from a cup – even if you start with a feeder beaker. Bottles should now be a thing of the past, and if you are still breast-feeding this may be limited now to morning and evening feeds.

If your child is still having large quantities of milk during the day, which helps her feel "full up" very quickly, she may not develop enough of an appetite for her meals. At this age two to three glasses of whole milk per day is more than enough. She may prefer drinking milk to eating solids, which is more time-consuming and less immediately satisfying in terms of feeling full. Encourage her to concentrate on solids at mealtimes and offer her some milk after she has eaten.

Drinking large quantities of juice can have a similar effect, especially as the sugar content in fruit juice is high. It may also cause diarrhoea and will increase the risk of tooth cavities. Drinking a lot of fruit juice now will give your toddler the expectation of high-sugar foods later

on. Limit her intake to 100g (4oz) a day. One very effective way of doing this is to dilute her drinks of fruit juice with water.

Eating together

When it comes to helping your toddler see what is expected of her at mealtimes, it helps if you sit and eat together, perhaps not at every meal but certainly once a day. At this age it is through imitation, and imitating the behaviour of those close to her, that your child is learning about her world and what happens in it.

Sitting together over a meal is a great time for family interaction and starting a routine. It also provides your toddler with the opportunity to learn how to behave appropriately at the table by imitating other members of the family. If you don't do this at home, it will be difficult for her to know how to do it if you go out to a relative's or a restaurant. And, while you cannot expect a toddler to tolerate a three-course, sit–down meal, you can help her join in and eat, and spend some of that time at the table contributing to the social occasion of the meal and family interaction.

Meeting your child's needs

What might seem a bit mysterious to you is that, in spite of all the physical activity that is so characteristic of the toddler years, your child appears to want to eat less. This is because her growth rate has slowed down in comparison to the first year. Over three meals, two drinks of milk and the occasional healthy snack during the day, her needs are easily met. Follow her lead and let her eat according to her appetite, while always offering her healthy choices.

You may also find that your child's eating habits are a bit erratic; she may eat very well some days and hardly at all on others. Don't worry about such discrepancies. Take a longer-term view, and assess what she has eaten over the course of a week. You will probably find that overall she has eaten about the right amount.

Making choices

Your toddler's sense of taste will be more developed now, and she may well start expressing a preference for one food over another. Try to encourage her to eat roughly the same foods as you and the rest of the family. This may mean a rethink of your own dietary approach, ensuring that you are giving her the right balance of nutrients. Keep the range of what you offer her to eat wide, and expect some rejections – you can always try a particular food again later.

To help your toddler feel that she has some autonomy over her food, you may wish to offer her a choice of foods at one mealtime. Allow her to choose between two items at first, say an apple or an orange, rather than giving her a handful of items to choose from.

Don't overreact when your toddler rejects your food: it is seldom more than a statement of not wanting it then. Never force-feed your child and try to avoid struggles by keeping mealtimes short – 15 to 30 minutes. If you feel your child has not eaten enough, offer her a healthy snack of cheese or fruit one or two hours later. Three small meals and two healthy snacks a day is fine.

Some children go through quite long phases of refusing certain foods. Don't worry about such phases. If the overall diet is balanced (even if it contains much of the same foods time and time again) and your toddler is happy, healthy, and growing well, then simply go on offering different items without comment.

Looking after your toddler's teeth

As soon as the teeth start to come in, they are susceptible to tooth decay. And by the start of your toddler's second year she will have enough teeth to warrant cleaning at

A healthy diet

Try to use as many fresh ingredients as you can for meals, because processed foods tend to be very high in salt, sugars, and artificial flavourings. Choose foods from the four basic food groups.

★ Meat, fish, eggs, and other protein foods

★ Milk, cheese, yoghurt, and other dairy products

★ Rice, cereals, potatoes, yams, sweet potatoes, bread, pasta, and other carbohydrates

★ Fruits and vegetables

Your child needs protein for growth, carbohydrates and fats for energy, while fruit and vegetables supply vitamins and fibre.

Fat and fibre issues

Remember that the low-fat, high-fibre diet that is suitable for an adult isn't suitable for a child who needs foods that are calorie-dense (weight for weight, they contain more calories) – full-fat milk rather than skimmed, for example.

As long as she is eating a proportion of fresh fruit and vegetables during the day, you don't need to select fibre-rich foods either. These are likely to increase the speed with which food moves through her system, not allowing enough time for all the nutrients to be absorbed. Small children who show signs of malnutrition or iron deficiency in developed countries have often been fed a low-fat, high-fibre diet.

least twice a day – morning and night – and visiting the dentist every six months for a check-up and advice.

You can help avoid cavities in your toddler's teeth by introducing teeth-cleaning. Cavities form when the naturally occurring bacteria in the mouth combine with sugars in the food residues left on the teeth, producing

an acid that attacks the tooth enamel. Avoid extensive snacking on foods, which means that the mouth constantly contains residual sugars. For healthy teeth, it is better to eat at mealtimes, followed by a drink of water or teeth-cleaning, than to snack constantly.

Although these are your toddler's first teeth they are very important, as they help form the mouth and create the space for the second teeth.

Sensible drinking habits

Another culprit in the creation of tooth cavities, or caries, in young children is drinking from bottles, which bathe the mouth in milk (which contains the sugar lactose), or drinking fruit juices (which contain the sugar fructose, even if they are labelled sugar-free).

Drinking from a cup is much better for the teeth at this age, and always offer water as a drink alternative to milk or fruit juices. Tap water is perfectly safe after the first birthday – you don't need to boil and cool it now. Don't give your child mineral water, however, because the mineral content is likely to be too high for her more sensitive system.

Communication skills

Your child will have been communicating with you for a long time before he says his first recognizable word. His language development began when he first heard your voice. He has been communicating with you through his body language and verbally through his babbling and his cries. He has also become adept at interpreting your tones and some of what you say, especially when associated with expressions of affection, or instructions.

What happens when your toddler starts to talk is the coming together of a lot of skills, which combine comprehension and the physical ability to make sound into verbal language. Your child will have been practising making sounds almost since birth, and you will be familiar with his making letter sounds repeatedly, like "b-b-b-b-b", babbling, blowing bubbles, and experimenting with the sounds he can make, and also varying the pitch and volume, perhaps shouting for attention. You can see how much your child understands, even if he cannot talk to you yet, by asking him "Where?" questions, such as, "Where are your feet?" He will probably have no difficulty in showing you!

First words

Although you can expect your child to begin speaking in his second year, there is a large variation between children, even those who are of similar intelligence. It is partly to do with personality and temperament: some children have more verbal personalities than others. In addition, boys tend to talk later than girls, and girls tend to talk more, but on average children produce their first word at around a year old. This may just be a repeated sound that has meaning for them, for example "woof" whenever they see a dog, or a picture of a dog. "Mama" and "Dada" are also common examples. Any words said may well be accompanied by a hand gesture to indicate the object, or to attract your attention to his attempts to speak. First words can cover a wide range of meaning at first, so that "woof" is not only applied to all dogs, but also to all four-legged animals. Also,

The crucial role of hearing in language development

There is one very important requirement to speech and that is the ability to hear. Even if your toddler can hear perfectly, he still needs to be able to distinguish different word sounds free from the interference of any background noise.

It is very important that your toddler engages in a lot of one-to-one communication, without distraction, so that he gets the benefit of hearing clearly not only what is being said but also the sounds of words. Not only will this help him to copy what he hears accurately, but it will also train his brain to distinguish what sounds make up each word. This will help him later when he starts to read, write, and spell. So, make sure that the television or radio isn't providing a constant background noise: turn it off unless you are actually listening to it or watching something. Your child isn't as able as you are to screen out noise when he tries to listen, and needs to hear words clearly.

Without being able to hear, it is impossible for a child to learn to talk, which is dependent on hearing and imitating sounds in a way that enables you to be understood. This is why hearing tests, at birth and again at around eight and 18 months of age, are very important. The earlier a hearing problem is picked up, the better for the child and

MUSICAL WRIST TOY
This toddler is exploring the various sounds that a simple musical wrist toy can make. Listening to words and music is crucial in language development.

his development. Even recurrent ear infections and glue ear can adversely affect your child's ability to hear, and consequently his language development. If your toddler has an ear infection, take him to the doctor's.

if you show a child of this age a picture of a dog sitting down, he may not identify it as a dog because the necessary four legs that help him define a dog are not seen. Your toddler may use one word to describe a range of objects without distinguishing between them, for example, "duck" may be used for all plastic toys and not applied to the real thing at first.

First sentences

First words are followed by two-word statements, which are often requests or commands; for example, "Go away" or "Want it". This will progress to simple sentences such as, "Tom wants teddy", as your toddler's understanding

and vocabulary build. Over your toddler's second year you can expect his verbal skills to develop from first words to telegraphed sentences, in which only the crucial nouns and verbs are spoken. This in turn helps his understanding because, now that he can communicate his interest in something more explicitly, he gets more detailed verbal information from you.

Television isn't recommended for this age group. Its fast-moving images are very attractive, but the speech is generally too difficult to follow, making it a language-free form of entertainment. So, if your toddler is spending a large amount of time watching television, it will probably have a negative effect on his language development.

Encouraging language development

The connection between language development and a later ability to read and write has been proved quite conclusively in research studies. Two or three one-to-one sessions daily between adult and child, of 10 or 15 minutes each, in which a baby or young child is talked to, read to, or sung to, without any background noise, has an enormously positive impact. Children who have received this sort of input show a reading age of almost 18 months ahead of their peer group at the age of seven.

The reason it makes such a difference is because the ability to hear different letter sounds, after your child has learned the individual letters of the alphabet and their sounds, makes it easier to identify them when they are seen written down. The words "fat" and "mat" have a very distinctive ending sound of "at" but, because of the different letter at the beginning, two very different meanings. Being able to distinguish between letter sounds becomes more important later when learning to spell.

It is fine for your child to hear two languages being spoken at home as long as specific individuals always speak the same language; for example, his grandmother always speaks Spanish, while you always speak English.

Having simple conversations

There is also a lot you can do to enhance language development generally. For instance, when your toddler attempts a word or two-word sentence, repeat it back to him to reinforce what he is trying to say. If he says "Cat gone", you can say, "Yes, the cat is gone. Where has the cat gone?" Keep the sentences simple. By doing this you reiterate his attempts so he can hear what he is trying

to say more correctly, and you are also continuing the conversation and introducing new ideas and concepts that he can build on. Do not overtly "correct" his speech, as this can inhibit him speaking.

To keep a conversation going with your toddler, point things out to him, listen to and acknowledge what he might try to say, and reinforce his efforts. When you are dressing him, talk about the clothes he is putting on, and name body parts. When you are shopping in the supermarket, talk to him and describe what you are doing. Although it feels a bit odd at first to have what are sometimes one-way conversations, dialogue will build rapidly and be fun for both you and your child.

Using rhymes and songs

Nursery rhymes and songs help fill the gap, and are also great for developing language skills. Some even have hand gestures, which help your toddler remember words and their sequences within a song or rhyme. They also help your child to focus, because with repetition comes a sense of anticipation, waiting for what comes next, which helps him learn to concentrate for longer on one thing.

Reading together

Reading to your toddler is an activity that many family members can take part in and is a role most grandparents particularly enjoy. It provides a great way to bond with your toddler.

Looking at books with your toddler is also a good way of developing language. To look at a book together, you have to sit close or have your child on your lap. This type of one-to-one time creates a good opportunity for language learning, and it is greatly enhanced by your attentiveness and closeness.

In addition, reading a book out loud means that your child has to listen to enjoy the story and, because it is an enjoyable and rewarding situation, he will do so.

Choose picture books with attractive illustrations and clear story lines written for toddlers. If you are unsure which books to choose, ask your local children's librarian or children's bookseller for advice. And be guided by your toddler – let him choose the book he wants. A book is something that he will be happy to return to time and time again, so you will get a lot of use out of each one.

Books follow a sequence of events with which your child will become familiar. He will learn to anticipate events in a favourite storybook that you have read to him several times before. He will also be able to respond to your questions about events in the story, and will point at pictures if you ask him about them.

Safety

As your toddler becomes more mobile and explorative, she needs constant supervision and you may need to reconsider safety measures. Never underestimate how quickly she can move once your back is turned, or how far she can reach.

In the home

Be especially careful with hot drinks: a pot of freshly made tea or coffee is hot enough to scald and scar a young child badly. Always put them to the back of a work surface or table. Use the back rings of the cooker when cooking, and don't underestimate the heat of the outside of an oven door – keep your child well clear. Keep electrical flexes out of reach, and make it a habit to turn off socket switches when not in use. Electrical socket covers are also a useful precaution.

Stair-gates deter your child climbing, but it is also worth teaching your child how to go up and down the stairs safely with you. Avoid rugs that can be tripped over. Small items, such as buttons, coins, and rings, present a choking hazard, so ensure they are out of reach. Move houseplants out of reach, too, as some can be poisonous.

Glass-topped tables, French windows or doors should be made of safety glass or covered with safety film. Fit childproof catches to any doors and cover guards to tables. Make sure cleaning materials, medicines, and sharp objects are not accessible.

Out and about

When out and about with your child, make sure that she is securely strapped in her buggy, and don't carry so much on the handles it could topple over with her in it. Car seats must meet safety standards, be correctly installed, and used for all journeys. Car doors usually have the option of child locking as standard.

You must be extremely vigilant with toddlers around water – children can drown in just a few centimetres of water. You also should begin teaching your toddler what is and isn't safe, without instilling unnecessary fear. Explain why you insist on certain rules and behaviour.

DANGEROUS HEAT
Avoid doing the ironing with your toddler in the room. An iron can cause serious burns to an inquisitive toddler, who will manage to grab it if her mother turns her back for a minute.

How toddlers learn

Toddlers need plenty of opportunities to play with toys plus lots of interaction with other children and attentive adults. What looks like the unstructured chaos of toddler play is actually the basis of learning. Your toddler will use these playtimes to develop her physical, emotional, and cognitive abilities through exploration.

How toddlers learn skills

By the beginning of the second year, your baby will have developed a wealth of skills on which to build new ones. He has progressed from being a small baby, dependent on you to meet all his needs, to a very definite personality in his own right, with new and emerging physical, cognitive, and emotional skills.

Where initially your baby's skills were geared to basic survival, now they are enabling him to explore and expand his world with your help. By the age of 24 months, your toddler will have more in common with an adult than with his newborn self in terms of abilities.

Increased mobility

This period is one of increased mobility for your baby. It is about exploring further afield through a newly developed ability to move from A to B. Initially this may be through crawling, but it also occurs through learning to walk upright, which enables greater movement and also frees up the hands. Once a skill like walking has been learned then progress is about becoming more adept at doing it. Part of your child's playing is the doing of something over and over again to become better at it.

As your child becomes more proficient at moving around, he is able to see things in context and develop his spatial skills further. For example, it's hard to imagine a chair in context unless you can move around it. Also, if your toy rolls behind a chair, and you can get to it, you learn that when things disappear from view they don't actually disappear altogether. This is part of a learning process that the psychologists call "object permanence", meaning that something continues to exist, even after you can no longer see it.

During your baby's second year he is using all his senses to gain in experience and understanding of his world. Physical skills are greatly increased through mobility, and mobility is increased through the development and practice of physical skills. As a consequence, your toddler's cognitive, or learning, skills are influenced by his new view of the world. And emotional development moves ahead as your child utilizes these new skills to interact with others, and learns to become more social.

Communication skills

The other great area of development during this time is in communication skills and language development. Comprehension, and a developing understanding of the meaning of what you are saying, comes long before the first words are spoken. It is not until the meaning of a word is understood that the spoken word follows, which is why repetition is so important. As you do something, constantly speak to your toddler, telling him what you are doing. Eventually it becomes clear that your child understands simple words through his response to what you say. Long before he can say "shoes", he will help you look for his shoes when you ask him, for example.

Individuality

The rate of your baby's development depends partly on opportunities provided to develop different skills, but also on the inclination and individuality of your child. Some babies love to sit and focus on one thing for a time, absorbed in something quite stationary, while others are always on the go and keen to get up and about. Some will manage to get to where they want through crawling, and show no inclination to walk, while others may spend a short time bottom-shuffling before moving swiftly to walking.

PHYSICAL COORDINATION
This 18-month-old toddler has no difficulty getting down from the bed while holding a towel over his head!

1 to 2 years: your toddler's milestones

Your baby's milestones during the next 12 months are an important indicator of his developmental progress. Although all children are individual, there are a number of achievements that you can expect of your child during this year.

Movement milestones

- learns to walk unsupported
- walks, stops, and turns
- carries something in his hand while walking
- climbs safely on to a chair

Hand and finger milestones

- self-feeds with a spoon
- graduates from a feeder beaker to a cup
- throws an object, even if not in a straight line
- rotates wrist to unscrew an item

Social and emotional milestones

- learns to be happily apart from you for longer periods
- plays alongside another child
- shows loving behaviour to a toy, pet, or another child
- may help you with simple tasks

Language milestones

- progresses from single words to two-word utterances
- responds verbally to questions you ask
- enjoys naming everyday objects when he sees them

Intellectual skills

- remembers simple events that occur regularly
- makes connections between live objects and pictures
- begins to understand the concept of possession

12 to 14 months

Your baby's increasing ability to interact with her world is becoming more and more evident now. She will take every opportunity to explore as she is developing physical and cognitive skills. Her newfound ability to move around her environment will help with this, sometimes bringing her wishes into conflict with yours! Provide a safe place where she gets the chance to explore her abilities.

Physical development

By now your baby will have been able to sit securely for some time. She has probably been standing too, either holding on to you or another person, or a piece of furniture. She may already have taken her first steps, either cruising from one object or person to another, or taken her first steps alone. Almost half of all babies learn to walk at around this time, although many will still topple over if they lose momentum. But, if your baby has been walking since 10 months, or doesn't bother for another six months, that is normal too.

Provide lots of opportunities to use and strengthen the leg muscles in preparation for walking. Start by holding her hands as she practises taking her body weight on her feet while taking a few tentative steps. Babies' heads are big, in comparison to their bodies, and heavy. Until the legs strengthen, balance is a little unsteady as a consequence. What she will do when she begins to walk, however, is to walk with feet wide apart, toes pointing out, to give herself as broad a base as possible to improve her balance.

Fine motor skills

Your baby's fine motor skills are also improving through practice. Learning to let go of something provides quite a dramatic shift in ability, and brings together a number of skills. Before, if you gave your baby an object, she would tend to clasp it and hold on to it until she dropped it accidentally, or had it taken from her. This was because of the reflex to hold on that she was born with. Initially so strong, this ability to cling so tightly diminishes over the months. Now, at the age of about 12 months, she is reaching out, placing her hand over the object, deliberately picking it up, moving it to another place, and letting it go.

Hand movements are becoming more sophisticated. Your baby is beginning to turn her wrist in order to place an object more specifically into the place she wants it to go. This movement is a bit haphazard at first, as the physical development of the bones, which allows for greater manipulation, occurs over the first few years, just as the child is growing in maturity and dexterity. All this picking up and dropping of things – maddening though it can be – is part of the activity needed to practise these movements.

Your baby now begins to stretch her fingers out into the right position to pick something up in preparation – she is anticipating what she intends to do. She will also stretch out her arm towards something that she wants, to convey to you what it is.

Learning to walk

When babies are learning to walk, it is much more useful for them to learn with bare feet. A baby can tell a lot about the surface on which she is walking through what she can feel through the soles of her feet – whether the surface she is trying to walk on is smooth and soft, or hard and lumpy.

Don't be tempted to encase your toddler's feet in anything but the softest-soled shoes, and allow lots of opportunity for safe barefoot exploration. It is essential that you get your toddler's feet measured for length and width to ensure that the shoes you choose fit correctly. Your toddler will only need properly soled shoes when walking outside, and you will probably notice that walking with feet encased in shoes demands a slight adjustment at first, when your toddler may seem to walk less well initially. Hard, unyielding soles do little to help.

Cognitive development

With the right balance of stimulation and time to assimilate new experiences, babies' cognitive development starts to move forward in leaps and bounds now, building on everything that has been absorbed over the first year.

Verbal development

Your baby's first words are evidence of her cognitive development, and the beginning of an amazing new stage where communication extends into verbal language. And, as babies continue to watch what happens around them, they learn that objects have functions. You may now see your baby using a toy telephone like a real one: picking it up, putting it to the ear and putting it down. Soon she will be saying hello – or an approximation of the word – into the mouthpiece, and appearing to wait. She may not understand what the purpose of the telephone is at first, but it will soon start making sense to her when you put her ear to the real phone to listen to someone at the other end. It is as if small pieces of the jigsaw puzzle are being accumulated before she is able to make sense of the overall picture.

A sense of touch

We are all born with a sense of touch, but its development is dependent on having the experience of touching and feeling things.

Our ability to distinguish between different textures comes from our experience of feeling them. Touching an object to see what it feels like also provides a baby or toddler with the opportunity to use her hands in a different way, not to manipulate an object but to find out something about it. She can learn to explore and experiment by touching different substances and textures, such as water or fabrics.

Emotional development

Every baby is individual with a unique personality. Ensuring that all the physical needs of your baby are met really helps a baby's emotional development at this stage. It's hard to concentrate on learning to walk, or to deal with new people in your life, if you are tired and cranky, or

Toy box

Stacking toys

These provide an opportunity to learn about sizes, and how things fit together. Playing with stacking toys like blocks also involves using the hand to pick up and put down. Show her how to stack two blocks, one on top of the other, and she will try to copy you. At first she will probably only manage two blocks – one on top of the other – but with playful practice she will soon progress to stacking three and four blocks at a time without any difficulty at all.

Push-down/pop-up toys

While such toys rely on hand–eye coordination, they also help your child learn about cause and effect. When I do this – push down – then this happens – it pops up. It engages her attention because she is learning that one event leads to another, but doesn't yet know for sure that it will happen every time. Show her how it works, then let her make her own efforts. Is it easier to push down with the whole hand, or just one finger?

Textured toys

Use a variety of textured items – egg boxes, joining bricks, shiny paper, crinkly fabric, soft toys – and allow your child to explore their different properties, while you supervise. Do they scrunch up, are they smooth to touch, do they stick together?

hungry. Whenever possible, plan new activities or experiences for your baby when she is well rested, to ensure that an enjoyable time is had by both of you.

By now, close attachments have also been formed to a parent, a caregiver, and other close family members. Often there is a specially close attachment to one or two persons if there is a parent and childminder sharing the daily care. It is within this secure emotional environment that babies continue their development and learning.

Developing a love of reading

Books provide a focus for a quieter time, allowing your child to begin enjoying the pleasure of stories and imagination. Fictional stories explore ideas that help your child learn about what happens next and how characters react to events. They also provide the first steps towards learning to read, which happens within the shared or solitary enjoyment of looking at books.

Enjoying stories

At this stage books are not about learning to read – they are about enjoying stories for their own sake, and learning to focus and listen, both of which are important skills for the future. But books are also for sheer entertainment and the joy of returning to old favourites, books to be read time and time again, which in turn creates security.

★ You will have to show your baby how to look at and take care of books. Choose sturdy, wipeable board books at first. Their pages are easier for little fingers to turn. Keep your baby's books somewhere that is easy for your baby to get at, so she can choose them on her own.

★ Look at them together, with you reading the words. Explain things more fully as they come up in the story, while you have your toddler's focus and attention, and take time to discuss the pictures. This process also provides a time for closeness between the two of you, and can be usefully done at any time of the day for its own sake or for a quietening-down period, perhaps before bed.

★ Make sure there is no background noise when you are reading to your baby. Turn off the television, stereo, or radio, so that it is possible for her to really focus on listening to your voice as you read the words or for you to answer her questions about the story or pictures.

1 *Sit with your baby held closely in your lap. Hold the book open so he can see the pictures clearly, and begin reading. Give your baby plenty of time to look at each page.*

2 *Respond to your baby's reactions to the pictures or the story. Enjoy his enjoyment in the tale, or the surprises the book contains.*

14 to 16 months

Once your baby starts walking, you may find that his explorer instincts open up a whole new world as you adjust to this new phase. Create a safe place for him to play, which allows exploration within a safe and secure environment. He is not being naughty, but his instinct to explore is stronger than his memory of what you've told him about not touching the electric socket!

Physical development

By now, if your child has learned to walk he will be getting steadier on his feet and can begin to walk – although slowly – longer distances. What he will probably also do is to rely quite strongly on using his arms for balance, occasionally holding on to you or to pieces of furniture as he makes progress. And, as he walks alone, his arms are held away from his body on each side to help him balance when standing alone. Instead of toppling over, he will probably sit down quite deliberately if he feels he is losing his balance.

Handedness

At this age your toddler will probably use both hands equally. Some toddlers may begin to show a preference for using either the right or left hand when playing, feeding, or drinking from a cup, but most children do not consistently use one hand rather than another until they reach about three years old.

The hand a child shows preference for is genetically determined. If both parents are right-handed, there is a 98 per cent chance of their child being so, too. When one parent is left-handed, there is a 17 per cent chance of a child being left-handed, and where both parents are left-handed, this increases to 50 per cent.

Advances in self-feeding

Being able to grasp an object has made self-feeding possible for some time, although being unable to turn the spoon into the mouth has, at first, made this a bit haphazard. As your child is more able to twist her wrist and turn the spoon towards her mouth, this gets easier.

Being able to drink from a cup also becomes easier for the same reason – bringing the beaker to the mouth then being able to turn it towards the mouth becomes more possible as this twisting movement improves.

Play activities that help develop this ability will also help your toddler achieve other skills that make her more independent.

Don't try to influence deliberately which hand your toddler uses: he will use the one that feels most natural to him.

Fine motor skills

Fine motor skills, smaller movements of the hands, are developing, along with hand–eye coordination. At first, toddlers tend to point with their finger, hand, and whole arm when they want something, but over time they learn just to use the finger to communicate their wishes to you.

Building bricks can be used in a variety of ways to help your child develop his fine motor skills. You can count them and group them as well as build with them. No doubt, when you play with him, most of the fun for your toddler is in knocking the bricks down that you have carefully stacked. But introducing the idea of balance to him by showing him how to build bricks is laying good foundations. The first time he manages to place one block on top of another is quite an achievement.

Cognitive development

Your child's attention span is beginning to lengthen and, if he isn't distracted by feeling tired, thirsty, or hungry, he can focus on an activity for a little longer. This is because he is beginning to develop memory, through repeated activity, so he is beginning to anticipate the pleasure of a book when you suggest it, for example, or going for a walk, or having a bath. And during an activity, if he is distracted for a moment and discontinues it, he will return to what he was doing after a pause.

Through the daily routine, your child develops an understanding of what might happen next. This understanding can then begin to be transferred to other events.

Verbal skills

At this stage your child will probably be saying, or attempting to say, a few words. Children vary enormously: some will say nothing at all for months then come out with a three-word sentence, while others will attempt to say individual words, however inaccurately, until they make themselves understood. Often a child will begin with one word, such as "dog" or "daddy", but apply it to all animals or to all men.

Emotional development

Babies who are cherished, cuddled, and kissed learn, by example, how to pass on similar expressions of positive emotion to others, and you may also see this extended to their toys. Equally, expressions of dissatisfaction may be displayed. Your toddler may get angry at a toy, but it doesn't usually last for long. Young children are often very responsive to the emotional environment in which they live. They may not understand it but they often pick up on your happiness or sadness – laughing with you, or stroking your face if you are sad.

The role of soft toys

A favourite toy, to which a child can form an attachment, can help some children make the transition from your company to being happily alone. It can become a "transitional object". Many young children find the presence of a familiar toy at bedtime quite reassuring.

Soft toys can also help develop a child's imagination, as they give their toy characteristics, or act out happy or sad times with it. They can also use their soft toys to act out feelings. Talking to your toddler about feelings through a favourite soft toy can help him learn how to empathize. Does she look sad? Why does she look sad? How can we make her feel happy?

You could get more than one of a favourite toy or blanket. Then, if the first one is lost or becomes worn out, it can be replaced by another that is exactly like it.

Toy box

Push-along toys

Pushing something along can be done for its own sake, or it can be incorporated into early, imaginative play – for example, putting a favourite soft toy into a miniature stroller or buggy, and taking it "for a walk".

★ A toy wheelbarrow in which things can be carried elsewhere is also fun, as is a toy vacuum cleaner that can be used alongside an adult using the real thing!

★ Some push-along toys are designed to make a musical noise when used, while others may include a dog on wheels (which incorporates the pleasure of a soft toy into imaginative play).

★ Some push-along trolleys come complete with a set of building bricks, which provide extra fun in being loaded and unloaded, and can be used to build towers.

Water play

Water play really begins from birth, when your baby enjoys his first bath. Water is great fun to play with, and has lots of interesting properties that make it useful for exploration. Just pouring water from one plastic beaker into another helps your child develop hand–eye coordination.

Bath and basin games

Provide a variety of different-sized plastic containers, even a plastic tea set with small teapot, which challenges coordination further when trying to pour from the spout. Playing somewhere where spills don't matter helps your toddler gain in confidence, as does helping to clear up a spill if it happens.

★ Lots of bath toys provide opportunities for pouring, while some also include other possibilities like turning a tap to allow water through or not.

★ Water play introduces the idea of different weights, a beaker of water feels heavier than an empty one, and provides opportunities to learn about other properties of water – for example, it always flows down and not up – and here you have the beginnings of understanding about why the rain falls down and rivers don't run uphill. Your toddler can also learn, through play, about the things that float, such as lolly sticks made of wood, and those that sink, such as a pebble.

★ The important bit is the fun and enjoyment your child gets out of learning about water, or the imaginative play about boats crossing the sea, but this sort of play is also making a contribution to a wider understanding of how the world works.

Paddling-pool play

Water play can be extended from basins and baths into paddling pools, where your toddler will learn to feel comfortable sharing space with other children, getting splashed, and participating in the rough and tumble of communal play. The confidence in water that this develops paves the way towards feeling confident in a swimming pool and, eventually, towards the confidence that precedes learning to swim.

★ Whenever your toddler is playing around in even a shallow pool, you need to provide constant supervision to avoid the risk of drowning accidents.

BASIN PLAY
This child is really enjoying playing with water in his own garden. He discovers that leaves float – unless you push them down – and that you can create exciting splashes by simply waving your hand about in the water.

16 to 18 months

Now that your toddler can concentrate for longer periods of time, she may get totally absorbed in playing a particular game – a developmental milestone for her. Don't expect her to take kindly to being told to finish off a game without adequate warning! Even then, she will need reassurance that she can play the same game again another time – and soon!

Physical development

With her walking skills getting better and better, and with her arms free, it now becomes possible to pick up and carry an object while walking. This usually requires two hands, so balance has to have improved enough not to need the arms for balancing. Being able to walk, and stand securely, also opens up the possibility of reaching for objects that were previously out of reach.

Don't underestimate how far a toddler can reach: make sure objects are placed far enough away to be out of danger. It's all too easy for a toddler to grab a hot cup of coffee left too close to the edge of a table. Accidents often happen because your child has made something of a developmental leap and you have not quite caught up with her.

Playing outdoors

Using their bodies in an energetic and expressive way helps children develop balance, coordination and strength, and much of this sort of play needs to be done outdoors. Make sure that your child wears suitable clothing when playing outdoors – clothes that you won't mind getting muddy or crumpled, and that won't catch when your child is trying to negotiate a slide with your help.

Learning to be adventurous on swings and slides doesn't come naturally to every child, and yours might need some encouragement. But when she sees other children having a go, and having fun, then this can encourage her too. This sort of play, if there are other children around, also helps her to learn about taking turns and taking care.

Take your toddler to the playground in your local park or to an indoor soft-play facility. In addition to pushing her on the baby swings, let her try out the small slides and mini climbing frames. Both will help her develop her hand–eye coordination as well as provide her with exercise and plenty of fun. She may well team up with another toddler of similar age, and they will chase each other excitedly around the playground.

Outdoor play can also include first games with balls. Choose a medium-size ball a bit smaller than a football and much lighter, so it won't knock your toddler over if thrown too hard, and your toddler can hold it in two hands. At first there will be very little hand–eye coordination, which is what makes actually catching a ball possible. This takes a lot of practice. But for now it is worth introducing the idea, and making a game of throwing, rolling, and catching balls outside.

Learning to throw

Once your toddler has learned how to let go, the next possibility is throwing. Although first attempts demonstrate that toddlers cannot throw with any accuracy, this will improve with practice. Give your toddler scrunched-up paper balls or soft foam balls to throw. Keep heavy objects out of reach of your toddler.

Cognitive development

By this stage your toddler's understanding has increased to the point of carrying out simple requests like "Give me the cup." Single requests are within her ability, but if you ask her to put down her book, fetch her shoes, and close the door, this would be beyond her ability because it requires her to remember a sequence of events in order. She would probably be able to do all three things, if you asked her to do them one at a time.

Your toddler's developing language may still be limited to one word at a time, but voiced in a different tone to convey different meaning. "Dadda!" might mean "Come here!" while "Dadda?", as she holds out a toy, might suggest "Help me." And "Dadda" said while pointing at a cup, might mean "I want a drink". Soon two-word sentences begin, so you might hear "Dadda, here!" or "Dadda, please?" or "Dadda, drink." Reinforce what you hear by asking, "Would you like a drink?" This way, you let her know you've understood her request, and help her to understand how to say things correctly.

Learning responsibility

At the end of a play session encourage your toddler to put the toys back into the box. At this age, doing this is just as much of a game as anything else, and if it is presented as such it starts to pave the way towards caring for things and putting them away after using them. We call it tidying up, and presume our child will find it boring – don't make that assumption and they won't either! Don't refer to it as

"helping me", either; it's a game and one she wants to play if you make it interesting, talking all the time – "Here's the red one. Can you find the green one for me?", "And… put it in the box! Now it's my turn." This will help her learn to value and take care of her possessions.

Emotional development

One change you may now notice is that your toddler will begin to recognize what pleases and what annoys you, and she may try out different behaviours to see what your reaction is. This is an extension of her learning about how she can influence her world, and is a way in which she learns to engage your attention. It is best simply to ignore any behaviours that displease you, so that she does not gain attention from doing them.

At this stage, she will want to please you, so it's worth encouraging good behaviour by giving her lots of attention when she behaves in a way that does please you.

Constructive scribbling

Making your mark permanent, even if it's just a streak of purple on a white page, is quite a thrill when done for the first time. It is very clear evidence that you can make something happen! And if this is joined by other colours, and eventually celebrated and pinned to the wall like a "proper" picture, it is a very rewarding process for a toddler.

Paper and crayons

First scribbles are very important – they are early expressions of creativity. Provide lots of paper – it doesn't have to be new; the back of junk mail is good, or discarded computer print-outs – and half a dozen colourful, thick wax crayons that are easy to grip for small fingers, in an easily accessible container for your child. You will need to make it clear that only paper should be drawn on, but if yours is a particularly expressive and experimental child then other

surfaces may be considered fair game at first. You can quite see why a nice white wall might be thought suitable, so you will need to be very clear about what's OK and what's not.

★ First scribbles are very important. They give her an idea of what she can achieve and, over time, using crayons in this way helps her learn to control the movements of her hand. Using the thicker wax crayons, allow your toddler to experiment with her own ways of holding the crayon when scribbling. It is best to wait until she is two years old before encouraging her

Becoming independent

You may also find that your toddler is quite happy to be independent of you in a group, occasionally checking to see that you are available to her if she needs you. Sometimes, however, in new situations, the need for reassurance is temporarily increased. You may find a period of clinginess arises, as a new adaptation is needed. This is normal behaviour while getting used to a new situation. Give your toddler the reassurance she needs, but don't become overprotective: it will pass.

Toy box

Building blocks

Building blocks that fit together take the possibilities of building blocks a little further. They require a bit more in the way of deliberate coordination, as the fit needs to be a little more accurate, and it takes more strength to push them together. But the rewards are greater, as the blocks stay together.

Playing with building blocks that fit together is great for boys and girls. With a little prompting from you, they will soon learn to use their imaginations to build a house, or a garage, or just put the colours together in particular patterns.

Activity toys

Activity centres or activity boards combine a variety of pushing, pulling, turning, and twisting movements that illustrate cause and effect. The reward for your toddler is the result but, along the way, she has developed her hand–eye coordination. This will also improve her skill with a spoon when self-feeding.

---

to hold a crayon in the proper way. Movements are large at first, covering wide areas of the paper, and become smaller later as her fine motor control – the small movements she needs to make in order to manage writing later on – improves.

★ Scribbling with crayons allows your toddler to practise twisting and turning movements of the hand. Her hand–eye coordination, as well as fine motor control, need to come together to do this. Encourage your toddler to have fun, enjoying the patterns she makes, so that she wants to continue to make more scribbles.

★ Don't concern yourself with which hand she chooses to use for drawing at this stage, as she may use both equally before she opts more and more for one rather than the other.

EXPRESSING CREATIVITY
Mum and toddler share some creative time while drawing, scribbling, and using imagination. This toddler makes a bold squiggly line right across the blue paper. He shows good hand control in his ability to make individual lines. His mother joins in the fun, choosing a blue pen to draw with. She encourages him to make more of his own lines with his orange pen. By doing this, he is further developing his hand–eye coordination.

18 to 20 months

Toddlers are naturally curious, and will learn to make important discoveries by themselves. If you constantly entertain your toddler, he won't develop his own ability to find things out for himself. Toddlers don't get bored if they have a good learning environment, even if they can't concentrate for very long yet, because their whole world is open to discovery.

Physical development

Your toddler may now be able to walk faster, and even run a little without stumbling, although children at this age vary considerably in what they can and want to achieve. If he is gently chased when playing, your toddler can speed up quite considerably and will also do so if excited. The large muscle groups in the legs have become much stronger through use, and give your child more control over stopping and starting when he is walking.

His movements are much more controlled generally, and may now include taking backwards and sideways steps. What also becomes possible now, with better balance and greater strength in the legs, is a kicking movement. At first, standing on one leg momentarily can be destabilizing and it takes practice to become proficient at doing so and then kicking out. Accuracy will be poor at first and, instead of actually kicking the ball, your child may effectively stand on it, which won't achieve his objective – yet!

Smaller movements

Because your child's fine motor skills are improving, he is more able to grasp a small object using his thumb and forefinger. This makes much smaller movements – such as undoing a large zip fastener – possible, although it may take some concentration and effort at first, and some children of this age will not be quite able to do it on their own.

All those activities that encourage pressing knobs, turning switches, and twisting handles, have helped, and now it is much easier for him to attempt something like posting a shape through its matching hole. Accuracy is improving all the time through playing, which practises these skills, and being able to achieve tasks independently – such as drinking regularly from a cup – all demonstrate his bringing together of motor skills.

Cognitive development

By now your toddler will probably have a vocabulary of between 50 and 200 words. The development of memory and of language are closely linked, so you may be aware of a big leap in his general understanding of the way the world works as his speech improves. What he says is now becoming more sophisticated, too. Whereas before it was more a question of naming objects – dog, car, shoe – or linking an adjective with an object – a red bus – now he may be using abstract concepts. He may also show that he is beginning

Sorting out shapes

A shape sorter, in which different-shaped objects must be matched to the same shapes in the side of a box, provides an extremely good opportunity for your toddler to enjoy developing spatial awareness and hand control. The shape has to be correctly matched, lined up, and pushed through.

Initially, this will be quite difficult for him to do, and you may have to line the piece up for him at first to demonstrate, allowing him to push it through. In order for him to want to try it needs to be rewarding, and over time, when it has become possible, he will return to the game again and again.

to understand that objects belong to people; for example, "my doll".

You may see how far your toddler's understanding has progressed when you make a complicated request to him, such as "Please go to the hall and get me your shoes." If he is able to do this, then he has understood a number of things – he has to remember where the hall is and how to find it, go there, find the right shoes from the rack, get them, and bring them back to you. This is a big leap in his cognitive skills.

Learning from books

By now your toddler will probably have quite a good selection of books, and visiting the local library to choose and borrow books is another activity that can be routinely enjoyed by you and your toddler. Have a

Musical activities

An appreciation of music can, in itself, be life-enriching for your toddler, and you may already share music with him by singing and dancing together at home. Musical toys can contribute to this enjoyment, and first toys – like a simple xylophone – can give enormous pleasure.

Sounding notes

Hand–eye coordination is required to hit the keys of a xylophone with the stick, and at first this will be a haphazard affair. But it does demonstrate cause and effect, and the possibility of influencing your environment through choice. The different keys provide different notes, and hitting them in a variety of sequences creates a range of musical effects. Don't expect a tune, though: this is about exploring noise! This activity will interest and absorb him as he listens to the sounds he produces, and listening skills are always worth practising.

Beating a rhythm

Other musical toys, such as a drum, tambourine, or hand-held bells, also produce noises, and allow your child to explore rhythm. Learning about rhythm, even indirectly, can be the beginning of learning how to keep to a rhythm, which is useful for other physical skills like dancing.

Identifying and copying a beat can be quite sophisticated, but it can also be very simple – 1, 2, 3, for example. You can copy the beat of a nursery rhyme – "Pat-a-cake, Pat-a-cake" – for example. Or you can pick out the beat of the syllables of your name – "Ti-mo-thy", for example, is 1, 2, 3.

You can also make simple, homemade shakers – a handful of uncooked rice or macaroni in a sealed plastic bottle makes a pleasant noise. And your toddler can use one of these while dancing to music or singing a song, picking out the rhythm with the shaker. This has the added benefit of allowing several children to participate, helping concentration and collaboration and promoting the idea of a joint activity.

MAKING MUSIC
These two toddlers are having great fun sounding notes on their instruments. They listen to the different sounds attentively and with pleasure.

special shelf or book box where you keep your child's books and where he can get them for himself. And always keep a favourite book in your bag when you are out and about, as it will give your toddler something to look at and talk about if you are waiting somewhere.

Find time at least once a day to sit and read stories to your toddler. This quiet, absorbing activity will give you some peaceful, restorative time together. If you have more than one child of differing ages, try reading one story to all of them at the same time. Ask them each to choose a story, and read each story in turn. This will also help them to learn about taking turns and patience.

Having stories read aloud encourages imagination and helps your toddler learn to focus on your voice while having fun. Talk around the stories you read, asking questions about the pictures, as well as reading the words. Always take your cue from your child: some children hate it if you deviate from the written word, as they love the rhythm and familiarity of a favourite story. With very simple picture books, even at this early age your toddler will probably start to memorize some of the words he sees written down. This early understanding of books and the written word will help him later on when he starts learning to read.

Toy box

Modelling clay

Making shapes out of soft, pliable, coloured dough can give your toddler hours of creative play. Clear a space on the kitchen table and show him how to roll the dough with his fingers to make sausage shapes. He could also have fun making flat shapes, using a child's rolling pin and some plastic pastry cutters or shape moulds.

Sand play

Sand has all sorts of interesting properties that can be explored. It trickles through the fingers or a toy. It feels gritty, and sticks to your hands. If you put a lot of sand into a large container, it gets heavy. If you make sand wet, it sticks together and will keep the shape of another object. Sand can mean hours of exploratory fun, alone or with an adult or another child. It also means using your hands in different ways, and using tools, which helps develop manual dexterity. Adult supervision is always necessary, as there is a risk of sand getting in toddlers' eyes.

If you have a garden, it's worth having a sandpit. Sand must be fine and washed. Any sandpit needs a lid, or cats and dogs will treat it as a litter tray (cat faeces can contain the toxicaris worm, which can be dangerous to your child's health).

You will need a selection of plastic containers or buckets to play with, and other plastic toys: hand spades, a sieve, a miniature broom or brush, shape moulds and cutters, and plastic cars or animals.

Emotional development

Although your toddler might begin to understand about an object belonging to him, at this stage of his development he is unlikely to get too upset if it is snatched away from him. Unless he has an emotional dependency on a favourite toy, he is more likely simply to reach for another toy to play with and continue his game. His interactions with other children are limited and, although he will enjoy being around other children of similar age, any playing he does is in parallel rather than interacting with them.

By this stage, he may smile at other children of all ages, and like to watch what they are doing and imitate them, especially if they are a bit older.

20 to 22 months

Even though your toddler is becoming increasingly independent, sometimes she attempts more than she can manage. Offer the help she needs rather than taking over completely, and praise her efforts even if she does not quite complete the task. The more she is able to manage by herself, the more her self-esteem will grow, and the happier she will be.

Physical development

By now walking, running, stopping, and starting movements are usually well coordinated and something you have begun to take for granted as your toddler becomes much more physically capable. Your toddler will also attempt to climb off and on objects, such as sofas and chairs, depending on how adventurous a personality she is, and perhaps even in and out of her cot or bed.

Climbing stairs will probably be attempted, on hands and knees. If you have stairs, teach your toddler to come downstairs backwards, on her hands and knees, from step to step, which is much safer than trying to come down facing forwards. If you are coming downstairs with her, she can walk down slowly, holding on to your hand.

Using her hands

Carrying something in her hands as she walks is probably routine now if it's not too large, and she may try to carry two items, one in each hand.

Her fine motor skills are now more developed, meaning that not only can she use her hands to greater effect, but she can also use tools more efficiently. This can range from digging in a sandpit with a shovel, to scribbling on paper and banging a drum. She may also try to do those tasks that you have always done for her independently, such as trying to put on her waterproof boots by herself or doing up the simple buckles on her new shoes.

Cognitive development

By constantly building on what she already knows and understands, your toddler continues to extend her understanding of the world. Now, if she puts a cup on her head she knows that is not its proper use – although she may experiment with pretending it is a hat – and she is expressing her understanding of this through her game.

She often demonstrates her understanding of what happens next through her anticipation of it: for example, if you put on her coat, she may go and stand next to the door ready to go out. If you pass her a book upside down, she will turn it the right way up and sit down ready to read or be read to.

Games that she has played in one simple way before may be experimented with, and used in a different way to see what might happen. Posting shapes, for example, may have been done routinely in the past, but now she might pick up the box and look underneath to see where it has gone.

Pretend play

The development of imagination is helped enormously by encouraging pretend play. Pretend play usually begins through imitation – so, for example, when you played peekaboo you pretended you had gone away by hiding your face and reappearing, and your baby copied you. This extends into other activities. She has seen you drive the car, so she will sit and pretend to drive a car by

Ball play

Throwing balls accurately takes practice, as does kicking a ball, but it's possible for your toddler to have a go at this age. Balls are quite interesting in themselves because, unlike other things when dropped, they bounce. Ball play is also a good family activity.

Make sure that the ball used for kicking and throwing is not too heavy, and that your toddler has plenty of space to practise in – preferably outside.

turning an imaginary steering wheel and making the noise, "vroom, vroom". She will pretend to pour tea from the toy teapot into a cup, and milk from a toy milk jug. Then she will put in sugar and stir it, before pretending to drink it. She remembers a sequence of events and pretends to do it as part of her game.

You may well be required to take part in pretend games, because you are given a plastic cup of pretend tea, and expected to "drink" it. All the time your toddler is playing these pretend games, she is beginning to understand the distinction between what's real and what's not.

Learning about nature

Playing outdoors gives a child the opportunity to experience the natural world. It's very different from playing indoors, with all its restrictions, and being outdoors makes it possible to try out new activities, such as playing with a ball, jumping in puddles, or running without any hindrance or worry.

It's also difficult to be aware of the weather when indoors – but when you are outdoors you can feel the wind and see its effect on the trees, for example. Walking in the countryside or a park also gives an opportunity to look at leaves, and other growing things, and also to see older children riding bikes, or scooters, or skateboards.

Talk about the leaves on the trees, the seasons of the year, how the temperature changes influence how things grow. Keep it simple, but point things out and name them. All of this will help her observation skills and her vocabulary. You can also point out things like the reflections in puddles and the shapes made by clouds in the sky, plus why we have a shadow that moves with us. All of this helps instil an appreciation and enjoyment of the environment in which we live.

Emotional development

Learning to think about others takes a long time, and can only follow self-awareness. As your toddler becomes more self-aware, physically and then emotionally, she can extend her feelings about herself to others. This starts with those who are closest to her, which is why you may see some evidence of this

Toy box

Tray puzzles

Matching shapes in tray puzzles is a development of shape-sorting, and a precursor to simple jigsaw puzzles. It is all about identifying and matching shapes. You may have to show your child what is expected of her before encouraging her to have a go.

★ Tip out the pieces and show her how you look at the piece and find the matching shape on the board; show her how you may have to move the shape around to make it match. Place the shape by its home so she can see how it matches up before putting it in place. Take your cue from your toddler. Some children welcome help, while others can't bear it and want to work it out for themselves.

★ Tray puzzles help train the eye and develop the ability to match shapes. This is a valuable skill for later on, when your child begins to identify letters through their shapes, and also words – the word "elephant" has quite a recognizable shape! Matching shapes does, eventually, help your child when it comes to learning to read and write.

in her relationship with you – on whom she is still so dependent – but not necessarily with others.

Close family members can create the emotional security that allows your toddler to consider the feelings of other people, as long as her attention is drawn to them. For example, if you point out that an older child is upset, your toddler may express sympathy by giving the child a hug and a kiss. Empathy – the ability to feel as the other person does – comes from experience, which takes time, so don't expect it yet!

Fun with painting

Your child can use paints in a variety of ways without using a brush – she simply needs hands and feet! You need thick water-based paint, and the three primary colours – red, yellow, and blue. You can experiment with one colour at a time, or by mixing two to make a third, or using them all together to make a gungy brown, which begins the exploration of the different properties of colour.

Finger painting
Finger painting is deliciously messy and very tactile, and gives your child a real hands-on experience of making her mark. You will probably need several sheets of paper to experiment with different effects.

Hand prints
Hand prints require a slightly different technique, and possibly some adult help to paint one hand at a time, all over, and then to carefully press down. First attempts will be undoubtedly splodgy, but eventually they will provide an opportunity to talk about fingerprints and individuality.

Footprints
Footprints require adult help if you are to avoid paint being trodden elsewhere, especially as balancing alone on one foot isn't possible yet. Footprints make a unique record of your child's growth, and you can compare children's hand and foot sizes, talking about whose is bigger.

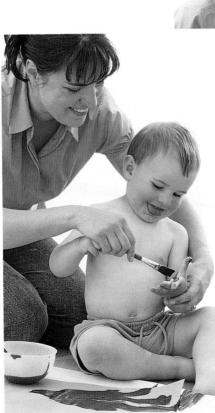

HANDS-ON EXPERIENCE
This toddler's mother helps him to paint thick dark-blue paint on to the palm of his left hand. Once his hand is thoroughly covered in paint, he spreads his fingers and presses his hand on the paper to make a print. She is helping him develop his own hand print, and he loves doing them!

22 to 24 months

Your toddler has become increasingly independent over the preceding 12 months, but he still needs your unconditional love and understanding. One feature of life with a toddler is a constant pulling away from and returning to parent or caregiver for support. Meeting a toddler's emotional needs means being constantly aware of his fluctuations, trying to understand him, and adapting to support him.

Physical development

The difference between the baby who couldn't walk just over a year ago, and the toddler who can now walk, run, and kick, demonstrates the amazing combination of physical skills that has led to these achievements over the second year.

Muscle coordination

Climbing off and on low furniture and on small climbing frames in the playground is probably routinely attempted and achieved. If you watch your toddler you can see that he is usually quite cautious, looking round to judge the distance and stretching one leg to find the ground and then the other. Some toddlers will also try to jump up and down, but their feet don't yet tend to leave the ground! All the time muscles are being strengthened and coordinated, and activities like kicking a ball become possible through practice.

Your toddler's ability to squat down and pick something up, then return easily to a standing position, is now quite proficient because of the increased strength and flexibility in his hip and knee joints. But his running may still be a little stiff, and he may still have insufficient strength and coordination to manage running around corners without slowing down.

Dexterous hands

Your toddler's hands are now much more dexterous.

★ She can manage smaller, manipulative movements, which makes her hands much more capable, using the whole hand to unscrew the lid of a jar, for example, or her finger and thumb to pick up something quite small.

★ She can use objects as tools more proficiently, or place things one on top of the other more specifically.

★ Fingers are used to point, poke, or prod – used singly or together – and your toddler can calculate how best to use her hands to achieve the result she wants.

Cognitive development

Physical experiences help to develop your toddler's cognitive skills. For example:

● Your child knows that the toy hammer is for banging with and would use this correctly now, instead of another toy.

● He knows that toy cars go "brrrrmmmm, brrrrmmmm" but a plastic cow goes "moooo".

● He can make connections between a toy car and the family car, a plastic cow and one in a book or in a field. He knows that each car has similar properties but that they are different: one is real, and the other is not.

And all the time he is talking about what he is seeing and learning, which means that you are reinforcing his knowledge with your questions or corrections in response. There is a massive shift in understanding as his language develops because of this, and because of his developing memory.

Language and memory

Memory and language are closely linked. It is much easier to remember something when it has a name than when it is just an abstract object. Make as much effort as you can to talk to and with your toddler, as this will help his cognitive development enormously. If you are reinforcing

Toy box

Crayons and paper

Having been introduced to the idea of crayons and paper at an earlier stage in his development, your child will probably want to scribble and draw regularly by now.

★ His hand movements are crude at first, but through his experimentation with colours and shapes he will learn that he can exert greater control over his movements and will gain in confidence with crayons.

★ Allow him to experiment with a variety of different crayons and felt pens (choose washable felt pens, in case of accidents). As he draws, tell him the colours and talk with him about what he is trying to express through his scribbles.

★ Don't assume that you can interpret what your child is trying to draw – let him tell you!

his efforts to communicate, it encourages him to go on trying. In addition, if you are repeating what he says and building on it, this helps. For example when he points and says, "Car", you can say, "Yes, that's your car. That's your blue car. Would you like to put your teddy in your blue car?" Not only are you responding to and reinforcing what he is saying, but you are giving him a lot more relevant information.

You are also helping him develop his ability to think about what to do next, which helps develop his imagination. On another occasion when he is playing with his car and

Imaginative play

Playing with first cars, trains, soft toys, and dolls, whether your child is a girl or a boy, provides them with opportunities for imaginative play. It also helps them to develop their own stories and events, which they can play out with these toys.

★ Toddlers sometimes act out their own experiences with their dolls, helping to make sense of events in their daily lives.

Playing with dolls and toy figures

You will probably find that your toddler concentrates quite hard while playing imaginatively with his toy figure or doll, and may talk about what is happening in his game, chattering away to himself.

★ Boys tend to talk less when they play with dolls or toy figures, as their games tend to include more action.

★ Both boys and girls will copy what they've seen happen in real life, and at this age will probably copy various parenting activities they have experienced in your company.

★ Your toddler may pretend to feed a doll, put it to bed, or give it a bath.

★ Looking after a sick dolly – giving pretend medicine, sticking a plaster on the knee, bandaging the arm – makes a great game.

★ Toys don't need to be sophisticated, either: an old shoebox and a tea towel make a very good bed and blanket for a teddy to sleep in.

Playing with cars

Both girls and boys enjoy playing with cars and trains.

★ At this age toddlers still tend to play alongside each other, although elements of social play are beginning to emerge. So sharing a group of cars may not work, but if each child has their own car they may happily play together, learning how to take turns. Look for opportunities to acknowledge and praise sharing, and "head off" any potential conflict before it occurs. Children need coaches not judges.

teddy, he will remember what you said. He will put the teddy in the car and move his language along, saying "Teddy in", for example. Then, over time, he may say "Teddy in car" or "Teddy in blue car".

Whenever you are with your toddler, whether playing, feeding, or putting on his shoes, talk to him and describe what you are doing, using lots of adjectives. Talk about putting on his brown shoes, one foot, then the other, and doing them up. Giving him a verbal description contributes to his understanding. Remember, too, to allow him time to respond to you, and the conversation will soon flow!

Using books

By now books will be part of your regular repertoire of resources. Although books are something that you can share with your child, also encourage him to use books on his own, perhaps suggesting that he looks at a book in bed while waiting for you to come and settle him at night, or when he is having a quiet time during the day.

In addition, start using books to look at pictures of something he has seen – an animal book after a visit to a zoo, for example. This gives you something to talk about and refer to, identifying the animals you have

seen. In addition, it introduces your toddler to the idea of books as a source of information.

Emotional development

As your toddler experiences more of the world, and develops the language to talk about his experiences, he also begins to think about how he feels and how others feel. This may become apparent first of all through expressions of his own feelings – happiness, anger, sadness – which can be overwhelming and may be expressed in a tantrum.

Managing feelings

For now feelings can be expressed in a variety of ways, and learning how to manage them, especially in a group, is the beginning of your toddler becoming socially able.

Unwanted behaviour towards another child can be because of an inability to manage feelings, and you will want to help your toddler deal with these. But it is only through experiencing mixing with other children that it is possible to practise managing feelings in a group, and to become emotionally aware.

Always remember that a hungry, tired, bored, or overextended toddler is much more likely to exhibit unwanted behaviours.

CAR CITY
This toddler plays with his toy car. He moves the car around an imaginary world, commentating on the action as he enacts it.

The third year

The third year of
your child's life is
a wonderful time,
however challenging
it sometimes appears.
You will start to get a
real feel for your child's
developing character
as his language skills
increase and he
becomes interested
in more social
environments.

Your child's development

During this third year of her young life, your toddler will develop into a physically dexterous, verbally competent, and emotionally expressive individual personality. She will also begin to experience just what a magical, and sometimes frustrating, place the wider world can be.

Emerging independence

This is a time when your child progresses from being almost completely self-centred and limited in her outlook to becoming more aware of other people and events around her. It is also a time spent juggling your child's growing desire for greater independence and opportunity with the limits of her actual abilities, which can often be out of line with each other, and she will frequently require your help.

Growing closer

This can also be the best of times for you as a growing family. Sharing time together provides all sorts of learning opportunities as well as being fun – whether you are visiting the park, reading a book, or even walking to the shops. Your child may also delight you with spontaneous outbursts of affection, disarming you with her endearing hugs, irresistible smiles, or infectious laughter; while you, in turn, can respond in an equally spontaneous way.

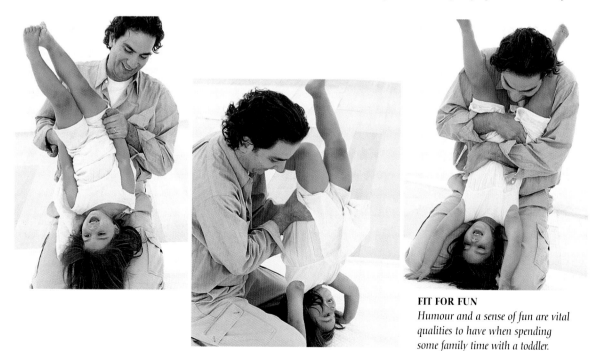

FIT FOR FUN
Humour and a sense of fun are vital qualities to have when spending some family time with a toddler.

Toddler characteristics

It is important not to confuse any family characteristics or potential personality traits with challenging toddler attributes. A stubborn or argumentative streak in a two-year-old is a typical form of behaviour for a child of this age, and is not necessarily setting up key character traits for later life. Even so, it can sometimes be challenging to live with a two-year-old child who just doesn't want you to put her shoes on!

Accentuating the positive

While it may sometimes seem at this stage as if your child's favourite pastime is saying "no", it may be because this is one of the words she hears most from the grown-ups around her! It helps to think about reducing the number of times you have to say "No" to your child: rephrase some of your answers using humour, or give her a gentle challenge: "Can you put your hat on before I open my eyes?" This is a good time to reinforce any positive behaviour with praise, and to start offering your child simple choices from two options. Remember, too, that your child saying "no" is a reflection of her growing sense of self, which is positive and important – her way of learning what it means to be an independent person.

Throughout all this period, your child needs your guidance, reassurance, and unconditional love. It's not easy, and can sometimes bring out the two-year-old in the best of us! So remember which one of you is the adult and retain your sense of balance as you make this journey from toddler to preschooler together.

About this book

During this year of enormous and exciting change in your child's young life, your support, encouragement, and love can do more than anything else to help her blossom. Understanding how your child develops is essential to helping you tune into her needs and give her what is best for her.

Section 1

The first half of this book tells you about how your child's development will affect both her physical and her emotional needs. For example, your child still needs lots of opportunities to use her body to become physically competent, but she also needs to balance this level of activity with enough restorative sleep to allow her to recharge those batteries.

Being one step ahead in terms of knowing what to expect from your child will help you understand her so that you can respond in the best and most effective way possible. And being able to meet her needs in this way will not only help her feel loved and valued, but boost your confidence as a parent, too.

Section 2

The second half of this book contains information about how and when your child is likely to reach each new milestone. Although the information is organized month by month, it's important to remember that the time-scale for every child is flexible. All children develop at different rates, and your child will progress in her own time at the speed that's right for her.

However, a certain amount of growth and development has to take place before each new skill can be acquired. So, for instance, don't expect your child to be able to manage her own buttons as she dresses herself until she has had time to try various activities and develop her skills of manual dexterity.

There are lots of practical things you can do to try to encourage your child along the way, and this section includes some ideas for games and activities that you can play with her. Giving your child the right kind of stimulation at just the right time will begin to build her confidence and self-esteem, and help give her the best possible start in life.

Family life

As a family, you have probably now settled into more of a predictable pattern and adapted to the emotional, physical, and perhaps financial changes that come with having children. Your toddler still has many new changes to adapt to and needs time and encouragement to learn how to handle them.

Parental responsibility

The enormity of being responsible for another life entails a very steep learning curve for most parents. Family life at the beginning of your child's third year should be settling into a routine and, as adults adapt to their individual and joint roles as parents, this time together can become amazingly rewarding.

Family relationships

Whether your child is an only child, has recently been joined by a new sibling, or has older stepbrothers or stepsisters, relationships with other members of the extended family are all-important for enriching your child's life: although his bond to you as parents is a primary relationship based on unconditional love, it's important for your child to have alternative sources of affection from people other than his parents. For example, he may be developing a particularly close relationship with relatives such as grandparents, or he may have a close bond with a caregiver or babysitter, which can be encouraged and supported by you.

The growing family

Every family is built upon different personalities and situations. A change in circumstances may occur for the first time in your child's life when a brother or sister is born. Your child's reaction to this new arrival will probably depend on a variety of things:

- his individual personality and temperament
- your family's particular circumstances
- the age gap between siblings
- how the situation is presented to him.

While your child may express no jealousy or rivalry towards a new sibling at first, he may find the situation becomes increasingly difficult as his sibling grows older and is more likely to interfere with his toys or games. Since there is no perfect age gap between two children, it all depends on the children concerned – their response cannot be guaranteed, whatever their ages!

Sibling rivalry

At this age, children are likely to express extreme love or hate for a new arrival – often within the space of the same hour! And, while some children may adapt easily and happily with no concern for the new arrival's apparent imposition, others can feel very threatened by this new change.

The skill as a parent is to know when to intervene or not. It is important to find time to really listen and respond to the concerns of each child, and to try to meet each of their needs while balancing what's best for the family as a whole. While children at the age of two may sometimes appear desperate to be independent, they do still demand – quite reasonably – a lot of time and individual attention. At the same time, it is also worth emphasizing to your toddler that he or she now has a special, exciting new role as an older brother or sister.

Special times

Try to minimize the possibility of sibling rivalry by ensuring individual time and attention for a period every day with your toddler. You may feel as if whatever you give is never enough, but you can feel reassured that if your two-year-old knows he always has some definite one-to-one time together that can be relied upon without interruption from the baby, this will make a big, positive difference to him. Choose something to do together that a baby couldn't possibly join in with to increase the sense of importance of this precious time together.

NEW ADDITIONS
Taking on the role of older brother can be an exciting time for your toddler, as well as being an uncertain period of great change. Give him time to adjust, and be sure to spend time alone together.

Twins and triplets

With such advanced reproductive technologies now available, the incidence of twins and triplets is increasing. Twins and triplets form their own unique relationships with one another, but their needs as individual children are still very important, and can sometimes present unique demands on parents. If you feel that you need extra support, organizations such as TAMBA (*below*) can provide you with practical advice to enable you to have the chance to spend some one-to-one time with each child and also with your partner.

Useful websites
www.tamba.org.uk
www.multiplebirths.org.uk
www.twinsmagazine.com

Social and behavioural development

At this age your child is still centred on herself and her own needs, seeing the world almost exclusively from her point of view. This works to her advantage in some ways as she focuses on practising her skills and abilities.

Learning to share

At this age your child is still very self-focused, and this is fairly typical behaviour for her age group. She isn't being selfish if she behaves in a possessive or ungenerous way, but if she can't yet grasp why she should share what she knows is hers, it can sometimes make it difficult for her to be able to interact, or share toys and activities, with other children of a similar age and at the same stage of development. You will want to

Acquiring social skills

Most of what children learn about respecting other people's feelings is acquired through example and by observing others. If your child is treated with fairness and consideration, and then sees this repeated in the extended family and wider community, she will, in time, begin to understand what it means to be socially well-adapted.

Likewise, in spite of her typical toddler attributes of self-focus and possessiveness, it is important to encourage your child to mix with other children to help her social development. For instance, if an older child who has already learned to be more thoughtful, considerate, and tolerant, plays with your child, she can in turn learn from the example of the older child.

encourage her to think about other people, of course, but it is not until a child is five years old or more that she can demonstrate any unsolicited or sincere concern for someone else's needs.

Nurturing generosity

Attempting to influence the behaviour of a child of this age by asking her to consider others doesn't have much of an impact since she genuinely can't yet empathize. Asking her to consider how she would feel if someone pushed her – as she has just done to another child – won't work. Keep it simple and reinforce the message, "We don't push other people".

This doesn't mean you shouldn't have conversations about feelings at another time, but when managing antisocial behaviour just insist that she doesn't do it. Also be sure that you always acknowledge and praise any kind and thoughtful behaviour when it arises spontaneously, thereby reinforcing what your child is beginning to learn for herself about being social.

Preschool groups

Learning to be socially well-adapted takes time, practice, and ultimately self-motivation; wanting to behave well to please you, rather than because you have to tell her, makes it much easier for your child to achieve. This is why meeting with other similarly aged children, perhaps at some sort of structured pre-school group, can really help. Your child will gradually learn what is expected of her and of other children, both from you and from the other adults outside of her family.

Other social skills

As your child begins to make this move out of the secure confines of her immediate family unit and into the wider world, she needs to become aware of other necessary social skills such as learning how to listen and cooperate. The primary way she learns how to do this is by example:
- how she is treated will in turn influence how she treats others
- if she is listened to when she speaks, she will learn to listen to others

- if she feels secure in her place, she won't have to fight so hard to be acknowledged

If a child is insecure about how she fits into a larger group, she needs reassurance and positive attention so that she doesn't feel the need to be demanding or inconsiderate of others. Children of this age are still very self-focused, striving to satisfy their own needs even if it isn't always socially acceptable.

Changes in behaviour

Social development is seldom a smooth progression, and all children can behave seemingly out of character on occasion. Whether it is in response to a specific incident, because your child is unwell, or sometimes for no apparent reason, the fact is that it is completely in character for a child of this age sometimes to be unpredictable in her behaviour.

Emotional development

At this stage, you will be increasingly aware of your child's emotional development. It is typical of this age group that a child will swing through a multitude of different emotions during the course of just one day. One minute your child may be insisting on doing things his way and refusing to do as you ask; the next minute he is clinging to your legs, refusing to let you move an inch without him.

Emotional inexperience

All young children show through their behaviour what they can't express in words. This may be because they don't yet have the language skills, or haven't previously experienced the emotion, so they don't actually know what they are expressing.

For example, if there has been no previous reason for, or experience of, jealousy when a new baby arrives, it's hard for a young child to understand just what he feels. This can make him act quite aggressively as a result. Therefore small children are dependent on the loving adults around them, such as grandparents, who do have the emotional experience and thoughtfulness to reassure them and help them find a way to express their feelings.

Explaining emotions

It can also be hard for a child to explain that he feels angry at having to share his toys, for example, because he doesn't understand that they will be returned to him. He may not know what emotion he is feeling, since he might not have had much to get angry about before now.

In this situation it helps to let your child know that you understand how he is feeling by trying to put the situation into understandable language for him. Keep it

simple but say something reaffirming: "You seem to be feeling angry about Sam using your crayons. I know that sometimes it's hard to share, but don't worry. I will make sure that Sam takes care of them and gives them back to you when he has finished his drawing."

Feelings matter

Showing your child that you understand, and can help voice his fears for him, may take the heat out of the situation. This is much more effective than telling him not to be so silly and ungenerous, which implies that his feelings don't matter and may, in time, prevent the development of a healthy sense of self-esteem. If you show him that you care about how he is feeling, he can understand that his emotions – and by extension himself – matter to you, and that you are there to help him.

Showing affection and pleasure

By the same token, it is also important to identify and talk about positive feelings with your child, such as acknowledging the pleasure he obviously displays when

he sees a grandparent, or explaining to him how much you enjoy the quick hugs and kisses he may impulsively give you from time to time. It all helps him to understand better the different range of emotions he instinctively displays.

Parenting skills

Your child can gradually begin to learn from you how to manage his emotions:
- begin by acknowledging to your child which emotion he might be feeling
- give him a sense of security by telling him that you understand why he feels like this
- explain to him what is and isn't acceptable behaviour
- distract his attention by encouraging him to move away and play another game with you
- get some paper and pens and suggest that you draw a picture for him of how he might be feeling – or show him different pictures of happy, sad, or cross faces – which may help him to refocus in a more positive way
- maintain your levels of patience. Don't forget that how you act towards your child will have a big impact on how he learns to deal with his emotions.

Intense emotions

It is worth remembering that experiencing some intense emotions is often more than your child can handle, so don't get cross with him if he doesn't appear to respond to your efforts to help him or to distract his attention.

Remind yourself that the reason he is able to express his feelings with you is because he feels secure enough to do so. What he needs at this point is to know that you can understand his feelings, even if he can't. This feeling of reassurance will gradually give him confidence that if his emotions don't overwhelm you then they are manageable, and that eventually he will be able to manage them for himself.

Coping with shyness

Trying to determine whether your child has an inborn shyness or is just displaying typical toddler tendencies can be difficult. Always accept his shyness rather than dismiss it, and tell him that you understand how he is feeling. Keep encouraging him and avoid situations where he might attract undue attention — always being late for nursery school, for example. If he needs your physical reassurance to begin playing alongside other children, stay only as long as necessary; once he feels comfortable, tell him that you are going to sit down. You may like to try role-playing games with his toys or teddies to help him understand that other children and adults may also feel shy.

Creating secure limits

Your role as a parent includes creating a sense of security by setting secure limits, but your child's "job" in many ways is to test them! Exploration is key to how your child learns about her world, and that means investigating everything: her physical abilities, her emotions, and exactly what you will or won't allow her to do.

Working out the limits

Part of the way your child learns about her environment, and the people she shares it with, are through the direct result of many of her actions. By exploring the secure limits you set, a small child will work out what is and isn't permissible in her family, and by extension the wider world outside her family. If you demonstrate the rules of society – not hurting other people, for example – your child will learn from the people she lives with that she is loved and protected. Praising your two-year-old,

distracting her, and helping her to avoid confrontations are also valuable lessons for her to learn. Children who have been brought up in a permissive way without limits may find it difficult to learn how to behave outside the immediate family.

Making your child feel secure

Setting limits is important because it makes small children feel secure – if a child gets out of her depth it can sometimes be an overwhelming experience. There are several different ways you can help your child to know what to expect:

- praise and encourage any good behaviour
- let her know in a loving way which behaviour is acceptable, and which isn't allowed. This provides her with a sense of security if, for example, hitting another person is off limits
- decide which limits are absolute in your family and trying to be consistent with these. For example, that food is only ever eaten sitting at the table, or that only a grown-up can touch the video player
- avoid confrontation by distracting her with a toy, or inject a sense of humour into the situation, rather than repeatedly telling your child not to do something
- reinforce the message, since small children have limited memories.

Learning to be independent

Your child will not only explore the limits you have set, she will also test her own limits – physically, emotionally, and intellectually. This is part of her attempt to become more independent of you, trying things out on her own while still needing your support and guidance. Getting the balance right can be tricky: some days your child will manage quite well with a simple task, but other days – perhaps if she is tired or slightly unwell – it may be beyond her. This constant fluctuation between a child who is managing well and one who needs support and reassurance (one minute rejecting your help and the next moment feeling clingy) is one of the characteristics of this age group and is what makes parenting such an intriguing challenge!

Curious explorers

Depending on their personality, some children accept limits more easily, while others are avid explorers whose curiosity often overcomes them. But children at this age aren't being bad, or particularly "naughty". Even when your child knows that something will arouse your displeasure, she is sometimes incapable of overcoming the urge to try it out, so great is her inclination to see what your reaction will be. This is evidence of how important you and your reaction are to her.

If you can't ignore such attention-seeking behaviour, focus on what your child has done, expressing your displeasure at her actions, rather than at her. Make it clear that deliberately spilling her drink is unacceptable and can have consequences: she may have to help clear it up, or not get a refill, for example. A child's persistence may even be a way of expressing a confidence in her growing ability to accomplish something. If some of the safe limits you have set are age- or ability-related, you may need to adjust them over time.

Managing the situation

There are several ways you can help your child to learn to accept limits that will benefit her development.

- **Limit the number of ways she can say "no".** Phrase a question so that you don't offer a choice if there isn't one: if it is time to go home, don't ask her if she'd like to go, merely state that it's time to leave in five minutes
- **Be consistent.** By making sure things happen when you say they will, your child will learn that there is no point in making a fuss
- **Make a game of it.** For example, see if your child can wash her hands before you finish laying the table
- **Reassure yourself** that, as your child grows, so will her ability to understand why things happen as they do: that you put her coat on when it rains to protect and care for her, not to restrict her.

Repeating the praise

If your child attempts something beyond her capabilities and doesn't succeed, keep praising her and giving her the guidance and support that she needs in order to realize that mistakes are in fact a creative opportunity to learn how to solve problems. If we give children the message that only successful accomplishments are worthwhile, and don't focus on the effort and care that goes into them, then they may put off trying to extend their abilities or testing their limits.

Managing behaviour

Managing your child's behaviour is about teaching him what you expect of him by giving encouragement and setting your own example. It is also about helping him learn, in time, how to manage his own behaviour without always referring to you.

Why toddlers need discipline

Teaching your child to manage his own behaviour is the beginning of self-discipline, something we all need to learn in order to function confidently in society and alongside other people. Self-discipline not only enables us to judge what is appropriate behaviour in a certain situation, it also helps us complete tasks for ourselves, concentrate on activities, deal with minor frustrations, and work towards the sort of self-motivation and self-esteem that makes us competent and independent people. Learning how to do all of this has to begin at an early age in order to instil a basic understanding of what is acceptable, and what is not.

Positive parenting

Understanding your child's behaviour is a vital part of positive parenting. Teach him by showing your love and encouragement, and through your own example. Feeling secure in the love and care of a parent frees up a young child's emotional life so that he can concentrate on the positive aspects of being a child, playing and learning in preparation for the time he can begin to take responsibility for himself.

LEARNING TO BE RESPONSIBLE
Give your child your attention and praise when she does what you ask of her, such as bringing her shoes to you. If you explain to her how helpful her behaviour is, she will probably want to do it again.

Appropriate parenting skills

When it comes to managing your child's behaviour, the skill of parenting is to go for balance.

● **Give choices.** Allow your child the freedom, within the parameters you set, to make choices that reflect his growing sense of independence. For example, if you ask him what he'd like to eat, limit it to an either/or choice to make his decision manageable.

● **Avoid over-controlling your child.** For example, don't hover over him in the expectation that he will play up to you.

● **Acknowledge positive behaviour** and gently correct unacceptable behaviour. When he chooses to behave well or share a toy, congratulate him on his ability or contribution – it will make him want to please you again.

● **Establish a routine.** This will help him learn to feel much more secure.

Learning by example

As your child progresses through his third year, you can expect him to have a growing understanding of what you ask of him. Children at this age have limited memories, but constant gentle reminders will finally pay off. He will know that there are things that he can't have to play with because they belong to someone else, or they aren't for playing with because they are easily broken. He will also hear you explain about learning to respect other people's feelings and property, and it is only fair that he, in turn, receives the same consideration. By having the same courtesy extended to him, he learns to treat other people and their possessions well; as is so often the case, children learn this skill by example.

Consistent teaching

At this age, help your child to understand by example and by giving him explanations. His improving language development and ability to understand allows you to

Rewarding good behaviour

Discipline and self-discipline ultimately help instil a sense of self-confidence in your child, as does your positive reinforcement of his good behaviour.

Make sure that you always notice when your child has behaved well, or successfully managed to complete something you have asked him to do. Let him see your appreciation for what he has done, rather than taking such an achievement for granted. Be specific with your praise, too. Tell him how pleased you are that he helped you clear up his toys, for example, or how quiet he tried to be while you finished talking on the telephone.

If he receives lots of positive praise – and hugs if he enjoys them – for his good behaviour, then your child will soon learn that he won't have to resort to behaving badly in order to get your attention.

talk through with him why you would like him to do something in a certain way. Follow your explanation by checking that your child actually does what you request, or help him in the most appropriate way. For instance, if you have asked your child specifically not to touch something, then you must ensure that he doesn't. Remove him from the vicinity, take the object away from him, or prevent him from reaching it. If he expresses his displeasure with a display of negative emotions, either distract him or calmly ignore him until it passes.

You also need to remember to be consistent. Don't confuse your child by insisting that all his toys need to be put away before dinner time one day and then overlooking it the next, or encouraging him to try undressing himself on his own one night and then not having the patience to let him try again. If you do need to make an exception, tell him why. It will be easier for him in the long run if you are consistent; otherwise he will have to test you out on everything every time, which is exhausting for both of you!

Tantrums

This is a very self-focused time for your child, and she is preoccupied with her own wants and desires. It is also common for a toddler to express her feelings volubly and physically if she feels frustrated or thwarted in some way.

What are tantrums?

Two-year-olds are renowned for their tantrums, but in practice this depends more on a child's individual personality and temperament, and whether or not she is developmentally able to manage her emotions. It can also depend on whether a child has learned early on that having a tantrum assures her of her parent's or her childminder's attention; she may now use tantrums as an emotional ploy to attract further attention.

Tantrums occur when your child is overwhelmed by her feelings, usually born out of frustration. When people don't understand what she is trying to say, or if she tries something beyond her capabilities and fails, it can be very frustrating. Inconsistency can also confuse a small child – such as being given some sweets to keep her quiet on one particular trip to the supermarket, and then being denied that special treat on subsequent shopping trips.

Equally difficult for a two-year-old is managing to calm herself down once she's reached a high level of distress, because she hasn't yet learned how. It can all be rather bewildering and overwhelming at times, and that is when a child really needs an adult's help.

Identifying tantrum triggers

Emotional outbursts are an expression of frustration, although some children react to distress and fear in a similar way. Learning how to manage frustrations and to see difficulties in context as they arise is an acquired skill and your child will need your gentle guidance to find out how. The older and bigger your child gets, the more difficult tantrums are to manage, so there are a variety of approaches that are worth considering to try and avoid tantrums becoming a regular occurrence.

● **Look out for triggers that you know from experience can lead to a tantrum.** Does your child find it difficult to manage new things towards the end of the day, or to share toys? Is her inability to do things beyond her

A passing phase

Perhaps the most important thing to remember about your child having tantrums is that they are a phase and they will pass, so make sure that you applaud and reward your child's good behaviour, rather than take it for granted.

Not always saying "No" to something can also help. If your child's request for something is made at an inappropriate time, instead of saying "No" you can say, "That's a good idea, shall we get some for later?" or "Yes, we will do that but after we have done this." In this way you can demonstrate that you have heard your child's suggestion, taken it on board, and allowed her contribution to be validated – all of which makes her feel good about herself, and valued. When children feel secure they tend to play up less and so have tantrums less frequently.

capabilities overwhelming her confidence? Avoid end-of-day demands, and find toys beforehand that she has agreed to share, putting the rest away for now.

• **Is she tired, thirsty, hungry, or unwell?** Don't expect too much from your child under these conditions. Making sure her physical needs are met means that your child is less distracted and can focus more easily on what is required of her emotionally.

• **Acknowledge the situation from her point of view.** It takes a certain amount of maturity, not available to your child yet, to cope when under stress. Even the most apparently inconsequential things can set off a child who is feeling vulnerable. The fact that her biscuit is broken may mean little to you, but to your inconsolable child it is the end of the world, so respect her feelings.

• **Sometimes a tantrum is inevitable.** Some children at this age actually seem to need an emotional blowout in order to let go. If this happens and it is too late for diversionary tactics, go into management mode. Make sure your child is safe, then stand nearby without focusing on her, and reassure her that you will be there when she calms down. After the worst has blown over, go and comfort her, as she will feel exhausted and upset, and let the issue pass.

Feeling reassured

Many children find having a tantrum quite frightening and will need your reassurance. Keep encouraging your child to do those things that she is capable of with enjoyment, working towards greater challenges so that her confidence grows and her self-esteem increases.

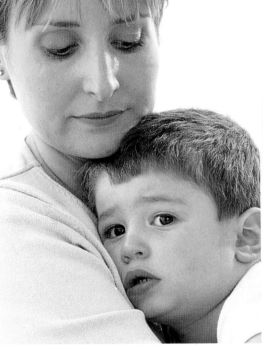

AVOIDING A CRISIS
Because you love your child, and his distress is something you'd like to avoid, giving him a reassuring cuddle and using humour may help to diffuse a difficult crisis. Or try distracting his attention by pointing out something of interest and steering the conversation in that direction.

Health and developmental check

A health check undertaken some time during your child's third year includes a physical exam to ensure that his growth is in line with what has been previously charted. Hearing, vision, and developmental checks are also routine.

A review of your child's health in his third year is a time to monitor his health, as well as his growth and development, and to make sure that there are no problems with his hearing or vision. If there are problems with his ability to see or hear, they need to be addressed and rectified as soon as possible. Your GP or health visitor will also listen to your child's heart and lungs, and you will be asked which illnesses he has had and about any recurrent problems such as ear infections. You will probably also be asked about what provision you have made for your child's dental care, too. This health check may include a blood test for haemoglobin, or lead levels, if any problem is suspected. This is quite a common procedure in the United States, but it is not undertaken in the UK unless clinically necessary. A urine test, though not routine, may also be required.

Fine motor skills

Your child's hand movements are becoming more precise. Turning the pages of a book one at a time, holding a pencil correctly, and using a cup with one hand, are all examples of the greater dexterity she is now developing at this age.

One thing that has benefited this phase in her development is her ability to focus on one activity for longer periods. This in turn gives her the ability and concentration to develop more creative tendencies, such as beginning to draw using her imagination and observation skills.

HOW TO DRAW
Your child's hand–eye coordination is becoming more precise.

General questions

The health visitor or GP will ask questions about your child's behaviour and eating and sleep habits. This is an opportunity for you to ask for information and guidance about anything that concerns you, and discuss any forthcoming changes in your child's life, for example potty training, the birth of a sibling, or sorting out childcare.

Percentile charts

In the meantime, routinely measuring the height and weight of your child, and charting it on a percentile chart from birth, will give you a good indication of his progress. The percentile divisions relate to the percentage of children of the same age that are within a specific growth band. The 50th centile marks the average, which means that, if you take 100 babies, 50 will be heavier and taller than the 50th line (above it) and 50 will be lighter and smaller (below it). The majority of children, 82 per cent, fall between the 9th and 91st centile. The charts are in two forms, one for boys and one for girls, since girls tend to be physically smaller than boys from birth. Children grow in fits and starts, so their progress doesn't necessarily follow the smooth curve of the chart. If your child is healthy and active, he is probably growing well and there is normally some fluctuation along the way, but if your child shows a big divergence between his height and weight – for example, 60 per cent height but 95 per cent weight – then you should consult your GP.

Social trends

There has been an increase in the average height throughout the developed world. This is known as the "secular trend". In the UK, researchers at the National Study of Health and Growth found that schoolchildren in 1994 were on average 1cm taller than in 1972. This follows a trend with five-year-olds in Britain today, who are on average 7–8cm (3in) taller than 100 years ago. The

"mid-parental height" may give an indication of what height children will be: add the mother's and father's heights together, divide by two, and add seven to work out your son's likely height in centimetres at 18 years old. For a girl, subtract seven from the result; girls tend to fluctuate by 8.5cm (3½in) either way of their mid-parental height.

Finally, your GP will probably check that your child has received all the relevant routine immunizations to protect him from serious illnesses.

CHECKING HEIGHT
Children tend to reflect the height of their parents: tall parents often have tall children. If you wish, you can work out roughly how tall your child will be when fully grown by using the "mid-parental height" (described above).

Potty training

Potty training is only possible when your child is able to control the muscles of her bottom and bladder. These muscles usually mature between 18 and 36 months, so it is generally recommended to start potty training after she is at least two years old.

Picking the right time

Potty training as a notion is a bit of a misnomer because you can't really train a child until she is physically ready. However, once she shows signs that she is capable developmentally and shows an emotional willingness, then the process should be a pretty straightforward one.

It is worth having the potty visible and available in the bathroom for some months prior to the start of formal training to allow your child the chance to get used to sitting on it and even occasionally managing to use it successfully, which is a good basis from which to start.

Night-time training

Even when your child is happily out of nappies during the day, she may still need a nappy for nap times during the day or at night-time. You can introduce the idea of going without a nappy by ensuring that she uses the potty before going to sleep. She may well have a dry nappy as a consequence, especially when she wakes from her daytime nap.

If she is waking in the morning regularly with a dry nappy, then you can probably try going without at night. Make sure you have a protective waterproof cover for the mattress of her bed, and check that there is enough light at night for her to be able to manage to use the potty or toilet – probably with your help at first, and then on her own as she grows older and becomes more experienced.

In addition to developing the necessary muscle control, your child may be showing signs of other skills:

- is she beginning to try to remove her trousers and pants without your help? It may help focus her attention by involving her in choosing some new pants to buy.
- is she able to sit down on a potty and get up easily?
- does she know when she has the urge to go, and can she tell you?

All these things make it easier for her to be successful when the time comes. In the past, to escape the tyranny of endlessly washing terry nappies, toilet training began at a much earlier age and involved a lot of time sitting on potties waiting for things to happen. There was a certain amount of success, but this depended on parents making a potty available at the right time rather than the babies being able to control their bladders and bowels. Studies show that many children who begin toilet training before 18 months old aren't completely trained until after the age of four, whereas those who started at around age two were completely trained before their third birthday.

Start looking for signals of your child being ready to try managing without a nappy:

- has she seen you or other family members use the toilet?
- is she aware of passing water or having a bowel movement (even if wearing a nappy), and then tells you?
- does she sit on and try to use the potty, perhaps before her bath in the evening?

Once you have some evidence that your child has an idea of what is going to be required of her once she goes without nappies, you can consider taking the next step. Avoid a time when your child is having to cope with other changes in her life, such as a house move, a new baby, or some other adaptation she needs to make. It will be easier for her, and you, without additional stresses to cope with.

FAMILIARITY
Let your child become familiar with sitting on a potty so that she'll be happy to use it properly when the right time comes.

Practical concerns

Make sure you have a potty that is comfortable to sit on, and for boys it's helpful to have one that has a higher splashguard at the front than at the back. You will also have to help your son understand that his penis will need to point inside the potty to be successful. It's easy for a boy to sit down quickly without checking and find he is weeing outside the potty, which is very dispiriting!

Once you think your child is ready, explain that without nappies she will need to use the potty. Because modern nappies are designed to prevent any feelings of wetness, it may not be until she is nappy-free that she can really make the connection between wanting to pass water, and what it feels like. You may have to tolerate several "accidents" or near misses before she learns this.

Once you replace nappies with pants, you may want to use thicker, terry-cotton training pants for a while. These can still feel rather nappy-like, so you may have more success moving straight to ordinary pants.

Getting into a routine

You will also need to give your child regular reminders that she might like to use the potty. Having asked her, don't sit her on the potty unless she says yes; otherwise she won't make the connection for herself. Sometimes she may say no, and two minutes later realize she does feel the urge to go, which is better than relying on you to tell her. Some accidents are inevitable, but if your child is ready to manage without a nappy these should number very few. Work on the principle of praising her efforts and successes, and, if accidents do occur, gently remind her that this is what the potty is for, change her, and make no fuss. Reacting negatively may make her resentful and less inclined to try again.

Finally, it is worth remembering that every child develops at a different rate and will be trained at their own pace, and that patience is key.

Sleep issues

Active, busy children who are growing rapidly still need lots of sleep to restore and refresh them. At this age, you can anticipate the sleep needs of a toddler to be between nine and 13 hours during a 24-hour period.

Physical benefits

Not only is sleep important to young children in order for them to have the energy they need to enjoy life, it is also during deep sleep that pituitary growth hormone is secreted in the brain. Therefore cell growth and cell renewal and repair in young children mainly occurs during sleep. It is also worth noting that children don't grow continuously but in spurts. During a growth spurt, which can happen virtually overnight, your child may need extra sleep. Inadequate sleep and wakeful nights can be detrimental to long-term health, as well as creating sleep patterns that become habits, so if your child is still a poor sleeper, try to rectify this now (*see also box on night waking, p.26*).

Family needs

Depending on each child's individual needs, you may find your child requires just one good nap during the day now, while some children will still need two naps. It also partly depends on your family routine: if you want your child to be happily awake until later in the evening so that you can all eat together after work, he probably needs at least one good nap of at least two hours later during the day to manage this good-humouredly. If, however, it is better for his schedule and his sleep needs for him to be in bed by seven o'clock every night, then a shorter nap earlier in the day will probably suit him better.

Checking sleep patterns

Although children vary in their sleep needs, your rule of thumb should be how your child manages during the day. If he is happy and showing no real behavioural difficulties, even though he only sleeps for eight hours at night with a short daytime nap, that's fine. But if he is consistently grumpy, finds socializing difficult, and is argumentative over everything, review his sleep patterns. No one manages well when they haven't had enough sleep, and it may be that increasing the amount of sleep he gets will help considerably. In addition, remember that during times of emotional and physical demand – illness, experiences such a new babysitting arrangement, family stress, even holidays – your child may need more sleep to compensate. New experiences can be very stimulating, even overstimulating, and, depending on your child's temperament, you may need to balance them with extra sleep to help him recuperate in between times.

A busy social life

During this third year, your child's life has probably become quite busy. It may be more social, perhaps with regular playgroup sessions or childcare arrangements away from home. All of this is very stimulating, which is positive, but which can also be quite physically and emotionally demanding. If he doesn't want to sleep, schedule in opportunities to recharge those batteries with some quiet times. Learning how to have a quiet

time by himself, perhaps with a book or a puzzle, is an important ability to acquire as your child matures. This won't be for a long stretch of time to begin with, but it does introduce to your child the idea of being self-motivated and self-sufficient.

Bedtime routines

With all his emerging independence and growing abilities, you may find that your child begins to present some resistance to going to bed. Depending on how your family life is organized, there may be some reason that needs to be acknowledged:

● is there a new baby who goes to bed at the same time as he does, without allowing any time for a one-to-one storytelling session?

● is he so overstimulated that he is unable to go to sleep easily?

● does his bedtime coincide now with a parent's return from work, with whom he wants to spend some time? It's always worth looking at what might be the cause of change in a child's behaviour, especially if previously it's been no problem.

Winding down

After the last meal of your child's day, allow some time for a quiet play before having a bath or shower and preparing for bed. The benefit of a routine is that the familiarity of events, which draw towards the inevitably of bedtime, contribute to a feeling of enjoyment about the end of the day. Finish the routine with one last milky drink if your child enjoys it, brushing of teeth, story and cuddle, and then bed. A predictable sequence of events may help your child realize that it's not worth making a fuss about something that will happen whatever he does.

Night waking

For some children, bedtimes and night waking are a problem, however, trying to ensure that bedtime is a peaceful routine may help to reduce the incidence of night waking. If a child is able to fall asleep peacefully alone, when he surfaces in his sleep or wakes briefly in the night he should be able to go back to sleep by himself without any need for intervention from you.

Babies have a sleep cycle moving from light to deep sleep of around 50 minutes, in contrast to an adult's sleep cycle of around 90 minutes. This means that small children move through light and deep periods of sleep more often, and if they haven't learned to settle alone the possibility for night waking is increased. Babies and toddlers who are perpetually assisted by rocking or feeding will have difficulty learning to go to sleep alone and this can become a habit. If this habit becomes entrenched, it means that a child can't be fully independent about going to sleep.

A consistent bedtime routine helps create a sense of security, which enables him to "let go" and fall asleep. Allowing your child to learn to go to sleep on his own is a positive step towards his growing independence.

If your child finds it difficult to relax, a massage can be a beneficial way to help him calm down. Use a specially formulated baby oil or lotion to massage his feet as he lies on his bed, the floor, or the sofa, or keep him warm after his bath and give him a soothing tummy rub. Gently massaging the shoulders helps release tension, and many children love having their scalps massaged, although you don't need to use oil. You could also try rhythmically brushing his hair, keeping it gentle. It partly depends on your child's preference, but if massage has been a part of your previous baby care routine reintroduce it now. For others it may be a new experience and take some adjusting to, so keep it short and light.

Getting to sleep

Some children will fall asleep straight away; others take a while to drift off. Reassure your child that lying in bed, perhaps thinking about positive things that happened during the day, is good, and that falling asleep will follow. It may be that listening to a peaceful piece of music, or just being aware of the family moving around close by, is more reassuring than silence. However, be quite firm that, once bedtime arrives, getting up again is not an option. Say you will pop back in 10 minutes to check on him and that he is not to get out of bed, but do remember to go back since he may deliberately stay awake. When you go back there is no need to do anything except say, "Sleep well." Lengthen the time before you next check on him and you should find he is asleep!

Changing night-time habits

Moving into his own bed will delight most toddlers. If your child needs time to make the transition from a cot to a bed, try putting the bed up before removing his cot, assuming there's room. Let him put his teddies in the bed or take his daytime naps there until he's happy to spend all night in it. It is also important to put up guard rails on the sides of the bed so that he can't fall out at night.

Now your child is physically able to get out of bed, you may find some new night-time habits arising! Getting into your bed in the night may begin on a regular basis. Lots of families tolerate this but it is at a price since everyone's sleep gets disrupted. Research shows that toddlers who sleep in bed with their parents tend to wake more often.

If it is a new habit, it may be linked to a recent event. Perhaps you nursed your child in your bed during a recent illness he had; though the illness has passed, his habit of being in your bed may not have. Maybe a new event has occurred – moving house or having another babysitter. Whatever the reason, give your child lots of time and attention during the day so that he doesn't feel the need to seek it during the night. Comfort him, but be firm about returning him to his own bed.

Bad dreams

Occasionally children have bad dreams, which usually occur during the second half of the night, when dreams are strongest. Dreams occur during REM (rapid eye movement) sleep, when the body is in such a state of deep muscle relaxation that movement is impossible. If dreams occur during the shift from REM to non-REM sleep, which can often be the case, your child may wake. If he is distressed, go to him immediately. He may fear returning to sleep, so stay with him awhile, reassuring him and check that he is not too hot or cold, but don't get him up. The occasional bad dream isn't significant if your child appears happy during the day, but it might make him anxious about going to sleep in case it recurs. Reassure him that his dreams can't hurt him and explain that everyone dreams. Check that he hasn't seen or heard anything inappropriate in a story or on television; some TV programmes can be quite scary.

Night-time accidents

When children move out of night-time nappies they may become anxious about wetting the bed. Play this down, ensure there is a waterproof cover on the bed, and, if it becomes an issue, return to night-time nappies for a while. Once he sees that his nappy is dry most mornings he will gain confidence. There is no point introducing anxiety at night for the sake of moving out of nappies.

Feeding routines

By now your child should be eating meals with the family, although you may want to adjust these occasionally to make them child-friendly and adapt some of your own eating habits to ensure that you provide your child with what is good for her.

Getting the right balance

Your child's diet should be healthy and balanced; keep in mind that the types of foods she eats now provide her with a blueprint for eating habits for the rest of her life.

Avoid fried foods that are heavy in saturated fats, and additional salt and sugar, opting instead for steamed and grilled foods. Use fresh ingredients since processed foods are high in salt, sugars, and artificial flavourings. Children need protein for growth, carbohydrates and fats for energy, and fruit and vegetables to supply vitamins and fibre, so choose foods from the four basic food groups:

- meat, fish, eggs, and other protein foods
- milk, cheese, yogurt, and other dairy products
- rice, cereals, potatoes, bread, pasta, and other carbohydrates
- fruits and vegetables.

Families who are vegetarian should be aware that milk and cheese also contain high sources of protein, as do soya and eggs. Large quantities of pulses and grains can be too bulky for children's stomachs; every mouthful needs to be as nutritious as possible. Egg yolk, spinach, and broccoli provide excellent sources of iron, and a vitamin and mineral supplement may also be beneficial.

Setting a good example

If you want your child to develop an appetite for fresh fruit and vegetables, set an example by eating plenty of these yourself. Don't expect your child to eat a banana if you snack on doughnuts or chocolate, or offer sweet treats (which promote sweet cravings and tooth decay) as rewards. Don't bargain with your child to encourage her to eat well; it could become a difficult habit to change.

Fluctuating appetites

Keep in mind that at this age your child's appetite may vary. Some days she will seem hungrier than on others, so it's sometimes useful to look at what she's eaten over

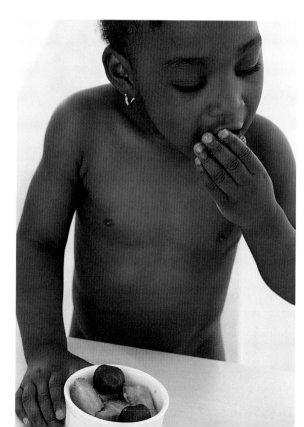

a period of days rather than just one. Although she will benefit from a nutritious, well-balanced diet, she isn't growing as fast as she was and so may not be as hungry. What is useful is to offer foods that provide a nutritional combination – for example, a piece of cheese provides calcium and protein. This works well for children with a picky appetite: offer calorie- and protein-dense foods such as avocados, beans, full-fat milk, peanut butter (if you are certain that your child has no nut allergies), or cheese. For those children whose weight gain is too fast, it's possible to use foods that offer nutrition but with fewer calories, such as fresh fruits and vegetables and wholegrain pastas (see also p.30).

Checking the sugar levels

You may want to think carefully about how much sugar is present in your child's diet. Often sugars are added by manufacturers to make processed foods more palatable to young children – for example, breakfast cereals already frosted with sugar. Sugar provides what is known as "empty calories", which have no nutritional value. An excessive sugar intake is also linked to the increased incidence of childhood obesity and diabetes.

Drinks

Water is the best and most refreshing drink to give to a thirsty child, so offer this as a first choice, and at mealtimes. Tap water is perfectly safe for toddlers to drink, and after the first year of life it doesn't need to be boiled and cooled before being drunk. Mineral waters shouldn't be given to young children because their mineral content could be too high in salts and other minerals. Bottled waters generally aren't necessary, and some of these aren't bacterially safe for small children, either. If you filter tap water, change the filter regularly in accordance with manufacturers' instructions and, if your household system includes a water softener, make sure that your child drinks the water from the mains tap only.

Brushing teeth

By two and half years old, your child should have all her first, or milk, teeth, including the second molars.

Regular teeth cleaning at least twice a day is essential to keep her teeth in good condition and prepare for the second teeth already developing in the gums. Supervise your child while she brushes since you will need to do some extra brushing for her, and don't let her use much toothpaste until she can spit it all out. Take her to the dentist for regular check-ups: eight per cent of two-year-olds have one or more cavities, increasing to nearly 60 per cent by the age of three.

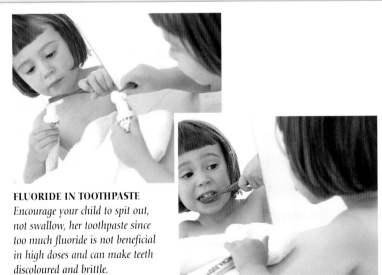

FLUORIDE IN TOOTHPASTE
Encourage your child to spit out, not swallow, her toothpaste since too much fluoride is not beneficial in high doses and can make teeth discoloured and brittle.

After the age of two it is possible to give semi-skimmed milk as a drink unless your child would still benefit from the calories in full-fat milk. Young children with small appetites but high-energy demands often need the additional calories provided by full-fat milk. In general, a low-fat diet isn't good for small children, who have small appetites and are only capable of eating limited quantities of food; they need calorie-dense foods. Unless your child is on a calorie-controlled diet for some reason and is monitored by a paediatric dietitian, don't deliberately reduce her calorie intake.

It's all too easy to give your child sugar inadvertently via commercially prepared fruit drinks. Make sure you dilute these concentrates carefully, and use them only as an occasional treat to flavour water. Fresh fruit juices are also high in sugars and fruit acids that damage teeth, so these should be diluted as well. Avoid giving a child with a poor appetite large sugary drinks with meals. Drinking these will stop her feeling hungry and prevent her eating properly. The same applies to milky drinks: offer them at the end of a meal, or as a snack. If your child has

between 500 and 900ml of milk (16–32oz) a day of milk as a drink or in cooked foods, all her calcium requirements for healthy bones will be met. But always try first to offer your child water as a drink with meals and to help quench her thirst.

Mealtimes

Eating together is one of the great social pleasures of family life, but it's all too easy to become a family who eats separately in shifts or in front of the television. If you want your child to enjoy her food, let her participate in the preparation of meals and mealtimes herself, then create the family occasion that helps her develop the social skills that will eventually enable her to socialize in the wider world. Family meals provide an opportunity to learn by example about table manners and consideration for other people eating together. And, while you can't expect a toddler always to tolerate a lengthy three-course meal with adults, you can expect her to enjoy some of it and participate – such as helping to lay the table, or carrying a dish out to the kitchen.

Mealtime schedules

Listed below are examples of drinks, snacks, and meals from the four main food groups. Aim to give four small portions each of protein and calcium, two or more small portions each of vegetables and fruits, and six

small portions of grains and carbohydrates through the day. This schedule should help children avoid snacking in between mealtimes.

Breakfast	Mid–am snack	Lunch	Mid–pm snack	Dinner	Bedtime
Cereal with milk Fruit Toast Waffle or a pancake Diluted juice	Fruit Yogurt Milk	Cheese sandwich Cracker Fruit or vegetables Water	Fruit Cheese Milk	Minced chicken, rice, and vegetables Stewed fruit or fromage frais Water	Banana or a biscuit (optional) Milk or water

At this age your child may express quite definite tastes in food and have numerous favourites. Build on these, offering variety where you can to keep meals suitable for all the family. In fact, your child may well opt to eat only a limited variety of foods as a gesture of independence. It sometimes helps to offer a choice between one or two items, rather than asking, "What would you like to eat?" Giving her a choice, albeit limited, helps her feel that she has some say in the matter. If you offer other substitutes, you create the possibility of endless choice, which can be confusing for many small children.

Mealtime manners

If you want your child to be able to behave well when you visit friends or relatives or eat out in restaurants, it's worthwhile giving her the ground rules at home. Sitting at the dinner table for long periods of time is difficult for small children, but impossible to do if they have never had experience of doing it at home. If mealtimes are enjoyable social occasions at home, then your child's anticipation is that this will be a similar experience wherever she eats. If she always eats in isolation, she won't experience being part of a group elsewhere.

Restaurant etiquette

It takes a bit of practice for small children to get used to eating out in restaurants, and the following points are worth keeping in mind.

- **Choose child–friendly places** that serve food without much of a wait.
- **Take a favourite book** or small toy with which your child can occupy herself if her interest in her food and surroundings starts to wane.
- **Avoid taking overly tired or hungry children** since they are unlikely to be able to cope well.
- **Stay relaxed and enjoy the experience** of eating out with your children. Many children respond well when they see the way other people behave in restaurants. If you praise your child for being grown-up, she is more likely to meet your expectations and behave well.

Language development

Two-year-olds can vary enormously in their language development. Some children are naturally talkative and may already be talking quite extensively, while others may still only be using single words.

Even children of the same intelligence can vary widely in their language development. This is due to a combination of a child's temperament and personality and the opportunities that are available to encourage and increase his language development.

More than just words

In some families, children and their parents or adult caregivers may rely on non-verbal communication, gestures, intonation, and a shared common knowledge of day-to-day life. The use of one word can be subtly changed by the use of intonation and even volume. A questioning tone will turn one word into a request – for example, "Drink?", to which you might reply, "Would you like a drink?" and receive the answer with a nod, of "Drink". Parents and caregivers become familiar with a child's efforts to communicate, and help him learn by listening and replying, often reiterating the question to indicate his effort to communicate has been understood.

Expanding vocabulary

At the age of two your child will probably understand much of what you say to him. By contrast, his own vocabulary now averages around fifty words or more. This vocabulary is growing rapidly, and he will soon progress from one-word statements to two- or three-word phrases. This improving development of language in turn promotes an increased understanding of a great

Hearing

The ability to hear is a very important requirement to speech. Without being able to hear, it is impossible for a child to learn to talk, since spoken language is dependent on imitating vocal sounds in a way that gets you understood. The sooner any hearing problem is picked up, the better it is for the child and his development. Recurrent ear infections and glue ear, in particular, which causes intermittent deafness, can adversely affect your child's language development.

Even if your child can hear perfectly, he still needs to be able to distinguish different word sounds apart from the possible interference of background noise. There is a potential risk to young children's hearing from continuous loud music – for example, at a sporting event. It is very important that your child has lots of one-to-one communication without any audible distraction so that he gets the benefit of hearing clearly not only what is being said but also the sounds of words. This will enable him to copy what he hears accurately and will also train his brain to distinguish what sounds make up a word.

This will help him later on in life, too, when he starts to read and write and spell. So make sure that the television or the radio isn't constantly providing a background noise, and turn it off completely unless you are actually listening to it or watching something. Your child isn't able to screen out noise as well as you can when he is trying to listen and he needs to hear your words clearly and precisely if he to increase the range of vocabulary he uses.

deal more words. Experimentation also comes into play as children provide their own meaning when seeking to apply language correctly. For example, for a while the word "Daddy" may be applied to all men or the word "dog" to all four-legged animals.

If your child tries to tell you something and you continually misunderstand him, it can lead to a great deal of frustration on his part. Communication is key to avoiding this build-up of frustration and feeling of inability. The best way to deal with this is to try to work within your child's frame of reference – acknowledge that he is attempting to express himself and ask him to show you or repeat himself so that you can carefully work out what he is saying.

Building up language

The use of two-word sentences usually follows about six months after the first words, and meaning is often added by non-verbal gestures such as pointing, or activities that express meaning such as the urgency of pulling on your sleeve to get your attention. Two-word sentences include things like, "Cup milk", "Teddy gone", "Car red", for example.

There is much you can do to help. Don't correct the mistakes naturally made when practising language, but reiterate and reinforce what is said. So, with the previous examples, you might answer, "Would you like a cup of milk?", "Yes, the teddy has gone. He's fallen down", "That car is red, and this car is blue". As you build on whatever has engaged your child's attention, keep things simple and focus on the pleasure of communication.

Sometimes the verbal stimulation of older siblings may also encourage a toddler to build up his vocabulary sooner and help him to focus on the pleasure he can gain from communicating with them.

Pronunciation

Reiterating what is said by repeating your child's words clearly and simply back to him also helps with his pronunciation. While it may sometimes sound very cute when a small child mispronounces a word, even if you can understand him, it is not helpful when he needs to be understood outside the immediate family. Persistent mispronunciation also creates problems when it comes to learning how to spell words. If your child can't hear and speak words clearly, he may have problems later on when he tries to write phonetically spelt words correctly.

Positive impact

The connection between language development and the ability to read and write later has been proved quite conclusively in research studies. You can help promote your child's language skills by spending short one-on-

one periods of time together at different points during the day – no longer than 10–15 minutes at a time – to explore a toy together, play or sing rhyming games, or look at a book without any background noise. Talking about an object or following a sung sequence or story can have an enormously positive impact. Children who have received this sort of input at this stage show a reading age almost 18 months ahead of their peer group when aged seven.

The reason it makes such a difference is because, after your child has learnt, the individual letters of the alphabet and their sounds, his ability to hear different letter sounds makes it easier for him to identify them when they are seen written down. The words cat and mat have a very distinctive ending sound of "at", but, because of the different letters at the beginning, two separate meanings. Distinguishing between letter sounds becomes even more important later when working out how to spell words.

Detecting problems

Since language development is so key to your child's intellectual progress, you will want to do all you can to encourage it and make sure there is nothing preventing it. Approximately one in every 10–15 children has problems with language comprehension or with the development of his speech.

Early detection and identification of a problem is important to ensure that language delay doesn't interfere with learning in other areas. If this is detected before school starts, the problems can be effectively addressed. Routine check-ups at this stage include hearing and developmental checks to ensure that, if any problem is detected, a referral can be made for a more complete evaluation (*see p.202*). Even if it's a minor problem that can be easily remedied, the problem can escalate if it is not picked up.

Stuttering

Stuttering is thought to affect the speech of about four per cent of pre-schoolers, but only one per cent of the adult population, so it is often just a phase and is more common in younger siblings. Stuttering can occur when the physical mechanism of speech isn't fully mature, which partly explains why it is something that children usually grow out of, but it can be frustrating and make a child withdrawn and lacking in confidence. Stressful situations can exacerbate the problem, but there is much encouragement a parent can give.

● **Listen attentively** when your child is trying to say something without rushing, interrupting, or finishing his sentence to maintain his confidence.

● **Children's thoughts are often quicker than their speech**, so make sure neither you nor any older siblings finish your child's phrases.

● **Slow down your child** by taking the pressure off him: nod slowly and speak at the same pace.

Effective parenting

There is much that you can do through daily activities to stimulate his language development. The most important thing is to listen and respond appropriately to your child and to make sure that you spend time listening to and talking with him. Look at books together that may explore new ideas and emotional content (*see also box, right*). Get into the habit of naming objects, and talk as you dress him – for example, say you are putting on his red striped T-shirt and green socks. This all helps build his vocabulary.

Imaginative play

The development of language and imaginative play are interlinked for a young child. Pretending to be Mummy going to the shops, for example, is one of the key ways in which young children learn to extend their language. The useful interaction between a child and his parent or caregiver, who can stimulate ideas on which the child can build, is also extremely beneficial. So learning to be imaginative is to the advantage of every child because it contributes to their creative intelligence.

Television and computers

Apart from occasionally allowing your child to watch an age-related programme, television isn't recommended since children find speech too difficult to follow, making it effectively a language-free form of entertainment. If your child spends a large proportion of his time watching television, it could have a negative effect on his language development, so monitor the time he spends watching it.

Even very young children can manage to use a word processor or computer. As with television, extended periods of unsupervised time can be detrimental, so spend just short periods of time with your child at the computer, letting him get a feel for it.

Reading

Books provide peaceful entertainment and encourage your child to focus on words – the ideas, emotional content, and new words stimulate conversation. Children's librarians will be able to help you choose appropriate stories.

★ Listening to stories helps concentrate on the human voice and trains the brain to hear different letter sounds.

★ Rereading the same books entails the necessary repetition of words and the opportunity to ask questions about events in a book and what happens next. This helps develop language, and fosters a healthy emotional development in your child through the bonding process. Stories also introduce new ideas and emotional concepts.

★ Reading to your child fosters a healthy imagination, helps build up relationships, and encourages a warm, caring, and verbally confident child.

Safety

Safety is still a big issue for this age group, especially since your child is becoming more physically independent. This new independence usually isn't yet matched by an ability to think ahead or judge what is dangerous.

Your child's sense of spatial awareness, which enables her to judge distances or surrounding areas accurately, is still developing and she has only a limited memory of previous events from which to learn. In addition, she has a natural curiosity and inclination to explore that often overcomes what you may have told her not to do. This isn't deliberately disobedient behaviour; it's just how small children find out about their world.

Take some practical steps to ensure that your child's environment is as safe as possible. Accidents sometimes happen, but you can avoid unnecessary mishaps with a little forethought and preparation. You will need to make sure that your home is as safe as you can make it. To avoid constantly having to tell your child not to touch certain things, make items such as electrical wall sockets safe, or move breakables out of reach, and get down to your child's level to see what other issues may arise.

It is important to instil a sense of self-responsibility about safety rules, too. These need to be reiterated again and again, but don't hover constantly over your child. It is also useful to decide which areas of safety are non-negotiable, such as always wearing seat-belts in the car.

Safety at home and out and about

★ Fit childproof catches to doors and drawers, and use safety glass or safety film on glass doors.

★ Allow your child to test things out with your guidance, since this is the only way that she will, in time, learn to make judgments about what she can and can't manage. Constantly berating her to "Be careful" implies that you feel she can't manage alone, so praise any tasks that she completes safely.

★ Establish non-negotiable family safety rules, such as wearing seat-belts in the car and always holding a grown-up's hand to cross a road. Rules such as these will hopefully instil a sense of caution and road awareness in your child.

★ Ensure that breakables and hot liquids are always out of reach.

★ Never leave a small child alone in a room with an unguarded fire.

★ Watch for "lookalike" hazards: pills and medicines that may look like sweets; or cleaning fluids that may seem similar to bottles of drink. Keep all household products and medication out of children's reach.

How toddlers learn

Over the next exciting twelve months of change, your child's outlook on life will open up as she gains a greater sense of independence and begins to explore the wider world. And, as her levels of understanding and communication improve, so too will her enjoyment of special relationships within the family and with other children.

How toddlers learn skills

The biggest change you will probably notice in your child's abilities as she enters her third year has to do with her understanding of her own world and her relationship to it, including the people around her.

New-found abilities

During this year your child's experience of the world around her will increase partly through the tremendous development she will make in her language skills. It's also important to ensure that your child has a warm, nurturing, emotionally stable environment in which she can safely explore the world around her.

You may find that your child is becoming interested in everything going on around her. By letting your child join in as much as possible with some of your everyday activities, she will learn new skills as well as enjoy your company. For example, let your child help you to tidy up in the house or to lay the table since this will help her hand-eye coordination and give her a natural feeling of independence.

At this age, it can be hard for small children to know how to wind down if they are tired or accept that something has to finish. You may find your child resists or rebels against ending a game she is enjoying because you have to go out, for example. It takes improving memory skills to understand that finishing something enjoyable doesn't mean that it can't be done again another day. Explain this to your child and allow her time to digest the idea.

2 to 3 years: your child's milestones

In terms of overall physical growth, which slows down between the second and third birthday, the most noticeable change is your child's body proportions. As her limbs lengthen and her muscles strengthen from being used, her posture becomes more upright, with a flatter tummy.

Coordination and balance

Your child's expanding physical abilities in turn give her increased coordination and balance. Now she can walk quickly, for example, or carry a toy in her hand as she walks.

By the end of this year you can expect your child to be able to:
- walk upstairs using alternate feet
- bend down to retrieve a toy without falling over
- pedal a tricycle
- use a crayon to copy a circle on a piece of paper
- turn the pages of a book one at a time
- rotate her wrist and unscrew jar tops.

Intellectual skills

Until this point, your child's physical development, and what she learned from it, gave her the impression that what happens in her world is the result of something she has done.

This self-oriented view of the world means that a child this age often takes things literally. She finds it difficult to differentiate between fantasy and reality: if you say, for example, "If you eat any more, you'll burst!" it is just possible, from her point of view, that this could happen.

Imaginative play also becomes important as your child tries to make sense of and seek explanations for events by acting them out, and learns to distinguish fact from fantasy.

By the end of this year your child should be able to:
- follow a two-part instruction
- speak in sentences of four or five words
- be understood by non-family members
- play imaginative games
- match an object to a picture in a book
- enjoy choosing or sorting toys
- understand the concept of "two".

Emotional development

With the development of the idea of the self, and of possessions, comes difficulty in sharing – either sharing you, or her possessions. As your child becomes more social, she'll start to anticipate events and express pleasure at certain activities, or begin to recognize particular children and grown-ups. Her emotional range is still broad, ranging from sheer

IMPROVING SKILLS
Your child's improving skills of observation and concentration will enable him to complete simple jigsaw puzzles.

delight to frustrated rage.

By the end of this year you can expect your child to:
- spend time happily away from you
- express affection to you and to other close family members
- show interest in other children.

Making sense of it all

The journey that you take with your child over this year happens in fits and starts, and the challenge for you is to help your child make sense of it all through opportunity and activity, with you as her guide.

24 to 26 months

Your two-year-old's growing independence and the pleasure he derives from his discoveries makes this an exciting time. You can still expect his emotions to reflect just how he is feeling – which can range from sunny smiles to tears in the space of 10 minutes. Help your child make the most of his eagerness to learn by encouraging him to improve his fine motor skills or build up his vocabulary through activities that you can do together.

Physical development

Your two-year-old's physical ability has progressed, almost literally, in leaps and bounds over the last 12 months and now he can walk, run, and climb. What he needs over this next period are lots of opportunities to use his body and explore his capabilities, building greater strength in his limbs and increasing his coordination.

Hops, skips, and jumps

Although your child may be unable to continually jump and hop at this stage, for example, it isn't long before he will incorporate an occasional hop, skip, or jump as he runs or walks. At first these skills have their own momentum, and will become easier with practice.

Social and emotional skills

Emotionally, your two-year-old will still appear quite selfish. This is our adult interpretation of his behaviour, of course, but his inclination will be always to put his needs first unless you keep gently encouraging him to think of others.

Sharing by example

Encouraging your child to share is part of his learning to consider other people. It will also help increase his

socialization process, which is learned primarily through imitation. If he is treated with respect and affection, he will learn to treat others in the same way. And if you are overly concerned with the feelings of others at the diminishment of his own, this won't encourage positive self-esteem in him anyway. Other people are just as important as he is, but not more so.

At this age you may also have the advantage of your child wanting to please you, so through your relationship with him he can learn to extend his consideration to others around him. Focusing on this aspect will help him develop the idea that if something is nice for him, then it would be nice for someone else, too.

Expressing emotion

You can expect spontaneous and genuine shows of affection from your child by this stage, especially if similar attention has been lavished on him. It makes it much easier for him to accept and value other people's feelings if he feels accepted and valued, too.

Try to watch the language you use when managing your child's emotional behaviour. He is not being bad or naughty if he doesn't want to wait his turn in playing with a toy or a simple game; he merely needs a gentle reminder or explanation of

Learning concepts

During this period you will be able to see your child's understanding evolve as you watch him play and as you talk and explain things to him. For example, if he sees you put his teddy bear inside a box and you then ask, "Where is the teddy bear?", he will soon comprehend what it means for something to be inside the box. Keep demonstrating and then explaining things to him, and he will gradually begin to understand more about how the world around him works.

FINDING TEDDY
Demonstrating concepts in a practical and interesting way helps your child understand how things happen.

how the process works or what his part in playing with other children is. If he can't manage to grasp what you mean at first, wait with him, or try suggesting that he play beside you until he learns that taking turns is a positive thing to do.

Language and intellectual skills

Your child will make enormous progress throughout this year as his language skills develop and he begins to gather and express information in ways other than physical exploration alone. This aspect continues, too, of course, but it is the bringing together of his language and physical skills – for example, "When I do this, this happens" – that really helps his cognitive development.

Understanding concepts

The continued development of his memory, together with improving language skills, allows your child to begin to form mental images of how things happen, which leads to an understanding of concepts. Concepts are more the abstract ideas about how the world works – for example, the concepts of up and down, under and over, in and out.

You can help develop this skill by talking to your child about going inside your house, or show him how you put one stacking cup inside another or your purse inside your bag, for example (*see also box, p.223*).

Simple requests

Your child will now begin to understand your simple requests. He may find it difficult to understand a

Toy box

Picture lotto
Choose a chunky picture lotto game that your child can grasp easily, and with simple images. Use only a few pieces to begin with; as he gets older he can memorize more pictures.

Cassette player
Some children's cassette players enable a child to record their own voice talking and singing, or are even equipped with headphones for listening quietly to a favourite tape.

Tricycle
Tricycles are good for indoor and outdoor play. Let your child get used to pushing himself along with his legs and learn how to steer before showing him how to use the pedals.

Activities to develop skills

Giving your child lots of opportunities to explore what his body is capable of can help his physical development and his self-esteem. Help him develop his memory skills, too, with tapes and picture games.

★ Outdoor playgrounds with swings and slides are good because there are usually other children to share the experience, which also helps your child learn about taking turns.

★ Steady, durable tricycles with handlebars to steer but no pedals can provide your child with a different opportunity to exercise his legs, and develop the coordination needed to steer the handlebars. Help him with a gentle push to get started or use a

DANCING FOR JOY
Physical playtime, both indoors and outside, is great fun and essential for children since it helps them grow and develop.

complicated instruction, such as going into the hall, finding both of his shoes, and bringing them to you in the kitchen. But simple requests to do one thing at a time are easily within his grasp, such as asking him to bring you his shoes. This activity fosters a sense of general helpfulness and also helps him learn to act for himself, which builds up his confidence in being able to manage small tasks, gives him a sense of self-esteem, and eventually leads to a degree of independence.

Making your own playdough

Making your own playdough saves time and money, and is fun. Your child may also enjoy helping you to mix and knead the dough once it is cool.

Cooked recipe:

200g (7oz) plain flour
100g (3½oz) salt
2tsp cream of tartar
1tbs (15ml) vegetable oil
300ml (12oz) water

- Put the dry ingredients in a saucepan and gradually add the water, oil, and a little food colouring to colour the dough. Cook over a low-medium heat, stirring continuously until stiff. Tip out, and then knead the dough once it has cooled down.
- Keep the dough in an airtight container in between playtimes. The salt will help preserve the mixture for a few weeks, and the salty taste will put off any children who may want to eat the dough.

tricycle with a long handle at the back to guide him along. Don't overdo the amount you help; provide enough momentum to get him started and confident. Once he has mastered this, he can try riding a trike using the pedals.

★ Matching shapes or pictures is an important observational and pre-maths skill. You may have previously given your child a shape-sorter posting box, and then moved on to a tray puzzle where he has to select and place a flat shape into its matching place on the board. Now this skill can be developed into a simple game of similarities and dissimilarities. This in turn helps extend language skills to communicate ideas, observations, and feelings.

★ A cassette player designed to be used by little fingers will give your child access to music and favourite stories on tape. You may also like to record yourself reading a favourite story for your child, and if there are stories with which he is familiar, he can look at the book while listening to the tape. This will increase the access your child has to the spoken word. Learning to listen attentively will be of great benefit to him, especially when he joins a group of children at nursery school or playgroup. Make sure the volume can't be raised above a certain level, to avoid damaging his ears.

★ Soft, squidgy modelling clay is a delight in itself, and your child may enjoy just squeezing it through his fingers before getting involved in more imaginative play. Creating flat shapes and making impressions in the dough with pastry cutters — or even just making hand prints — allows him to explore all sorts of interesting possibilities with playdough.

ROLLING OUT DOUGH
Rolling playdough – either between the fingers or with a rolling pin – gives a child a huge amount of pleasure. Make sure you also provide a blunt plastic knife or pastry cutters to cut the dough.

26 to 28 months

Over the next few months your child will begin to focus for longer periods on interactive activities that help expand her attention. During this time she will be capable of experiencing stronger emotions and will also be able to master skills through repetition. Although at first she may remain interested for only a comparatively short time, gentle encouragement will help make her efforts all the more worthwhile.

Physical development

While your child's gross motor skills – such as walking and running – are improving, so, too, are her fine motor skills, enabling her to use her hands in specific ways to accomplish tasks.

Fine motor skills

At birth, your child's wrist and palm consisted of only three bones, in comparison to the 28 bones in an adult's hand. It isn't until the cartilage in a child's hand ossifies into bones that the brain's ability to influence the supporting muscles can mature. Once this happens, using tools (in your child's case, these are usually toys) becomes easier, whether it is a stick to beat a drum, a crayon for drawing, or a spoon for feeding herself.

As a baby, your child began by swiping at an object, then was able to grasp it with her whole fist, and now she can delicately pick up something quite small between her thumb and forefinger. Not only that, her ability to pick something up, twist her wrist, and place it carefully down again, is physically quite an achievement. Initially, every effort was put into trying to place and balance just one block on top of another, for example. Practice has made this easy, and now she may try to balance as many blocks as possible before they topple over – or are deliberately

knocked down! Thus her ability to pick up an object in her hand has matured immeasurably: she can now do this with greater accuracy and judge far more easily where to place the block so that it will balance.

Playing in the park also increases your child's motor skills, although she still needs close supervision since her energy levels and her expectations of her abilities can still get her into unexpected difficulties.

Social and emotional skills

The emotional range of a two-year-old is broad, extending from sheer delight to frustrated rage depending on your child's personality.

Managing emotion

While being able to express emotions freely is considered a healthy ability, what a child must learn is to manage her emotions and know which feelings are appropriate. This takes practice and she will need your help.

Children may feel overwhelmed by the force of their emotions sometimes, hence the full-blown tantrum. These situations need specific management skills (see pp.18–19), but it also helps to keep in mind what might trigger such extremes of emotion. Some children cannot manage emotionally as well as others when they are tired

or hungry, for example. It is worth remembering in the middle of an emotional maelstrom that your child is also capable of expressing positive emotions, such as happiness. So finding an activity to share that she

Repetition

You may find your child requests the same story book over and over again. Children of this age love repetition, and sometimes object if you deviate from exactly what is written. They may also remember or recognize the odd word, and notice it again if they then see the word printed somewhere else. You will probably find they like playing the same action songs, rhymes, and clapping games over again, too.

MEMORY GAMES
The visual stimulation and simple phrases of action games help develop a child's language and listening skills.

really enjoys and that allows her to express her happier side will help her self-esteem, and also increase your own pleasure.

Language and intellectual skills

Your child's understanding of the world continues to improve through her developing language and memory skills. Memory also helps in the development of her attention span as she begins to understand the concept of sequences of events.

Cause and effect

If you say you are going to read a story to your child, her memory of what this involves, and the pleasure she knows she will derive from it when it happens, will make her more willing to focus on the book for the time it takes to read a story. She can then use this knowledge about what books involve, and how to enjoy them, to look at books by herself, developing her concentration and lengthening her attention span.

Over the last two years you may have collected numerous children's stories, from treasured first board books and favourite picture books to more sophisticated stories – all of which provide unique access to an imaginative world that helps your child learn about new ideas, cause and effect, feelings and facts, as well as developing concentration, learning how to listen, and extending the range of her vocabulary. This is the beginning of understanding about learning to read, so it is important to encourage your child to develop a natural curiosity about books and stories, and to make the experience of reading a pleasurable one.

Improving concentration

You can also see the effectiveness of your child's memory at this age if you interrupt her activity to ask her a question about something else. She can focus on you and your question and then return to whatever it was she was doing. This is because she can now not only remember what she was doing, but what stage she had reached doing it.

Part of being able to develop this technique involves what psychologists call "selective (or focal) attention" – the ability to switch off from outside stimuli and concentrate on one thing at a time. One of the benefits of this is that concentration becomes easier if you can ignore other noise.

Some children can achieve a better level of concentration than others, so if your child finds it difficult to focus on something, reduce any background distractions or mask them by playing classical music at low volume. But remember that if you want your child to focus one-to-one on listening to your voice, either in conversation or by having a book read, make sure there is no background noise at all.

Toy box

Scrapbook materials
Choose round-ended scissors that are easy to open and shut with one hand, and a water-based glue that actually sticks but which can be washed off hands and clothes.

Painting equipment
Choose paint specially designed for young children and that will wash out of clothing. Thick finger paints in bright colours are the best choice. If you buy brushes, choose large brushes that are easy to grasp.

Books
Although your child will love reading the same stories over and over again, make sure you keep her stimulated by occasionally borrowing other books from your local library to vary the complexity of pictures and introduce new types of stories.

Activities to develop skills

Finger paints and glueing paper are a lovely way for children to make their mark. Be prepared for a mess and dress your child in old clothes, or use overalls. You can also help improve your child's coordination and imagination by encouraging her to continue playing with blocks, and try to spend time reading stories and looking at pictures together.

SHARED ACTIVITY
To begin with, your child may need a little help and encouragement to try finger painting.

MESSY HANDS
Praise your child's efforts, even if her first attempts are splodgy, and she'll soon gain the confidence to experiment.

GLUEING PAPER
Glueing paper is a skill in itself: your child needs to learn to adjust the amount of glue required to stick something down.

★ Find time every day to sit and read books with your child. If you have children of different ages, it is possible to share a range of books, reading to your two-year-old while feeding your baby, for example, or choosing a book with enough of a story for an older child to enjoy as well. Carry a couple of favourites with you in your bag in case you have an unexpected wait somewhere.

★ Encourage your child's hand skills and hand–eye coordination by helping her make a scrapbook or a book of discarded or duplicate photos. Get her used to scissors by letting her cut coloured paper into broad strips and squares, and include stickers and water-based glue. First attempts are often a messy business, but that's all part of the fun.

★ First attempts at hand painting don't need pristine paper – use the back of any junk mail or redundant computer printouts – but you do need to allow plenty of scope for experimentation. Help your child enjoy the process for its own sake, with colours and shapes; then, when the masterpiece is dry, stick it on the wall for everyone to enjoy. You can also chop a potato in half, cut a simple shape like a circle or cross, into the surface, and let your child dip it in paint to make potato prints. Or try using a sponge dipped into paint.

★ Coloured blocks in different shapes and sizes will encourage your child's imagination. She may deliberately choose blocks of all one colour, subconsciously sorting them to bring a sense of order. Rather than just put one block on top of another, she may start to build different shapes and create her own games.

28 to 30 months

The human body is designed for motor activity, and young children in particular need to develop important physical skills such as coordination and balance, as well as improve their stamina and strength. In addition, the chance to master their physical abilities and skills helps enhance young children's self-esteem, muscle development, and coordination. It is important for children to have the opportunity to participate in physical activities under adult supervision, and to be encouraged to do so.

Physical development

Your child needs plenty of physical activity to help expend some of the enormous amounts of energy he exhibits at this age. The amount of exercise he gets helps his spatial understanding and, by extension, his balance and coordination skills.

Ball games

Playing outside with a ball can give enormous pleasure to an energetic two-and-a-half-year-old. Kicking the ball requires balance and coordination, while throwing it is really an extension of letting go, with a little force behind it. Catching, too, is a skill that has to be learned. Your child's first attempts will be inaccurate and haphazard, but with practice and praise he'll improve in time.

ACQUIRING THE SKILLS
Developing ball skills helps improve hand–eye coordination and increases the pleasure of new achievements that encourage physical self-confidence.

Body and brain

Getting plenty of exercise not only burns off excess energy, it establishes a positive body image and a sense of self-esteem in your child's mind.

In addition, the connections built between neurones in the brain, known as neural pathways, are formulated by persistent physical, as well as cognitive, activity. This is why, once learned, we never forget how to ride a bicycle unless something interferes with those specific neural patterns imprinted in our brains. Therefore, a child needs practice in the larger physical skills – running, kicking, climbing, or pedalling a tricycle – to become competent, as well as build strength and use energy.

Exercising together

With concerns growing about today's rising rates of childhood obesity, our sedentary lifestyles, and children's lack of exercise, it is as well to foster an enjoyment of exercise. Let your child walk rather than take the car, allowing him to sit in his buggy if he gets tired, or park further away from the shops than usual and walk there.

Social and emotional skills

You may find that as your child becomes more social he starts to anticipate events and express

pleasure at one activity over another. He may also begin to express his excitement when he sees a friend he recognizes or enjoys playing with.

Other relationships

Forming attachments outside the immediate family circle is evidence of your child's widening emotional development. He is starting to make relationships based on his own positive feelings about being a person, independent of you.

It is important to try and validate your child's emotions, even if doing so sometimes seems at odds with your feelings. With his improving language skills, articulating how he feels about someone, or something, becomes a greater possibility. He may not know what he feels at first, but you can help him explore his emotions. Don't disregard him, tell him not to be silly, or ignore the situation if he appears hesitant about playing with another child, for example. Gently determine what it is that he doesn't feel comfortable about.

Expressing pleasure

In the same way, when a person or an event generates particular pleasure, ask your child what it is that feels good about the experience. Use this opportunity to talk to him about feelings, but keep it simple. By being attuned to your child's feelings and acknowledging them, and encouraging him to articulate them when he's ready, you are paving the way to him being able to learn how to explore and express his own feelings.

Other people's feelings

If your child can learn at this early age that his feelings are valued, it will eventually enable him to consider other people's feelings in the same way. Respecting your child's feelings in turn teaches him that respecting another individual's emotions is equally important.

Language and intellectual skills

Since memory is such an important part of what helps children develop intellectually, it is worth helping your child improve his memory skills.

Show and tell

At this stage it is still easier for children to remember language that is reinforced by physical activity, such as action songs (*see also box, p.227*). In the same way, when you tell your child how to do something, show

him at the same time – turn the page of a book carefully, or close a door gently, for example. This is especially important when your child grapples with abstract concepts.

Creating an impact

For all of us, remembering routines that happen every day is harder than remembering one-off events. You may notice that if you ask your child what he had for breakfast – even if it was only an hour ago – he may look at you blankly since the food he eats every day is not of

Activities to develop skills

Encourage young children at this age to engage in pretend play, since it is an absorbing way for them to develop their imaginations – likewise with toy cars and train sets, and plastic bricks and models.

⭐ Playing out the simple routines in their lives helps children make sense of events and prepares them for more complicated pretend play,

which in turn stimulates their imagination. Pretend games are also the way in which young children begin to develop an understanding of what is

TEA FOR THREE
When pretend games happen, they are often the end result of remembering something that has happened before and exploring what might yet happen.

real and what is not – the difference between fact and fantasy. Playing with a tea set, for example, involves all sorts of remembered events of preparing and drinking tea – it may even be too hot to drink! Children recognize that drinking tea or coffee is a social event, usually drunk sitting down, sometimes with a friend. A child will act all of this out in his game, usually talking it through as he does so. He'll probably be equally happy playing on his own with some toys, or with you or perhaps a friend.

⭐ Toy cars or a simple train set can give both boys and girls great pleasure, so always encourage imaginative play. What may differentiate girls and boys in the way they play with these toys is how they develop this into their own particular imaginative game: pushing

much consequence to him. But if you ask him what he had for tea on his last visit to his grandma's house, he may easily remember when he returns there and point to a cupboard, for example. Children are very much "of the moment", and remembering the mundane holds comparatively little interest for them. Something that may have been planned, discussed, and involved a change in the normal routine becomes an exciting event, and thus has a greater impact on a child.

Toy box

Balls
Buy a medium-sized, lightweight ball that your child can easily wrap his arms around to hold securely. Soft tennis balls are another option.

Tea set
A brightly coloured, well-made plastic tea set will give hours of pleasure. Make sure the pieces are sturdy

enough for little hands, and not so flimsy that they keep toppling over.

Plastic bricks
The chunkier the plastic pieces are, the more chance your two-year-old will have of being able to use his coordination skills and the strength in his hands to fit blocks together without becoming frustrated.

---

the cars around, imagining different scenarios, and acting them out. You can buy special mats with a road layout marked on them for an added focus for play, but these aren't essential items.

★ Larger plastic bricks are easier for little fingers to use. A good selection of bricks is an ideal toy for both boys and girls of this age, and can be played with in a variety of different ways: building toys, houses, and scenes, and incorporating play figures and animals encourages all sorts of imaginative play. Children's creativity is stimulated when they are allowed to use their imagination. Take your lead from your child to assess the degree of help needed and always encourage creative play; resist any urge to teach him or control his playtime in any way.

BUMPER TO BUMPER
A good selection of toy cars provides opportunities for shared play as your two-year-old may begin to play with, rather than alongside, another child.

CAPTURING THE IMAGINATION
Although by no means an exclusively male pastime, playing with toy cars may hold boys' interest for longer and from an earlier age.

30 to 32 months

During these early years you are your child's first teacher and her most sensitive guide, and time spent together is invaluable. Even when life is very busy, finding a moment to spend time alone together to give your child your undivided attention will give you both pleasure. Reading is one important way that you can provide physical reassurance and comfort, the familiarity of a favourite story, and the one-to-one attention your child needs to flourish.

Physical development

Given the opportunity, it's amazing what a difference practice can make to your child's ability to use her hands proficiently.

Hand skills

It may be interesting to note that most Chinese children at this age are competent at using chopsticks, since they have had to learn to do so in order to feed themselves – something those of us who find chopsticks hard to use may think extraordinary!

What you can expect of your child now, though, is that she uses her hands to do a variety of different things, from carefully turning the page of a book to holding a pencil or unscrewing a jar. Practising undoing poppers on clothes, for instance, can help her fine motor skills and develop her independence. Help her by selecting the sort of clothes that enable her to manage dressing as much as possible by herself. This will also help her competence and her self-esteem.

Growing in confidence

Another measure of your child's increased physical skills is her ability to balance blocks one on top of the other. When your child was in her second year, learning to balance just one block at a time on top of another seemed quite a feat. But now that she is in her third year, she should be able to manage to stack at least six blocks.

This maturing of fine motor skills helps in all sorts of ways, including encouraging your child to develop the self-confidence to try other things that were once quite difficult. Seeing her own progress, and enjoying the pleasure and satisfaction that it brings, encourages her to try other new activities.

Social and emotional skills

Your child has probably developed quite a clear idea of what possessions are, but she still needs reminding that she can share what she has.

A child's viewpoint

Understanding what's "mine" at this age can result in a certain amount of possessiveness in children. However, all this is really just part of how they view the world around them from their own, very singular, point of view. What is needed is for you to act as a guide to your child: by helping her open up her focus and incorporate a wider viewpoint.

Learning respect

Most of this social behaviour is learned by example, so if you want your child to share you will also have to watch your own possessiveness! Saying "Don't touch that, it's precious" may be a way of avoiding something getting broken, but it also conveys the idea that if

Awareness of self

Your child probably now knows that she is a girl – or he is a boy – and can distinguish between the sexes, although she may not always know why. She will also be able to refer to herself as "I" and may be able to describe herself in simple sentences: "I am hungry", for example. This growing awareness of self began months before, but its expression is now becoming clearer, and as your child's language skills become better she may be able to convey her thoughts more easily.

ROLE MODEL
While traditional gender stereotypes are no longer the norm, children often tend to look to role models of the same sex.

it's yours, your child can't have it. So, by extension, if that toy is your child's, why should she let another child have a turn with it? It helps if you can take the time to explain why it is important to respect other people's possessions so that she will respect yours while still being able to share.

Language and intellectual skills

By now your child's vocabulary may include as many as 200 to 300 words. She may also be using connecting words between phrases such as "and", while also adding details through description. Bilingual children may initially have a smaller vocabulary base and tend initially to mix words from each language when they speak, but they will soon catch up with their peers.

Asking questions

With this acquired vocabulary comes the question, "Why?" This process of questioning is valuable to your child since it helps her understand and is likely to continue for many months. Answer simply, allowing for development of thought and further questions from your child, rather than overwhelm her with a complicated explanation. Answering a two-year-old's incessant questioning is an art, and there can't be many parents who haven't resorted occasionally to saying, "Because I say so!" However, be prepared for the comeback, "Why?" You may even want to respond with your own question in a friendly tone: "What do you think?" Your child now also understands quite complex instructions from you, although she may choose not to respond!

Developing conversations

Attending a playgroup or a nursery school is an important opportunity for children to enjoy interacting with each other and develop their own communication.

Your child may also keep up a running monologue to herself to help her organize her thoughts, or have pretend conversations with a teddy bear or doll. It can bring you up short when you hear your child say sternly, "No!" to her toys!

Speaking clearly

Children of this age may still speak unclearly or mispronounce words. This may be connected to the development of facial muscles, and can be helped by making sure that you give your child lots of foods that require chewing. This helps exercise the same muscles needed for speech. If your child still mispronounces most words, it is important to check first with your GP that she hasn't suffered any hearing loss. Also check that any background noise is turned off when you spend one-to-one time together.

Toy box

Dolls

You can now buy dolls with appropriate clothes that are specially made to help young children learn about the process of dressing and undressing yourself. Playing with dolls will stimulate a child's imagination and also encourage role-playing games.

Picture dominoes

Make sure that the dominoes are large enough for young children to pick up and put down easily.

Jigsaw puzzles

Choose puzzles with a maximum of six or seven pieces so that the task of fitting everything together is not too daunting a task for your child. Well-made wooden jigsaw puzzles with clear, simple pictures are most appropriate for small fingers and hopefully will hold a child's attention.

Activities to develop skills

Simple jigsaw puzzles are an excellent way of training your child's eye to recognize matching shapes and to look at how things fit together. You can also help her manage a small task and improve her fine motor skills by giving her a doll to undress. Try playing singing games to improve her ability to listen to different sounds and follow rhythms.

★ Introduce the idea of rhythm to your child by beating time. Pick out the rhythm of different words, or combinations of words, for example, the rhythm in your child's name: Martin becomes "Mar-tin", Samantha becomes "Sam-an-tha", and so you introduce the idea of syllables with a game. Maybe an older sibling could play an instrument while you and your two-year-old beat time clapping your hands or tapping glasses filled with different measures of water.

★ Getting dressed and undressed is a routine part of your child's activity, and something she may be happy to attempt on her own. It can provide the chance to learn to undo various clothes fastenings – poppers and zips, which require small, precise movements of the fingers. But these are skills of great value, and something your child needs to be competent at doing in due course. It also allows her to develop the sort of confidence needed to be able to manage small tasks alone, which will stand her in good stead when she has to manage away from one-to-one support – perhaps when she starts nursery school.

★ You may also like to try playing picture dominoes and matching games with your child. Matching pictures demands observation and memory skills and improves her ability to spot similarities. While she is still too young to play this game on her own, she may enjoy playing alongside you.

BRAIN TEASER
Children love the challenge of completing jigsaw puzzles and can become quickly absorbed in their task.

★ Simple jigsaw puzzles take the process of matching up shapes to another stage, since they require good observation skills. Children can get great satisfaction in trying to find the right piece and put it in the right place. Learning to look at something in this very specific way is also good training for the identification of letter shapes later on. Jigsaw puzzles also require focus, concentration, and a logical thought process, but it doesn't feel like that to a child – it's just a game!

MAKING MUSIC
Encourage an older sibling to play a simple tune so that your two year-old can copy the rhythm by tapping glasses.

32 to 34 months

Quiet times are important for small children to have as part of their normal routine. It allows them the opportunity to be imaginative, creative, and develop new ideas of their own. Don't be tempted to fill every waking moment of your child's day with a planned activity or an organized event. It's important for him to be allowed to be creative and to learn how to develop his own imagination.

Physical development

Your two-year-old can now build on the strength he has developed so far in his limbs to climb up and down stairs, walk on tiptoe, and control his hand movements more accurately.

Balance and flexibility

If you live in a house with a flight of stairs, your two-year-old may now be getting used to going safely up and down them, although never leave him to climb or descend the steps on his own.

If you do not have stairs in your home, your child will inevitably have had less practice at this skill. However, he is probably now beginning to climb stairs stepping up one foot at a time rather than taking just one step at a time.

Improving motor skills

Jumping with two feet may now be possible for your child, although he may still be rather flat-footed. You might like to suggest games that encourage him to walk on tiptoe in bare feet. This activity strengthens his feet and gives flexibility and balance. Your child may also be getting more competent at washing and drying his hands. Some fine motor skills, such as eating with a spoon or fork, are also improving, but may still be a little haphazard.

Social and emotional skills

Attention-seeking behaviour in two-year-old children can take different forms, and having a tantrum is often one of them.

Displaying emotions

At this age, tantrums in children can be due to changes or events, or a learned response. If they surface in a previously peaceable child, consider why his behaviour may have changed, and teach him firmly but calmly that his behaviour is not appropriate.

Emotional frustration

It's important to try and work out why a child responds to situations in this antisocial way. This can be difficult if having a tantrum gets him what he wants in the short term. Tantrums are usually linked to a child's frustration and an inability to communicate effectively. A two-year-old cannot do all the things he wants, or fully understand that there are things he cannot have. Check to see if he is overtired or hungry, or if he feels threatened in some way or needs more positive attention.

Positive attention

It is worth remembering that children have an emotional need for a lot of attention and, while positive attention is better than negative, they tend not to make that distinction – any attention will do if a child feels he isn't getting enough.

The challenge of parenting is being attuned to your child so that you can try to accommodate his needs as they change. The basic principle is to

Hand–eye coordination

At first, threading cotton reels or large buttons demands good hand–eye coordination and a considerable amount of concentration. However, this is a rewarding activity since it affords the chance not just to thread objects together, but to choose the sequence of colours and shapes.

THREADING COTTON REELS
If you don't have time to make your own shapes by cutting circles and squares in coloured card with a hole at the centre, you can buy coloured reels and thread.

try to ignore negative behaviour and to be generous in your reward of good behaviour. So, when you have to deal with any aggressive behaviour in your child, make sure that you pay attention to, and reward any occasions of, positive behaviour with praise.

Also give your child specific feedback on his behaviour so that he learns what is and what isn't considered desirable. You might say, for example, "Thank you for sharing your books", or "I like it when you play gently with your sister."

Language and intellectual skills

Your child may now be beginning to grasp the concept of simple number sequences and different categories.

Number sequences

Your child's knowledge of numbers began when you first sang number rhymes to him, although it wouldn't have been clear then what these words represented. Through your frequent repetition, your child may have learned to "count" to five, or even 10, although in reality he has been repeating a sequence of sounds.

Now he will begin to use these familiar words to represent the more tangible concept of counting. The development of this understanding begins with forming groups, or sequences, of objects. Just counting three cars or two spoons is a start. Your child may also grasp the idea of different categories soon: 10 plastic animals in total, but three cows, five pigs, and two horses. You may even find him repeating numbers and number sequences in his games.

Activities for developing skills

Imaginative play is very important for young children. Through it they learn to work out certain abstract concepts, act out story lines, "try on" different ideas, explore feelings, and ways of behaving – all within their own imaginations.

★ Playing with other children is a learned skill, and is all about socializing, taking turns, and thinking about others. Help your child learn these skills by playing simple board games that are appropriate to his age group and encourage him to take turns. In addition, playing a counting game enables you to help him learn about numbers plus their names and sequences. If you play board games, focus on the pleasure and excitement of playing the game, irrespective of who wins, so that winning is not your child's only achievement when playing. It is more important at this

age to have fun than to focus on the desire to win.

★ Reading books are probably a regular feature in your child's life now, not just at bedtimes but also at other times of the day. Remember that small children enjoy clear, attractive pictures and, by this stage, will probably listen to quite a sophisticated story line. Looking at books alone is still something to be encouraged. If you are unsure which books might be appropriate for your child, ask a children's librarian to recommend different titles, authors, and illustrators. Some children's libraries may also have some special

SOCIAL GATHERING
Children may need a little encouragement to begin playing with each other, but they soon become involved in imaginary games.

storytelling sessions and other entertaining book-related activities that your child can enjoy.

★ All young children should be encouraged to play games that rely

Nursery rhymes

Have you ever wondered why parents pass down favourite nursery rhymes through the generations? Perhaps it's from an intuitive knowledge that talking to your child helps him develop speech, but the repetition of nursery rhymes is also a very useful preparation for reading. The constant repetition of the rhymes in early life means that your child becomes familiar with different word sounds. They also engage his attention, helping him pick up information about language and how it works.

Toy box

Simple board games

Focus on simple games with your child, such as buying a durable board game that is clearly marked as being appropriate for his age group. Go slowly and patiently as you play with him, and you may find that he soon begins to pick up the rules of the game.

Dressing-up box

It is worth keeping a large box full of a selection of old grown-ups' castoffs and dressing-up clothes for children to play with. Encourage them to think imaginatively about how they can adapt the clothes to suit who they want to pretend to be.

on their own internal resources, and dressing-up games help to stimulate this ability. Dressing up also makes a game of developing the necessary skills your child needs to learn in order to be able to dress herself.

A big square of material can instantly become a princess's cloak, a magician's cape, a magic carpet, a baby's blanket, or Red Riding Hood's granny's shawl. Adults' clothes and accessories such as old hats or high-heeled shoes are another great attraction. Shop-bought outfits, perhaps based on popular fictional characters, are also an option, as are doctors' and nurses' outfits and other costumes. As your child grows, he may find more and more enjoyment in his repeated imaginative games, especially when other children are prepared to join in and play with him.

ROLE-PLAYING
Most children love dressing up, and enjoy wearing the odd grown-up castoff as they act out their pretend role-play games.

34 to 36 months

Your almost-three-year-old is becoming much more obviously her own person now, with her own developing interests and opinions. Her personality is also becoming more clearly established, and, while she may share certain characteristics with other family members, she is learning to experiment and express her own ideas. However, your child still needs all your encouragement, affection, and security, so don't entrust her with older siblings without you being there to supervise, for example.

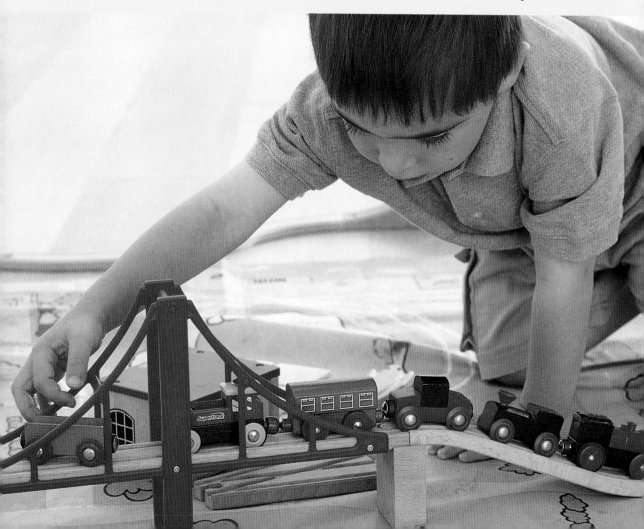

Physical skills

As they near their third birthday, most children are now physically proficient in the large motor skills of running, walking, and climbing. If you feel that your child isn't perhaps as physically competent as her peers, it may be that she needs more practice to develop these skills.

Individual development

Some children may seem physically less able than others because often they are impatient to get from one place to another, or achieve a specific task; they may manage better if they slow down and take things more gently. Other children can be very impulsive and don't allow themselves time to assess physical risk, so, again, they may need some encouragement to slow down a little. If they show little natural fear or reservation, they may need help in understanding that what they are doing could put themselves at risk.

Structured activities

For a parent, it may feel like a natural inclination to reduce the level of physical activity in a child who appears less physically able, but guard against this tendency as it won't help the child. In fact, increasing the amount of structured activities to help your child learn to manage physical skills more easily will be to her advantage. As long as it could help her in an uncompetitive and fun way, think about whether she may benefit from joining a gymnastics or dance class for young children at your local sports centre. Remember to keep giving her lots of encouragement to raise her self-esteem.

The concept of time

Your child may be advanced enough in her understanding now to grasp the abstract concept of time – before and after, for instance. She may now understand you if you say she can get down and play "after you've finished your lunch". This understanding is possible because of her developing experience and her memory of what happens during the course of her day.

MEALTIME
Repeated activities such as mealtimes and bedtime help define the course of the day for young children.

Social and emotional skills

Your child should now be reasonably happy to be separated from you with a familiar carer for an extended period of time, although some children may be able to manage this progression with less anxiety than others.

Separation

In order to be able to separate happily from you, your child needs to be able to hold on to the thought of you and know that you will return to her, something which is learned partly through experience. How you handle the separation will also convey to your child what is expected of her. If you appear confident that she will manage and be safe without you, you will convey to her your confidence in her ability to manage. If you are anxious or diffident, she may well pick up on this emotion, which might make it more difficult for her to feel confident without you.

Practical measures

Whether your child is about to start nursery school or is getting used to being with a childminder, there are

Activities to develop skills

Your child's first scribbles with wax crayons have now become more deliberate, controlled, and influenced by what she is trying to achieve. She still enjoys learning through play, so continue to keep her stimulated.

★ Picture lotto is a wonderful game for all kinds of reasons. It can be played by two or more people so it encourages the process of sharing, taking turns, and developing conversation. It also helps develop a child's visual memory skills.

★ Bath time is a good wind-down at the end of the day, but it can also include pleasurable activities such as pouring water from one container to another, playing with bath toys, singing songs and rhymes, and chatting with you about the events of your child's day. Foam letters can also provide an easy way to introduce first letter shapes that can be touched and moved around. Handling something actually helps a young child memorize it better, so these large letters and numbers can help your child identify and remember them. Choose letters that are lower case, not capitals. Introducing the letters to your child just by naming them is enough at this stage. Then let her add them to her collection of toys in the bath to have fun with them.

★ By the end of your child's third year, outdoor play will not only be a source of pleasure for her but a way in which she can run off some of her abundant energy. It is much easier

PICTURE LOTTO
This game helps improve a child's observational skills as he matches pictures and develops an eye for slight differences in shape, colour, or form.

to tolerate inactivity and focus on something if there has been a chance to expend some energy first. A daily excursion to a park, almost whatever the weather, is a change of scene and an opportunity to exercise those growing limbs. Regular exercise also encourages a child's appetite, and helps her sleep well.

★ Your child will probably now love to make pictures with paints, crayons, or even washable felt-tip pens. While she may still sometimes use either hand, it is likely that she will now use just one hand rather than the other. Movements are still big, but she may be able to copy some basic shapes – a circle, square, or even a triangle, for example. Help her develop a good pencil grip by giving her triangular-shaped crayons, since they will encourage a tripod grasp.

PAINTING SKILLS
As well as improving their control and flexibility, painting helps a child learn to express himself through shape and colour.

some practical measures you should keep in mind to make things bearable: ensure that your child understands exactly who is going to care for her and that she realizes they are a familiar face; be confident yourself that you trust and feel relaxed with whoever is left in charge; reassure your child that you are coming back; and then leave her on a positive note.

Other practical measures to help your child feel secure include giving her a photograph of you or perhaps allowing her to take a security object along with her for a while.

Maintaining trust

Don't be tempted to try to avoid a scene by slipping away from her without saying goodbye, since this will betray her trust in you. Even if she appears unable to manage without you, remember that she will be fine and will soon learn that she can manage her feelings without you being present, which in turn will build her confidence.

Feeling secure

While most children will separate quite happily once they feel secure – and are also happy to see their parents again – if you find that your child has been upset while you've been away, don't leave her for more than 20 minutes at a time until she really feels settled in her environment.

Language and intellectual skills

Your child should now be able to converse with you in short sentences rather than just in phrases, and she may now be able to continue talking about a topic for a short period.

Personal references

Your child will probably now refer to herself as "I" rather than by her name, say "you" rather than use the third person, and refer to friends and family by name. This demonstrates how her cognitive skills have advanced over the year identifying herself as an individual within her family, and referring to herself as such. By the age of three most children's speech should be largely intelligible to

people who are unfamiliar with the child. If, however, your child is becoming more difficult to understand or is saying less, have her hearing checked by your GP or health visitor.

Visual memories

As her language skills improve, you will notice how good your child's memory and observation skills are becoming. Children have very visual memories, so if your child has a broad range of vocabulary you may be surprised by how much detail she can give you about something she has seen or heard. Encourage your child to develop this skill by asking her to describe events or experiences in more detail and ask simple questions about what she saw or how she felt.

Toy box

Picture lotto

If you have already begun playing a simple version of picture lotto with your child, you may want to buy a slightly more sophisticated version of the game if she is becoming proficient at it. Or make your own version of picture lotto using pictures cut from magazines and glued on to square pieces of card.

Foam letters

Many toy shops now sell containers of foam letters and numbers that

will stick to the side of the bathtub when wet. Choose large rather than small pieces.

Pens and paper

Buy chunky pens or triangular-shaped crayons and bright paper to give your child many hours of fun.

Index

Acknowledgments

Chapter one: The first six months
Text by Katy Holland *For Patrick and Stanley*

Chapter two: The second six months
Text by Tracey Godridge *For Cora, Eden and Noah*

Chapter three: The second year
Text by Harriet Griffey *For Josh and Robbie*

Chapter four: The third year
Text by Harriet Griffey *For Josh and Robbie*

The authors would like to thank Pippa Duncan, Claire Legemah, Susannah Steel, Julia North, and Glenda Fisher for all their work.

Credits
Proof-reader: Nikky Twyman

Indexer: Hilary Bird

Jacket designer: Katy Wall

Models:
Chapter one: Jo with Jade Salliger, Jason with Kasia Wall, Linda with Mackenzie Quick, Simon with Oban Murrell, Rachana with Arianna Shah, Penny with Anastasia Stephens, Thimmie with Emily Pickering, Andrea with Joel Peters, Rachel with Zoe Nayani, Rachel with baby Best, Isabelle with Carla Wicker-Jourdan, Alison with Phoebe Lee.

Chapter two: Tali with Gil Krikler, Denise with Kymani and Kymarley Woodstock, Helen with Joseph Jack and Leo Stiles, Mulki with Wyse Ali, Janis and Maureen Lopatkin with Mia Lopatkin, Mr & Mrs Kiyomura with Eri, Michelle with Charlie Terras, Ivor with Ruby Baddiel, Rachel with Zoe Nayani, Maria with Jasmine Leitch.

Chapter three: Lilian with Gregory Maya, Tracey with James Coleman-Ward, Faith Knight with her dad, Janis and Maureen Lopatkin with Mia Lopatkin, Mrs Sugiya with Nana and sister, Lina with Anna Maria Sheridan, Shelley with Sadie Goswell, Penny with Evie McCann, Kay with Ben Whiteley, Lynn with Esme Spencer, Carol with Hannah Tennant, Michelle with Charlie Terras, Nicki with Max Riggall, Tina with Lewis Oakey, Fiona with Ellie Messer, Sarah with Phoebe Berman.

Chapter four: Simon with Lauren Murrell, Deborah with Aaron Bright, Mr and Mrs Perez, George with Sophia Sirius, Tony with Christina and Louise Aquino, Sima and Tim with Danielle and Tal Randall, Gaynor with Oliver Benveniste, Sue with Anya Dziewulski, Deborah with Sadie Seitler, Meena with Shaun MacNamara, Jane with Luke Rimell, Cheryl and John with Yasmin Weekes, Orlean with Ethan Stennett, Sibel with Lara Peck, Teresa with Isabell.

Hair and make-up: Tracy Townsend

Consultants
Warren Hyer MRCP is Consultant Paediatrician at Northwick Park and St. Mark's Hospitals, Harrow, and Honorary Clinical Senior Lecturer, Imperial College of Science, Technology and Medicine.

Penny Tassoni is an education consultant, author and trainer. Penny lectures on a range of childhood studies courses and has written five books, including *Planning, Play and the Early Years.*

Picture Credits
Picture researcher: Cheryl Dubyk-Yates

Picture librarian: Hayley Smith

The publisher would like to thank the following for their kind permission to reproduce their photographs:
(abbreviations key: t=top, b=bottom, r=right, l=left, c=centre)

Sally & Richard Greenhill Photo Library: Sally Greenhill 44c. **BSIP ASTIER:** 15tr. **Robert Harding Picture Library:** Caroline Wood/Int'l Stock 18bl; Ruth Jenkinson 78bl. **The Image Bank:** Tosca Radigonda 29tr. **Mother & Baby Picture Library:** Moose Azim 10bl. **Pictor International:** 14br, 37tl. **Science Photo Library:** John Greim 11tr; Ruth Jenkinson 13tl; Publiphoto Diffusion 16bl; Peter Yates 31bl; Hattie Young 12bl. **Corbis Stock Market:** Norbert Schafer 17br; Pete Saloutos 36bl; Steve Prezant 89tr. **Superstock Ltd:** 27tr; **Bubbles Photo Library:** Jennie Woodcock 86br. **Retna Pictures Ltd:** Ewing Reeson 231bl. **Gettyone stone:** 191tr.

All other images © Dorling Kindersley. For further information see: www.dkimages.com